Deleuze and the Immanent Sublime

Also available from Bloomsbury:

Thinking Between Deleuze and Kant, edited by Edward Willatt and Matt Lee
Kant, Deleuze and Architectonics, by Edward Willatt
Deleuze and Art, by Anne Sauvagnargues

Deleuze and the Immanent Sublime

Idea and Individuation

Louis Schreel

BLOOMSBURY ACADEMIC
LONDON • NEW YORK • OXFORD • NEW DELHI • SYDNEY

BLOOMSBURY ACADEMIC

Bloomsbury Publishing Plc, 50 Bedford Square, London, WC1B 3DP, UK
Bloomsbury Publishing Inc, 1359 Broadway, 12th Floor, New York, NY 10018, USA
Bloomsbury Publishing Ireland, 29 Earlsfort Terrace, Dublin 2, D02 AY28, Ireland

BLOOMSBURY, BLOOMSBURY ACADEMIC and the Diana logo are
trademarks of Bloomsbury Publishing Plc

First published in Great Britain 2024
This paperback edition published 2026

Copyright © Louis Schreel, 2024

Louis Schreel has asserted his right under the Copyright,
Designs and Patents Act, 1988, to be identified as Author of this work.

For legal purposes the Acknowledgements on p. viii constitute
an extension of this copyright page.

Cover image © Studio ANF / Andreas Fischer

All rights reserved. No part of this publication may be: i) reproduced or transmitted
in any form, electronic or mechanical, including photocopying, recording or by means
of any information storage or retrieval system without prior permission in writing from the
publishers; or ii) used or reproduced in any way for the training, development or operation of
artificial intelligence (AI) technologies, including generative AI technologies. The rights holders
expressly reserve this publication from the text and data mining exception as per Article 4(3)
of the Digital Single Market Directive (EU) 2019/790.

Bloomsbury Publishing Inc does not have any control over, or responsibility for,
any third-party websites referred to or in this book. All internet addresses given
in this book were correct at the time of going to press. The author and publisher
regret any inconvenience caused if addresses have changed or sites have
ceased to exist, but can accept no responsibility for any such changes.

A catalogue record for this book is available from the British Library.

A catalog record for this book is available from the Library of Congress.

ISBN: HB: 978-1-3503-4488-4
PB: 978-1-3503-4492-1
ePDF: 978-1-3503-4489-1
eBook: 978-1-3503-4490-7

Typeset by Integra Software Services Pvt. Ltd.

For product safety related questions contact productsafety@bloomsbury.com.

To find out more about our authors and books visit www.bloomsbury.com
and sign up for our newsletters.

For Anne, Alva and Lotta

Contents

Acknowledgements		viii
Introduction		1
1	Self-organization and feeling of life	13
2	Conatus – power – faculty	35
3	The metaphysics of individuation	55
4	From transcendental to dynamical structuralism	75
5	Psychic individuation	99
6	Passibility	121
7	*Erewhon*: Infinity and the sublime	139
Notes		166
Bibliography		191
Index		201

Acknowledgements

In the past ten years, there have been some philosophers and colleagues whose work has so deeply influenced my thinking in this book that it could not be truly acknowledged in citations alone. Many of the metaphysical and epistemological ideas discussed here derive from the rich work of Jean Petitot, Rudolf Bernet and Gerard Visser, which has done a great deal in framing my thinking. Much of my insight into the philosophy of Deleuze, Kant and Bergson was enabled by the exceptional work of Johan de Deckere, Boris Demarest and James DiFrisco. They have been a continuous inspiration throughout my journey. To Jesse Lopes, I am thankful for his Cartesian probings and Fodorian cogency, which have long guided me in the final stages of writing. Special thanks also to Florian Vermeiren, Henri Somers-Hall and three anonymous reviewers at Bloomsbury, who all greatly helped me refine my writing. When thinking about the earliest stages of this book, Arthur Cools, Timo Skrandies, Reinhold Görling and Sjoerd van Tuinen will always come to my mind. I am forever grateful for their continuous support. For my past years at Ghent University, I am especially thankful to Bart Vandenabeele for his guidance and encouragement. I should also like to thank my colleagues and friends who made Düsseldorf, Antwerp and Ghent a joyful home for intellectual work.

I consider myself very fortunate in having briefly known Johan de Deckere. There is much in this book that grew out of the brilliance of his work. I also wish to express my deepest gratitude to my father, Yves Schreel, for showing me the ways of philosophical thinking and for igniting my passion for truth. Finally, thank you Anne, Lucas and Arne, for saving me from myself. I dedicate this book to you, Anne, love of my life.

Chapters 1 and 2 include some material from my earlier-published paper, 'Conatus and Feeling of Life: A Genetic Shift in Kant's Faculty Doctrine?' (2022), *Deleuze & Guattari Studies*, 16(3), 402–27. https://doi.org/10.3366/dlgs.2022.0484.

An alternate version of Chapter 6 will appear as 'Passibility: The Pathic Dimension of Subjectivity' (2024), *Phenomenology, Neuroscience and Clinical Practice. Transdisciplinary Experiences.* Ed. Francesca Brencio, Berlin: Springer.

Introduction

The idea of sublimity has fascinated thinkers from classical civilization to modern times. For the classics, it meant the ecstatic experience of a cosmic transcendence actualizing itself in man's theoretical and practical endeavours. For the moderns, it manifested the voice of human reason, awakening man's awe at his ideal vocation. But what becomes of the sublime today, in a philosophy that discards the old oppositions between body and mind and embeds human reason in the creative evolution of life? How can we think of this sublime force that drives the mind to incarnate its exalting ideas? In this book, I aim to show how Gilles Deleuze's life-long engagement with the sublime grappled with just these questions. Its core argument centres on Deleuze's understanding of the sublime in terms of psychic individuation – a creative, self-organizing process that animates the mind from within. What emerges is an exploration of how and why Deleuze considered the sublime to be the great discovery of Kant's *Critique of Judgment* that was to define the transcendental philosophy of the future.

*

In the history of philosophy, the sublime is traditionally understood as a feeling of exaltation or elevation (*Erhebung*) that is associated with awe, astonishment, wonder, ecstasy, ravishment, grandeur, but also repulsion and fear. What unites the key philosophical theories of the sublime – ranging from Longinus to Burke, Kant, Schopenhauer and Hegel – is the idea of a paradoxical experience of feeling at once *overwhelmed* and *exalted*, which is intimately connected with a human striving for *transcendence*.[1] Already in Longinus' original treatise on the sublime, *Peri hypsos* (First Century AD), the sublime is understood as a feeling of 'elevation' that is connected to an irresistible human desire (*eros*) for all that is 'great' and transcends us as finite, imperfect beings. For Longinus, this feeling of *elevation* or *exaltation*, as expressed in his notion of *ekstasis* (literally: going outside or beyond oneself, self-transcendence) is always coupled with feeling *overwhelmed* or *overawed*. In this sense, sublimity also implies a certain violence, an encounter with something superior leading to a feeling of submission and inferiority – a feeling Kant would link to our moral feeling of respect (*Achtung*). For Longinus already, it is only *through* this feeling of being overwhelmed that an elevating feeling of the grandeur and nobility of the soul (mental exaltation) can be attained.

In modern thought, this paradoxical feeling of transcendence (feeling overwhelmed and feeling elevated) was related to the power of human reason. Kant defined the sublime as a 'feeling of spirit' (*Geistesgefühl*), a feeling in which the mind hears within itself 'the voice of reason' and senses its 'receptivity to Ideas'.[2] This characterization is an important and subtle point. The feeling of being overwhelmed or overpowered may not be understood as literal fear of natural phenomena (mountain ranges, volcanoes, stormy oceans, etc.). Rather, for Kant, vast and powerful phenomena trigger within us our *moral sensibility*, which senses inferior and humbled in the face of *moral judgment*. In a sublime encounter, one senses the kind of *violence* that our reason, in self-inflicting moral judgments, can exert upon our feeling. This is the kind of violence we also fear when others judge us and when we feel guilt or shame. There is a veritable violence inherent to the exertion of moral judgment, which leads to a painful humiliation of our self-love (*Eigenliebe*) and self-conceit (*Eigendünkel*) and has a certain depressing effect.[3] This idea, that the exercise of our cognitive powers has certain *sensible effects* on our state of mind (*Geistesstimmung*), is one of the central insights of Kant's practical philosophy and forms the very basis for his analysis of sublimity.[4]

What is remarkable about our moral sensibility is that we can feel not only *repulsed* (fear, humiliation) but also *attracted* (awe, respect) to one and the same moral judgment.[5] Indeed, moral judgments have something of a heroic, sublime character precisely in that they require overcoming self-inflicted humiliation in our attraction to what is Good (*das Gute*). For Kant, it is this dual structure of moral feeling (repulsion and attraction) that is awakened in a purely contemplative way in the feeling of the sublime. Feeling overwhelmed *and* elevated is triggered by sublime natural phenomena, but really these feelings derive from our sensible way of relating to Ideas of reason (such as the Good). For Kant, the feeling of the sublime is thus intimately bound up with the way in which human beings *undergo* the exercise of their practical reason in the form of a calling, a demand or a destiny.

*

While for Kant it is our moral exercise of reason that grounds the feeling of the sublime, for Deleuze this exalting feeling is that of the *creative* mind – and how it can surpass itself. Indeed, for Deleuze, 'to think is to create' and to create is the highest *telos* of thought.[6] But this relation between thinking and creativity is quite perplexing, not to say enigmatic. First of all, creativity is not primarily a matter of rationality. Contrary to rationality, as it is usually understood, creativity is not primarily a matter of using laws or rules that are applicable to the world in general. Instead, creativity has something to do with a capacity to deal with situations independently of a given framework of laws and rules, and possibly to transform such frameworks altogether. One might therefore say that creativity is a capacity that comes both before and after laws and rules have been set.[7]

But even to speak of creativity as a capacity is problematic too. Because creativity itself is not a faculty that is present in a subject or an organism. It belongs rather to what we will call in this book *individuation*. Just like creativity, individuation is not some capacity or faculty 'in' an individual subject or organism, such as movement, perception or memory. Instead, the subject and the organism are 'in' phases of individuation. And individuation is creative in principle. We should say therefore that creativity is a property of individuating processes, which take place in different degrees in the realms of life and mind. Indeed, while creativity is usually thought of in psychological terms, to Deleuze biological evolution and even life itself are also fundamentally creative. In this expanded sense, creativity means *the capacity to generate new forms*, while the nature of these forms may be either biological or psychic.

Through this philosophical lens, a fundamental duality then emerges between creative processes of individuation and the static things they create.[8] Among the latter, we may count individual organisms but also their organs and functional parts. Even the homeostatic self-maintenance that regulates the dynamical persistence of the organism falls on the side of the static. That is because homeostasis presupposes a limited range of possible changes in the structure of the organism (or in the structure of its organs, tissues, cells, etc.). By contrast, individuation is not a static but a creative process, generating new realities that did not subsist beforehand, not even in the form of pure possibility. Individuation is an open-ended dynamic creating elements that are novel in the strongest sense, since it shifts the whole *range* of possible changes in the organism's structures, and even those structures themselves.

Our philosophical duality is thus that between the *structure* and *organization* of a living or psychic system, on the one hand, and its *evolution* and *development*, on the other hand. Individuation involves changes not merely *within* the framework of an established organization, but rather a sequence of discontinuous changes that transform the very organization of the living or psychic unit. Framed in this way, however, it is not easy to formulate precisely what individuation is, since it may not be reduced to an individual living or psychic system. At this point, some preliminary metaphysical clarifications may help.

*

In Deleuze's metaphysics, the central organizing idea is that reality itself is the continual creation of unpredictable novelty and not the successive realization of pre-existing possibilities. Instead of the Newtonian worldview of a deterministic reality in which all possibilities are pre-existent and time has no creative effect, Deleuze developed the Bergsonian view that reality is itself fundamentally creative evolution, the continuous creation of new possibilities. To develop this alternative view of an inherently creative reality, Deleuze's metaphysics divides reality into two fundamental planes: one pre-individual plane of Nature (*natura naturans*) and one individual plane of material, living and psychic things (*natura naturata*). But how might one give a robust meaning to the concept of a *pre-individual* Nature that is deprived of natural beings?

Deleuze's central idea is that insofar as every individual being has a *form* or a *structure*, one must conceive of an *a priori* space within which this form individuates itself. In this sense, Euclidian space has traditionally been given an ontological primacy, and many thinkers have conceived it as the body of God. In Newton's metaphysics of space, for example, absolute space or pure extension exists prior to and independently of matter as an affection of God himself, because God is omnipresent or everywhere.[9] The most salient philosophical source of this view was the neo-Platonic tradition, which conceived absolute space as neither a substance nor an accident, but as an emanative effect of God.[10]

But Deleuze's conception of pre-individual Nature stands in stark contrast to the conceptions of space in Newton and Kant. Following a tradition that runs from Leibniz to Spinoza, Fichte, Schelling, Bergson, Hermann Weyl and others, Deleuze defends the view that matter is not a *passive* given in pure extension, but rather it is an *active* process in an intensive space that is prior to and constitutive of extension. In this framework, pre-individual space is conceived in terms of Anaximander's indefinite *apeiron*: a primordial, unbounded field in which matter exists as a flux of 'pure intensity' or 'pure energy'. If we ask ourselves, as the first Greek philosophers did, what is the origin and first cause of all existing things, then we should imagine an original energetic flux, a 'boundlessly indeterminable' original matter, that is in an initial state of complete symmetry – a disordered *apeiron*. As material, living and ultimately psychic forms *individuate* and evolve, this original state of symmetry and disorder becomes increasingly *differentiated* and thereby becomes asymmetrical, ordered and heterogeneous.

It is important to note that Deleuze develops this theory of individuation within an ontology of pure immanence. This means that all natural entities have a common, unitary ground with which they remain in some sense identical. Spinoza called this *natura naturans* ('naturing nature'), which is an unlimited productive power. All entities exist by virtue of this common, primordial ground, and this ground is somehow *immanent* to them – it is not therefore a transcendent God or a Neoplatonic One from which they emanate.[11] In Deleuze's interpretation, *natura naturans* can be understood as an immanent, self-individuating causality in Nature that is unbounded and unlimited, in contrast to the ordered states of nature we usually experience. Generating an infinite multiplicity of forms and creatures, *natura naturans* is Nature itself in the creative process of individuation, whereas *natura naturata* ('natured nature') is its *expression* into finite, ordered beings and states.

With such a notion of immanent causality, individuation can be seen as a cosmic process of self-organization and complexification of matter, at work at different levels of organization in nature. As we will see, this immanent causality of Nature expresses itself in finite, constituted individuals as a *conatus*, which is an innate striving of any entity to continue to exist and to enhance itself. This *conatus* is a kind of innate 'optimizing principle' that strives to regulate and direct the affections of body and mind.[12] As such, it can have two modalities: either it is present as a creature's power to *exist* and to *act*, or it is present as its power to *think*. But in Spinozism, *all* conative powers – whether vital or psychic – are mere manifestations of Nature's all-encompassing, productive power. To the Spinozist, even the power of thinking, from which Ideas emerge, is not superior to a power of existing and acting in which all things participate.[13] Indeed, the *conatus* implies the presence of a self-transforming infinite power within every finite being – the possibility of individuation across different creatures and at different levels of organization.[14]

This is how the dual character of Spinoza's Nature – *natura naturans* and *natura naturata* – returns in Deleuze's postulation of reality as both creative and ordered. Our representational understanding of nature allows us humans to see *natured* nature as organized, stable and ordered in certain ways. But to Deleuze, individuation is reality itself and accordingly any organized, stable thing, form or order must be thought as a product *of* individuation. This goes against the natural tendency of representational thinking, which attempts to reduce individuation to the order and stability of mechanisms that can be fixed and controlled. But while *natured* nature allows the subject to represent reality as ordered and structured in some way, *naturing* nature prevents it from ever attaining any kind of complete understanding or control.

This metaphysical scheme of things leads Deleuze to distinguish between an *a priori* intensive space and time, within which creative processes of individuation unfold, and an *a priori* extensive space and time, which is related to the actualized properties of these dynamics. Accordingly, Deleuze distinguishes between two irreducible ways of apprehending reality itself: a metaphysical mode, which intuits Being as a genetic process or creative becoming, and a representational mode, which apprehends qualified and ordered things in extension.

What is largely unknown is that Deleuze connected to this a new way of conceiving the intuition of the sublime – a topic he repeatedly returned to throughout his work.[15] On his view, the feeling of the sublime is an intuitive opening onto the ontological reality that is inherent to the creative becoming of individuation. The sublime here thus becomes an experience of individuation, and through this experience we are no longer locked into the representational world of our subjective consciousness. Aside from representational conscious beings, we are also an element of the creative nature in which our body is included. This experience of inclusion is for Deleuze an ontological one, meaning that our mind is now opened onto *another Being* than the stable, ordered world of common human experience. The bodily and psychic forms of a living creature stand in relation to the individuating power that generated it as to a massive pre-individual potential that the individual has actualized and closed off. But living creatures always maintain a relation to this infinite, self-transforming power, as a kind of pre-individual reservoir of potentials that can plunge them into the exalting element of individuation. The feeling of the immanent sublime then becomes an ecstatic intuition of the energetic indetermination driving individuation: an intuition of reality as 'a fundamentally open Whole'.[16]

*

To grasp this novel interpretation of the sublime, we will have to investigate the focal point of Deleuze's transcendental philosophy, which is to understand how creative *thought* may emerge and how it may individuate creative Ideas. To embark upon this endeavour, Chapter 1, 'Self-Organization and Feeling of Life', will begin by introducing the central ideas underlying Deleuze's *genetic* interpretation of Kant's faculty doctrine. In his reconstruction of Kant's Critical philosophy as a whole, Deleuze makes the remarkable claim that the cognitive and practical faculties are genetically grounded in the affective, enlivening dynamics of the reflecting powers of the mind. On this view, the aesthetic 'feeling of life' (*Lebensgefühl*) should be understood as a generative dynamics of the cognitive powers in which all determining judgment, that is, all thought, is rooted. Following recent organicist readings of Kant's faculty doctrine, I argue this creative dynamics may be understood in terms of the *circular causation*, which Kant ascribes to the self-productive power of living self-organization. Accordingly, the generative function of reflective judgment may be understood in terms of a spontaneous striving to integrate the faculties into a living, self-organizing whole, a generative striving that comes to the fore in the subject's feeling of life. Indeed, in both his accounts of self-organization and feeling of life, Kant puts forward a movement of circular causation that is purposively animated from within by a self-productive and self-maintaining tendency.

Chapter 2, 'Conatus – Power – Faculty', goes on to argue that this self-productive and self-maintaining tendency of the cognitive powers should be understood as a *conatus* of the power of judgment. This *conatus* forms the causal potential of the power of judgment to integrate the mental powers into a self-organizing, generative whole. Drawing on Kant's reading of Leibniz in the *Lectures on Metaphysics*, it is shown how Kant establishes an intricate relation between (a) the cognitive powers, (b) the acts that are causally individuated by the powers, which are representations, and (c) a *conatus* or '*vis activa*' that is the causal potential of the powers in the sense that the *conatus* is a spontaneous, generative striving towards *self-activity* (and hence towards representation) that is inherent to each power.

To examine how this Leibnizian framework may be applied to Deleuze's faculty doctrine, Chapter 2 will raise the following pivotal question: what does it mean to embody the subject's cognitive powers in the stream of life? For Kant and Leibniz, the conative force that animates the spontaneous striving of the cognitive powers belongs ultimately to the human *soul* or *spirit*. For Deleuze, however, who adopts a resolutely Spinozist and Nietzschean reading of Kant's faculty doctrine, the mind's conative striving has its roots in a primordial unconscious striving of the *body*. For Deleuze, all conscious thought, feeling and desire are genetically and ontologically animated by the energy of an *unconscious will to power*. Deleuze will call this fundamental active force (*vis activa*), which actualizes itself in mental acts, a 'virtuality'. For him, as for Leibniz, this virtuality is – despite its lack of actuality – a positive, existing force that belongs to the essence of both life and mind. But Deleuze will find in Spinoza and Nietzsche an important naturalist amendment to Leibniz and Kant: 'a devaluation of consciousness in relation to thought: a discovery of the unconscious, of an *unconscious of thought* just as profound as *the unknown of the body.*'[17]

To get a deeper understanding of how a vital *conatus* may determine psychic individuation, Chapter 3, 'The Metaphysics of Individuation', takes a step back and outlines the basic metaphysical commitments of Deleuze's philosophy of individuation. The chapter begins by sketching what I take to be its main metaphysical conjecture: *there is a continuous creation of unforeseeable novelty, which seems to be going on in the universe.* This conjecture entails two distinct theses. First, it entails an ontological priority of generative processes of individuation with regard to constituted individuals. As such, Deleuze's metaphysics entails a veritable *ontological difference* between generative processes of individuation and individuals considered as static products of such processes. Secondly, the conjecture entails the thesis that individuation cannot be the result of a fixed totality of possibilities, but instead must involve the continual creation of new possibilities. This thesis entails that individuation brings forth something unforeseeable and new, such that it does not simply enact timeless, pre-existing possibilities, but rather it involves the creation of new, unseen possibilities.

If individuation is a pure process rather than a discrete substance or thing, then its individuating dynamism must be understood as having its own kind of *force* and its own kind of *acting*. Drawing on Deleuze's reading of Henri Bergson and Gilbert Simondon, we will explore the idea that individuation generates and organizes variable degrees of *energy indetermination*, which manifests itself in *life* in the form of metabolism and memory, and in *mind* as an indetermination of *will*. Restraining our focus initially to the level of biological individuation, we will first examine its metabolic and mnemonic dimensions.

For Deleuze, biological individuation emerges from pre-individual intensive fields, in which potential energy is harvested in a state of maximal asymmetry. These intensive fields are like local islands of vital indetermination in a global ocean of physical determination.[18] It is my view that in this state of indetermined and potential energy – this non-actualized virtuality, this *restrained* and yet *striving* force – we have found the vital potential at the heart of individuation. We will then see how this virtuality of potential energy may *actualize* itself in creative acts of *differentiation*. Moreover, we will be attentive to the fact that individuation as creative *movement* always 'alienates' itself in the material *form* that it creates: by actualizing itself, by differentiating itself, it loses contact with the rest of itself.[19]

A second essential requirement for individuation, other than an external source of potential energy to dissipate, is the presence of reciprocal dependency relations *within* the system. We will initially explore the idea of reciprocal dependency relations in Chapter 1, when considering Kant's conception of self-organization. But in Chapter 4, 'From Transcendental to Dynamical Structuralism,' it is shown how Deleuze's proposal for a transcendental structuralism expands this notion to include not only organisms but also psychic systems. The key idea underlying Deleuze's proposal is that the foundations of structuralism are not only transcendental but also *topological*, rather than logical. Deleuze speaks of a 'transcendental topology' which conceives psychic structure in terms of a topological order of proximities defined by differential relations of emergence. Psychic structures would emerge in a topological space, divided into regions by a system of energetic differences and singularities. These intensive differences between the elements of a structure are generative relations of reciprocal determination. As such, the structuralist principle of reciprocal dependency relations becomes in Deleuze's transcendental structuralism a *morphodynamic* principle, which generates ideal structure. To demonstrate the significance of this proposal, we will turn to Jean Petitot's *dynamical* structuralism, which has meticulously developed Deleuze's topological foundation of structuralism.

With the introductory explorations in transcendental philosophy laid out in Chapters 1 and 2, and the theoretical foundations laid out in Chapters 3 and 4, Chapter 5, 'Psychic Individuation,' examines Deleuze's conception of the sublime in terms of psychic individuation. In its usual, empirical exercise, thought is organized for Deleuze by an overarching identity principle and representational logic of recognition, which organizes conscious experience in terms of generic concepts and categories. As such, representational thought is fundamentally concerned with shaping our experience of the world as a *typified* world. As the chapter shows, this representational dimension of thought has led to a fairly widespread rationalist and computationalist conception of thought, according to which thought is essentially in the business of inferential rule-following. In the wake of Leibniz and Kant, rationalists and computationalists assume all humans have an innate faculty of thought that is a veritable cognitive *instinct*, an innate conative drive towards logical inference. This conception of thought will play an important role in our analysis because psychic individuation is defined in contrast to it.

For Deleuze, psychic individuation brings to life, *in thought itself*, a different conative tendency or cognitive instinct, which is critical and creative. Faced with singular and contingent events, thought undergoes a qualitative shift, a veritable leap, which *forces* it to leave its abstract realm of preconceived possibilities and to realize itself by adopting a different mode of sensibility: a sensitivity to singularity. Thought is then elevated towards a transcending and properly sublime exercise, in which it transgresses its pre-existing possibilities. As Chapter 5 shows, Deleuze conceives this individuating element of thought as an infinitary dimension of *learning*.

Unlike a common misconception, learning is not subordinate to the acquisition of knowledge: it is not the mere method that leads to knowledge. On the contrary, learning is an a-conceptual exercise of thought, which exerts constructive and creative acts in relation to singular problems, and which thereby determines new Ideas. I distinguish what I call 'finite learning,' which is enacted for the purpose of attaining knowledge and which must follow certain pre-given rules, from 'infinitary learning', which is a constructive, autopoietic *rule-making* capacity and is enacted for the purpose of continuing to learn. Finite thinkers think *within* boundaries, whereas infinitary thinkers think *with new* boundaries.

Chapter 6, 'Passibility', is entirely devoted to Deleuze's view that the link between creative thought and individuation emerges from an intensive field of energy indetermination, which constitutes the thinker's sensibility. With this notion of sensibility, however, we are facing an interpretative difficulty: Deleuze conceives of sensibility in a 'pure' state, independently from the qualities and extension with which it is always mixed in our conscious experience. Grasping intensity for itself, it would seem that sensibility is somehow cut off from the external world. If we follow this hypothesis, it would detect, with extraordinary acuteness, certain changes in its bodily interior, especially oscillations in the tension of its instinctual drives, and these modifications would become conscious as affective feelings. Inspired by Deleuze's reading of the phenomenologists Erwin Straus and Henri Maldiney, Chapter 6 explores this aspect of sensibility as it relates to the organic body and to the inorganic life, which is its conative instinct for individuation.

Finally, Chapter 7, '*Erewhon*: Infinity and the Sublime', aims to lay out the ramifications of Deleuze's philosophy of individuation for his genetic conception of the sublime, and to offer a concluding confrontation with Kant's Analytic of the Sublime. The aim of this final chapter is to show that both the Kantian and the Deleuzian interpretation of the sublime rely on a particular view of space and time, and on a correlated metaphysical view of its infinity as an actual (Kant) or a virtual (Deleuze) whole. In Kant, we should distinguish the mathematical concept of potential infinity, which is applicable to Newtonian space and time, from a neo-Platonic, metaphysical Idea of actual infinity, which

Kant applies to the universe as a self-contained world-whole. Similarly, in Deleuze we find a properly metaphysical concept of infinity, which is rooted in Anaximander's concept of *to apeiron*, and which Deleuze applies to the space and time of thermodynamics as a self-individuating virtual whole. Confronting these differing views of space, time and infinity, Chapter 7 shows how Kant and Deleuze are led to develop separate, yet interconnected conceptions of the sublime.

1

Self-organization and feeling of life

What is truly created, from the living being to the work of art, thereby enjoys a self-positing of itself, or an autopoiesis by which one recognizes it.
— Gilles Deleuze & Félix Guattari[1]

The fate of the faculty doctrine

Kant's doctrine of faculties has long stood in ill-repute. Whereas most philosophers value the *constitutive* dimension of Kant's transcendental system (the doctrine of the constitution of objectivity by means of *a priori* principles), many have been critical of its *cognitive* dimension (the idea that it is a subjective consciousness which is constitutive). Critics often argue that because the constitutive principles are characteristics of our human representational consciousness, Kant's theory leads to a transcendental *subjectivism* (a recourse to a foundational subject), which threatens to degenerate into a psychological or psychologistic account of the origins of knowledge.[2] For instance, Peter Strawson's *Bounds of Sense* famously denounced 'the imaginary subject of transcendental psychology' as 'incoherent in itself' and as masking, rather than explaining, the real character of Kant's inquiry.[3] In the same vein, prominent philosophers such as Hermann Cohen, Gottlob Frege and Moritz Schlick have argued that explaining the possibility of objective knowledge by elucidating the mental acts and faculties that are supposed to give rise to cognition leads to confusing psychological genesis with true epistemic evaluation.

Among twentieth-century philosophers, Deleuze's attitude towards Kant is distinguished by his explicit appreciation of the faculty doctrine: 'Despite the fact that it has become discredited today, the doctrine of the faculties is an entirely necessary component of the system of philosophy.'[4] In his reading of Kant, Deleuze emphasizes that the subjectivity of constitutive principles is not an empirical or psychological subjectivity but rather a 'transcendental subjectivity'.[5] In fact, one should distinguish two sides to subjectivity, only one of which is relevant to transcendental philosophy: Kant postulated the existence of an ideal, formal subject constitutive of the ideality of space and time and accessing a dimension of objective meaning distinct from the empirical subject of mundane psychological intentions, beliefs, opinions, habits, associations, etc. Much like Husserl, Kant maintained the normative autonomy of both logical and mathematical ideality with regard to factual consciousness and its dependence upon a universal, purely formal subjectivity. Empirical subjects and factual consciousness participate in this ideal subjectivity insofar as they share a universal form of intuition and understanding – the same transcendental constitution – and are accordingly capable of making the same judgments about the meaning of objects in the world. But Kant's talk of cognitive faculties as conditions of meaning constitution is not concerned with the empirical or psychological conditions of constitution.

In his reading of Kant, Deleuze thus emphasizes both the theme of meaning constitution and that of constitutive cognitive faculties. But Deleuze also refers to *pre-subjective* constitutive structures: there must be some cognitive principles and tendencies in nature before human consciousness, and these principles and tendencies have a *genetic priority* over culture and transcendental subjectivity – they come first both phylogenetically and ontologically. For Deleuze, even the higher faculties of the human mind, such as language and reason, have their roots in the corporeality and vital functions of living beings. In this sense, Deleuze *desubjectivizes* the transcendental dimension of Kant's faculty doctrine: at various levels of reality, he posits natural processes of self-organization and individuation, which are generative of cognitive structures at both the animal and the human level. Like Derrida confronting Husserl's transcendental philosophy, Deleuze thus sets forward the problem of *transcendental genesis* as the guiding thread in his confrontation with Kant's philosophy.[6] Deleuze does grant Kant the discovery of the transcendental: both time and space as ideal forms of intuition and meaning itself must be constituted by *a priori* transcendental acts. But in order to be truly constituting, transcendental subjectivity must itself be constituted by a process of transcendental genesis.

In Deleuze's view, it is Kant's *Critique of Judgment*, which laid the first foundations for a doctrine of transcendental genesis. At this ultimate point, Kant is led to the deepest level of transcendental subjectivity, namely the 'transcendental life' of the subject, which is distinct from yet also entwined with the universal structures of both cognition and volition. It is this genetic level of transcendental subjectivity that we want here, in our first chapter, to better understand through the resources of Kant's third *Critique*. Following recent organicist readings of Kant's faculty doctrine, I will argue that transcendental genesis may be conceived in terms of the circular causation, which Kant ascribes to vital self-organization. Accordingly, I will argue the genesis of the cognitive powers themselves can be understood in terms of a spontaneous striving to integrate the powers into a living, self-organizing whole, a generative striving that comes to the fore in the subject's 'feeling of life'.

What is transcendental genesis?

Before proceeding to these rather technical philosophical matters, let me begin by clarifying what is meant here, precisely, with the problem of transcendental genesis. Traditionally, transcendental philosophy distinguishes *innate* faculties from *acquired* faculties. For Kant, for instance, the faculty of visual perception belongs to the first kind, whereas the faculty of swimming or playing world-class tennis would belong to the second. Acquired faculties realize certain latent potentials, which require specific, contingent circumstances such as a repeated, progressive practice. Innate faculties, by contrast, are present in *every* subject and correspond to elementary organic functions (sensation, movement, perception, etc.) and cognitive functions (memory, imagination, language, reasoning, etc.).

The idea of innate faculties made a famous comeback in the twentieth century with Noam Chomsky's theory about how the human mind is intrinsically, genetically structured into innate faculties such as, notably, the language faculty. Chomsky famously rejected the behaviourist idea that language could be an acquired habit and claimed our language faculty could only be explained in terms of innate, inborn mental grammar.[7] More precisely, Chomsky argued that children learning a language would never be able to *infer* grammatical rules from raw data of spoken language and they would never be able to distinguish grammatically correct and incorrect statements if they did not dispose of some kind of innate grammatical faculty: a 'universal grammar' that *precedes* and *enables* a child's learning of and eventual competence in the grammar of a particular language.[8] Thus, even though language is of course *learned* and *acquired*, Chomsky claimed this can only be explained by presupposing some innate grammatical structure of the mind (so-called deep structure), which itself determines particular grammars (with so-called surface structure). The classic transcendental idea is here that we must possess some *innate* language faculty for the learning of a particular language to be possible in the first place: learning behaviour occurs via the modification of an innate, already present functional organization. In Chomsky's own words, 'an actual language may result only from the interaction of several mental faculties, one being the faculty of language.'[9]

On Kant's view, other notable examples of innate cognitive faculties include spatial cognition (the capacity of locating something in three-dimensional space), conceptual cognition (the capacity of thinking about things in general, that is, in terms of universals, concepts, types, etc.), moral cognition (the capacity of determining one's will based on reason itself, without intermediary of feelings of pleasure or pain), aesthetic sense (the affective sensitivity to arrangements of form, colour, music, etc.) and judgment (the capacity of applying conceptual rules to particular sensory data), which for Kant is identical to rational thinking itself and is the central faculty of the human mind.

Now, to say a faculty is *innate* does not mean merely that it is inborn or intrinsic to the mind but also, and more importantly, that it processes data in accordance with specific context-invariant rules that reflect the internal structures of the faculty. Thus, to say a faculty is innate means two things: (1) it is inborn and (2) it has certain intrinsic, *a priori* rule-based procedures.

According to Deleuze, the most important feature of Kant's doctrine of faculties is not their being innate or inborn, but rather their *priority* over sensory experience. In fact, much like Chomsky, Deleuze starts from the assumption that *every* faculty – also the most universal and innate, such as the language faculty – emerges from a *genesis* or an *acquisition* that follows certain genetic principles of formation or structuration. It is central to Deleuze's transcendental empiricism that faculties are ontogenetically determined: faculties are *a priori* cognitive structures that develop in response to external environmental influences. But what is meant here with *acquisition, learning* or *genesis* is quite subtle. Let us briefly consider the example of spatial cognition.

In what is undoubtedly one of Kant's most important and fascinating thoughts, space is a 'pure intuition,' which means that it is a mental *a priori* form, which our perceptual apparatus uses to process sensory information. Contrary to what our natural attitude suggests, the perception of the spatio-temporal 3D structure of the world is not a *passive reception* of external structures (which surely exist), but rather an *active projection* of the mind onto the world. In Kantian terms, space is a 'form of intuition' through which raw sense data are first 'given', and can subsequently be processed or 'synthesized'. What is usually taken as Kant's 'nativist' (as opposed to Hume's 'empiricist') view amounts to the claim that this form of intuition is not *derived* from sensory experience, but rather it is an innate feature of the subject's constitution, which allows it to receive sensations in the first place.

In fact, several prominent neuroscientists today believe this Kantian vision is fundamentally correct: spatial cognition, the capacity to perceive things in a three-dimensional frame, is essentially *a priori*, meaning it is not *derived* from sensorial information but rather used as an *a priori* format, in which this information can be processed.[10] But the fact that this faculty of spatial cognition is *a priori* does not mean that it is *inborn* – it only means that our sense of space is prior to sensation and to all object cognition. In other words, our sense of space is not derived from the senses, as empiricists would have it. But the priority of spatial cognition does not logically or factually imply that it is inborn. Indeed, one can reject empiricism without having to be a nativist. It is logically consistent and factually warranted to say spatial cognition is *a priori* and *learned*, rather than inborn. Today, much is known about the early development of spatial perception: in human infants, stereopsis (the major contributor to depth perception) is developed by about ten weeks. Kant was essentially right in claiming our faculty of sensibility constitutes space as an *a priori* form of sensibility. But we should add that it is ontogenetically *developed* and place it in the body – giving spatial cognition a *desubjectivized*, physiological basis.[11]

This example gives us a first idea of what is meant by transcendental genesis: it refers to the ontogenetic development or learning of a cognitive faculty. This turns the Kantian *a priori* into an ontogenetic *a priori*, which is rooted in the evolutionary past of our species, and which therefore links the transcendental conditions of cognition to the evolutionary structures inherited in phylogenesis. As Jean Petitot puts it, 'The fact that space as a sensorial format would be a result of biological evolution does not undermine its *a priori* status because the *a posteriori* of phylogenesis is the *a priori* of ontogenesis.'[12]

Everything hinges, then, on our understanding of the generative character of the learning and development involved in transcendental genesis. Two key questions arise. First of all, should we say, following Chomsky, that learning and development are determined by universal, *a priori* rules such as those entailed in universal grammar? And secondly, should we simply locate generative principles in the mind, as the innatist hypothesis does, or should we trace them in the relations between the active subject and reality – rather than in the mind itself? In other words, should we simply assume the generative capacities of syntax *a priori*, or should we trace the latter in our active engagement with reality, such that the *a priori* itself may be emergent, and open to growth and development?

To consider these questions, let us briefly return to Chomsky's example of the language faculty. As noted, for Chomsky, a universal grammar consists of a set of context-independent, invariant rules that underlie and make possible all the different human languages. As such, universal grammar specifies what language learning and competence must achieve if it is to take place successfully. Chomsky compares this to the biophysical structure of the organism: we know that from embryo to mature organism, the growth and development of this intricate organic structure is deeply genetically constrained. In the same way, human and animal cognitive structures should grow and develop according to certain genetic, innate rules that underlie and make possible this very growth and development.[13] Of course, such innate principles do not determine *which* language a child should learn – the innate rules must be a *species* property and, in this sense, form a universal grammar.

Despite its allure, this comparison between syntactic rules and the genetic rules instructing the ontogenetic development of organisms also hides a difficulty at the heart of Chomsky's theory. For genetic instructions are not laws of nature nor are they legislated or programmed by any external authority. They too have emerged and developed throughout the whole of evolution. But how can the same be said of the universal grammar underlying the development, learning or acquisition of the human language faculty? In other words, how can 'innate' or *a priori* cognitive structure *itself* be the result of genesis and development? To answer this, we need a generative principle that is capable of accounting for evolution and development at the level of faculties themselves. Universal grammar, for instance, would somehow have to allow for *both* rule-governed activity and *rule-changing* activity, where the latter stands in a creative, generative relationship to the former.

On Chomsky's innateness hypothesis, it is unclear how to understand this genesis of deep structures or faculties themselves. The universals of language are for Chomsky not themselves acquired by learning or development. Universal grammar is not, for instance, rooted in structures of perception and action – for that would relapse into empiricism. Hence, for Chomsky, the only way out is to take the innatist stance and to explain the language faculty in abstract terms that preclude any historical, evolutionary or physical (neurobiological) genesis.

One may wonder if Chomsky's life-long reflections on creativity may prove more fruitful in this context. But on his view, creativity is itself fundamentally predicated on a system of rules and forms, in part determined by innate human capacities.[14] What Chomsky calls 'rule-governed creativity' derives from what he considers to be the infinitary character of grammar, namely the fact that a language can 'make infinite use of finite means'.[15] Rule-governed creativity is to Chomsky a formal property of grammar, an *a priori* principle inherent to it, based on its purported recursivity, which entails that any language is capable of producing an infinite number of expressions from finite means. But such syntactic creativity leaves language and the syntactic system *itself* entirely unchanged, and in this sense, it is not a candidate for the generative principle mentioned above. Rule-governed creativity does not develop syntax itself and although it is highly generative, it is 'creative' only in a restricted and mechanical sense.[16]

A principle of transcendental genesis should account for genuine *rule-constructive* and *rule-changing* creativity. But what might such a principle consist in? Before proceeding to this question, let me indicate what it *cannot*. If anything, Kant's Critical philosophy has shown that a principle of transcendental genesis cannot be of a merely empiricist nature (principles of learning such as association, generalization, induction, classical or operant conditioning, etc.). I believe any transcendental philosopher should agree with Kant on this point, and Chomsky and Deleuze align in this regard. Transcendental genesis cannot be reduced to learning in the traditional empiricist sense, that is, to the transfer of structure *from* the environment *to* the organism. By contrast, for the transcendental philosopher, cognitive mechanisms of acquisition, learning, complexification and novelty-generation must be due to a process of *internal* selection. Transcendental genesis is a process with powerful *internal* resources and cannot be based on the induction of external structures.

As Massimo Piattelli-Palmarini has shown, the situation is analogous to that in evolutionary biology: there is no place in contemporary evolutionary theory for an 'internalization' of external templates or for the generation of rich internal structures dictated by external blueprints.[17] Instead, only mechanisms of *internal* selection based on genetic predispositions can be mechanisms of development and learning – mechanisms which involve a process of internal selection acting on a vast repertoire of highly specific genetic dispositions and structures already present in the organism *before* any encounter with the outside world. Put plainly, the environment does not *supply* structure, but rather it steers and constrains a selective process generating structure from *within*. With these conceptual clarifications in place, let us see now how Deleuze found in Kant's *Critique of Judgment* the first foundations for a doctrine of transcendental genesis.

Kant's horizontal faculty doctrine

Kant has what Jerry Fodor would have called a 'horizontal' faculty doctrine.[18] I mean by this that all the faculties discussed by Kant in his model of the mind are essentially *interactive* cognitive processes, such as thought and decision-making. Fodorian 'vertical' faculties, by contrast, are non-interactive in the sense that their processes occur independently of other cognitive processes. These include low-level faculties such as the visual, auditory, tactile and other kinds of sensory experience, memory, but also language. Horizontal faculties, by contrast, comprise the high-level capacities of forming concepts, rational beliefs, inferences and also making free choices and taking decisions. To Fodor, this distinction also entails that vertical faculties are innately specified, automatic and computationally autonomous, whereas horizontal faculties are creative, interactive processes, which are therefore much harder to study or understand.

To account for our horizontal cognitive organization, Kant distinguishes two fundamental kinds of capacities, namely 'receptivity' and 'spontaneity'. Receptivity is the mind's capacity of being affected by something and as such it essentially requires an external stimulus to start producing representations. By contrast, 'spontaneity', which Kant ascribes to our faculties of understanding (*Verstand*) and reason (*Vernunft*), does not need such an external stimulus to act. Instead, it can initiate its activity from within, without any external trigger. In the metaphysical terminology which Kant inherited from Leibniz and Wolff, this spontaneity of our faculties derives from a *conatus*, which is a spontaneous striving towards self-activity.

On first approximation, the spontaneity of the faculties of understanding and reason concerns their capacities of generating *a priori* concepts and ideas *spontaneously*, that is, without deriving these from experience. On second approximation, spontaneity refers to Kant's term for cognitive processing, namely 'combination' (*conjunctio*) or 'synthesis'.[19] Kant characterizes synthesis as a spontaneous act of 'going through' and 'putting together' representations given by intuition in order to form concepts, judgments and for any cognition to arise at all.[20] Synthesis in general is, to Kant, the 'first origin of our cognition'.[21] This means two things. First, Kant conceives the spontaneity of the faculties as a power that is responsible for enacting a unifying synthesis of those representations that are either given to it in sensibility or that are actively produced by itself. In this sense, spontaneity is responsible for the information-flow processes that constitute cognition. Secondly, thought or cognition cannot be regarded simply as *analyzing* a given complex informational whole into its decomposable constituents. Such an act of analysis would never be possible if there were not some more primordial capacity of generating, within the mind, synthetic representational wholes.

In the context of Kant's faculty doctrine, then, the question of transcendental genesis refers specifically to the generative power of synthesis: where does this synthetic power of the mind get its spontaneity from? How can we account for the horizontal organization of our cognitive faculties? In his first two *Critiques*, Kant does not explicitly address this question. Instead, he focuses on the presupposition that there must be *a priori* rules that regulate and determine the information flow between faculties so as to generate well-founded, objective thought or cognition. One of his key concerns in doing so is to refute empiricist accounts of synthesis by mere association.[22] Association can of course also generate unity among representations, but this is a wholly *passive* process that *results* from exposure to environmental regularities. One might, for instance, associate thoughts of losing hair with thoughts of raising children, if one only had started losing hair after getting children. By contrast, synthesis is a fundamentally *active* process that depends not on environmental regularities but rather on the mind's spontaneity. It is the *product* of actively processing representations in terms of concepts such as causality, possibility, contingency, etc. – something which association never does.

For Kant, then, concepts or categories provide *a priori* rules that constrain and determine the interaction between the faculties. Kant's fundamental aim was not to inquire how such a horizontal interaction is possible *in the first place*, but rather to inquire under what conditions *a priori* conceptual rules may be applied to experience. That is, if *a priori* conceptual rules are not themselves of an empirical nature (i.e., they are not derived from experience), then by what right might we claim them to have any objective validity and apply to empirical reality? The synthetic approach we find in Kant's horizontal faculty doctrine thus pivots on the idea of non-empirical, *a priori* rules that form a kind of transcendental syntax: *a priori* concepts provide abstract rules for the synthesis of representations that we can use in an infinite variety of different empirical situations. It is by virtue of these rules that we can compose structured, unified representations, which in turn can be analysed, that is, decomposed.

A genetic shift in Kant's faculty doctrine

In his reconstruction of Kant's Critical philosophy as a whole, Deleuze makes the remarkable claim that the higher faculties of understanding and reason, and the *a priori* principles that define them, are genetically grounded in the affective, enlivening activity of the faculties as they engage in aesthetic, reflective judgment: 'aesthetic common sense does not complete the two others; *it grounds them and makes them possible*'.[23] According to Deleuze, both the *a priori* syntheses determined by the faculty of understanding and the *a priori* syntheses determined by the faculty of reason presuppose a more fundamental organizational level of the mind, which consists in the spontaneous, unregulated interaction of the cognitive powers as they mutually engage in aesthetic reflective judgment. Indeed, Deleuze proposes this spontaneous interaction of the cognitive powers may be understood as a *generative* dynamics in which our horizontal cognitive organization is rooted. Indeed, in Deleuze's view, the faculties of understanding and reason would never take on a spontaneous, determining role were not all the cognitive faculties together in the first place capable of this free subjective 'harmony':

> In fact, determining judgment and reflective judgment are not like two species of the same genus. Reflective judgment manifests and liberates a depth, which remained hidden in the other. But the other was also judgment only by virtue of this living depth. (…) The point is that any determinate accord of the faculties under a determining and legislative faculty presupposes the existence and the possibility of a free indeterminate accord. It is in this free accord that judgment is not only original (this was already so in the case of determining judgment), but that it manifests the principle of its originality. According to this principle, despite the fact that our faculties differ in nature, they nevertheless have a free and spontaneous accord, *which then makes possible their exercise under the chairmanship of one of them according to a law of the interests of reason*. Judgment (…) never consists in one faculty alone, but in their accord, whether an accord already determined by one of them playing a legislative role or, *more profoundly*, in a free indeterminate accord, which forms the final object of a 'critique of judgment' in general.[24]

Whereas the reliance on *a priori* rules or laws allowed the first two *Critiques* to start from the presupposition that our cognitive faculties are equipped with *a priori*, preformed determinate accords, the third *Critique* no longer assumes such a preformed accord based on an *a priori* lawful structure.[25] Instead, to Deleuze, Kant's inquiry now revolves around the problem of 'a genesis of the faculties in their original free agreement'.[26] This spontaneous accord is original and genetic in the sense that it precedes the possibility of a determining relation among the cognitive powers. In reflective judgment the powers do not interact based on *a priori* logical or moral rules or laws, which determine their interaction. Rather, the cognitive powers are integrated in a *spontaneous* and *unregulated* manner, and for Deleuze it is precisely this spontaneous, unregulated integration of the powers, which forms the genetic 'living depth' in which all determining acts of understanding and reason are rooted.

Deleuze's genetic interpretation, which attributes to reflective judgment a genetic depth that was still lacking from Kant's faculty doctrine in the first two *Critiques*, consists of two ideas that are central to the purpose of this chapter.

Cognition and feeling of life

First of all, reflective judgment is understood as isolating and manifesting a necessary subjective, affective component of all cognitive and practical mental life, which itself remains unnoticed in determining judgments. For Deleuze, the notion of reflective judgment must be seen as a reconsideration of Kant's previous account of the power of judgment in the *Critique of Pure Reason*. Here, Kant had already put forward the power of judgment as the essential unifying power constitutive of determining, cognitive judgments: it mobilized concepts and constituted their predicative force by linking them to intuitions. In the third *Critique*, however, Kant introduces a dimension of our receptivity to representations that cannot become an element of cognition (*Erkenntnisstück*), but that can only be *felt*. More specifically, Kant introduces the idea of a 'feeling of life' (*Lebensgefühl*) that is derivative of our receptivity to representation itself. This feeling is not derivative from *intuition* (as in the first *Critique*), nor from representations of understanding or reason, but strictly and solely from the spontaneous interactions between the faculties of imagination and understanding.[27] Indeed, if in the third *Critique* the realm of affective feeling becomes worthy of transcendental inquiry, it is not to consider the sense of merely empirical sensations of pleasure or displeasure, but because against all odds the horizontal interactions of the cognitive powers themselves become intrinsically connected to aesthetic feelings of pleasure and displeasure.

The transcendental analysis of our receptivity to representation certainly does still appertain to the 'receptivity', which Kant had isolated in the Transcendental Aesthetic of the first *Critique*.[28] It is not that the first *Critique*'s 'sensation' (*Empfindung*) and the third *Critique*'s 'feeling' (*Gefühl*) would designate two different ontological domains. Rather, with the analysis of receptivity in terms of *feeling*, Kant opens up *another dimension of the subject's 'sensibility'* (*Empfänglichkeit des Subjekts*): one which is distinct from its cognitive power ('which contributes nothing at all to the cognition of the object') and which accordingly does not appertain to the problematic of the Transcendental

Aesthetic *stricto sensu*.²⁹ What is at stake in the transcendental analysis of aesthetic 'feeling' is how certain apprehended spatio-temporal forms can trigger a *spontaneous* and *unregulated* interaction of imagination and understanding, which produces a stimulation of the subject's *'feeling of life.'* As Deleuze puts it, in reflective judgment a given representation is related to the subject only 'in so far as it affects the subject by intensifying or weakening its vital force'.³⁰ Although this reference to the *Lebensgefühl* in Kant's account of reflective judgment has received relatively little attention, the principle of an increase or decrease of the subjective life of the faculties provides for Deleuze the general perspective for understanding the reflective functions of judgment and the introduction of a new transcendental principle in Kant's philosophy.

In the metaphysical terminology that Kant inherited from Leibniz and Wolff, the power of judgment may accordingly be understood in terms of a *conatus*: it enacts a recurrent, self-referential *effort* or *striving* to integrate the powers into a living, self-organizing whole. Just as the Spinozist *conatus* corresponds to a living sensibility that strives to conserve and enhance a creature's existence, the striving of the power of judgment corresponds to an inclination to preserve a dynamic interaction of the powers that is 'reciprocally expeditious' (*wechselseitig beförderlich*).³¹ Accordingly, the *conatus* of the power of judgment may be understood as a spontaneous striving to produce and maintain a reciprocal integration of the cognitive powers. It is this conative striving, which comes to the fore in aesthetic pleasure as a *Lebensgefühl*, for the latter has its 'ground' (*Grund*) in 'a state of the powers of the mind reciprocally promoting each other' (*der Zustand einander wechselseitig befördernder Gemütskräfte*).³² Just like the organism's power of self-organization, this *conatus* of the reflecting power of judgment is an animating dynamics without any pre-given *telos*. The *conatus* of reflective judgment is a purposiveness 'without a concept': 'a purposiveness without an end' (*Zweckmäßigkeit ohne Zweck*).³³

The idea of transcendental genesis

The second and perhaps most striking idea in Deleuze's reading is that the third *Critique* does not simply complement the two others but rather unveils a genetic 'ground' that remained hidden in the two other Critiques.³⁴ Whereas the reliance on *a priori* laws allowed the first two *Critiques* to start from the presupposition of preformed faculties with *a priori*, preformed determinate accords, the third *Critique*, by contrast, no longer assumes an accord of the faculties based on an *a priori* law-like structure. For Deleuze, this means that the third *Critique* reveals to us a completely different domain than that of the two other *Critiques*. As he writes:

> In the aesthetic of the *Critique of Judgment*, Kant poses the problem of a genesis of the faculties in their original free agreement. Thus he uncovers the ultimate ground still lacking in the other Critiques. The Critique in general ceases to be a simple *conditioning* to become a transcendental Formation, a transcendental Culture, a transcendental Genesis.[35]

Kant's inquiry now concerns a free and spontaneous accord in which the interaction of the faculties does not rely on preformed *a priori* rules or laws, but rather in which they generate their own purposive lawfulness in the face of contingencies. As I understand it, this interpretation of reflective judgment hints at the unity of the third *Critique*, *both* the Critique of the Aesthetic Power of Judgment and the Critique of the Teleological Power of Judgment being concerned with conceiving self-organization as a process of immanent purposiveness, that is the purposiveness immanent to a self-organizing whole. In accordance with Kant's understanding of organisms as natural purposes, then, the *Gemüt itself* would be a self-organizing natural purpose if and only if:

i. Its parts are only possible (with respect to their existence and their form) through their relation to the whole.
ii. Its parts are combined into a whole by being reciprocally the cause and effect of their form.[36]

This means that for the *Gemüt* itself to be a natural, self-organizing system, it is required that its heterogeneous parts (that is the different faculties) 'reciprocally produce each other', and thus produce a 'whole' out of their own reciprocal causality.[37] In my view, it is exactly such a principle of circular causality that Kant's reconsideration of reflective judgment was after: a genetic principle that is capable of both spontaneously generating and maintaining the organic unity of the *Gemüt*.

In recent decades, several Kant scholars have pointed out that Kant indeed conceived the systematic unity of the faculties as an *organic* unity.[38] For instance, in his work on what he calls Kant's 'transcendental organics', Boris Demarest proposes the following organicist interpretation of the faculty doctrine:

> These faculties relate to each other and the whole of the *Gemüt* as organs do to each other and the organism they make up. (…) First of all, this suggests that the workings of a faculty and the a priori's it involves can never be fully grasped

in abstraction from the workings of the others. (...) [It] suggests further that the *Gemüt* is constituted in a dynamical process of self-production. (...) As a result, the faculties (*Vermögen*) can be conceived of as the result of the activity of the dynamic powers (*Kräfte*) of the *Gemüth* as they face contingencies in their cooperation.'[39]

Such a genetic interpretation of Kant's transcendental philosophy indicates an important step beyond the limitations of the first *Critique*'s transcendental framework. Although Kant accepted the idea that the empirical content of science could historically evolve, he did not accept the idea of a historical development of its *a priori* principles. For this reason it has often been argued that transcendental philosophy cannot truly explain the historical development of knowledge. Whereas Kant's claim that rules exist prior to experience is still widely valued, his claim that some rules are *definitive* because they reflect immutable structures of human reason is generally taken to be narrow and false. For example, the allegedly immutable system of categories or pure concepts of understanding is related to dynamics and appears to have no bearing on statistical laws of nature. This challenge facing Kantian transcendentalism to move from a static to a generative conception of the faculties and their *a priori*'s did not derive from the developments of science alone, however. The challenge was formulated already by the early pioneers of German Idealism, such as Maimon, Fichte and Schelling, who sought to convert the subjective formal *a priori* into a formative power and who replaced the spontaneity of understanding with a generative force of organic development. Before examining how such a generative force may be ascribed to the faculties, we will now turn to Kant's conception of the formative power of organic development itself.

The generative power of self-organization

Circular causality

As is well known, for Kant, the essential and 'inscrutable' property of living organisms is their '*formative power*' (*bildende Kraft*), which is distinct from the mere '*motive* power' that is characteristic of inert matter.[40] Kant conceives the formative power as a natural force that is responsible for generating and sustaining the organized, teleological *structure* or *form* of organized beings. This structure consists of a reciprocal determination between the parts of the organism and the organism as a whole. For Kant, this structure is not that of a mechanism and eschews the laws of geometry and physics, because the latter could not account for the systematic *unity* of the structure and the cohesive, organic connection between its parts. As he puts it in a central, well-known passage in §65 of the third *Critique*:

> An organized being is thus not a mere machine, for that has only a *motive* power, while the organized being possesses in itself a *formative* power, and indeed one that it communicates to the matter, which does not have it (it organizes the latter): thus it is a self-propagating formative power, which cannot be explained through the capacity for movement alone (that is, mechanism).[41]

Although Kant was convinced that a true knowledge of nature (life included) should be described mechanically, and organized beings certainly do possess motive power, he argued that the origin and functioning of organic self-organization could only be understood in *teleological* terms. An organism, Kant writes, is 'possible only as a purpose'.[42] Our judgment of life '*necessarily* carries with it the concept of it as a natural purpose'.[43] But what exactly is teleological about the self-propagating formative power of organisms? What is it that makes this formative property not susceptible to mechanical explanation? To understand this, we have to see how this formative power has the causal power to organize matter.

Kant explains the meaning of the concept of organization as the production of a 'whole' in which each part is 'not merely a means, but at the same time also an end, and, insofar as it contributes to the possibility of the whole, its position and function should also be determined by the idea of the whole'.[44] This means that the formative power has the causal capacity to generate a particular kind of organic *structure* in which whole and part are purposes for each other. However, Kant is clear that this teleological structure of the organism does not mean that it has come into being on the basis of a rule that is external to the configuration of its material parts themselves – for in that case it would be a designed artefact that derives from an external, rational causality. The teleological structure is *intrinsic* to the organism and is related precisely to the organism's formative power. Kant specifies the latter as a specific kind of circular causality: the formative power is what drives the reciprocal causal influence among the different material parts of a system. Let us examine this idea of a reciprocal, purposive causality more closely.

First of all, in organic systems the causal influence of parts on other parts has the remarkable effect that *the parts produce each other*. In other words, reciprocal causality is responsible for a self-productive dynamic. An organism produces and reproduces its biological macromolecules, cells, tissues, organs, and vascular, nervous, immune and metabolic systems as the parts, of which it is composed. These different material parts and their capacities (their functions) are not *pre-given* but rather they are *produced* by the organic whole itself. The interrelation of the parts is not the product of an external designer who conceives the purposive idea of the structure as a building plan. Rather, in a natural purpose 'it is required that the parts produce themselves [*hervorbringen*] together, one from the other, in their form as much as in their binding, reciprocally, and from this causation on, produce a whole'.[45] With regard to the functions of the different parts, this means that the dynamical interaction of forces in an organic system does not merely cause the way in which each part *exercises* its functions. Rather, the reciprocal dynamics are also a *generative* cause of the very *existence* of those functions in the first place.

A second important aspect of this self-productive capacity of the formative power is that it causes a specifically organic kind of *structure* or *form*, which Kant calls a 'whole'. That is to say, the formative power causes the 'form' and the 'combination' of the parts to be such that each part 'exists only *through* all the others'.[46] This means that parts do not merely co-exist but that their existence is reciprocally dependent upon the others. In a machine, the parts exist only *for* one another in that each is the condition of the other's functions towards a common functional end. In an organism, however, the parts exist *for* one another but also *by means* of one another.[47] For example, one might say that a gear of a watch remains that same gear if separated from the watch: the gear, outside of the watch, is still the same (formed) bit of metal. An organ, however, separated from the rest of the living body, loses all its characteristic properties, behaviours and effects: cut off from the body, the organ is dead. As such, the parts of an organic system are essentially internally related. They reciprocally adapt themselves to one another and to altered external circumstances, in function of the preserved equilibrium or continued activity of the whole.

Finally, a third teleological effect of the formative power is that it causes not just the form and combination of the particular parts, but it also causes the form of the organic whole itself and generates a reciprocal relation between the particular purposes of the parts and the general purpose of the whole.

To summarize, the fundamental features of self-organizing natural purposes are, according to Kant, morphogenesis, self-regulation (homeostasis), reproduction and the adaptive relation with an environment (plasticity, external finality).

Self-organization and autopoiesis

For Kant, what makes self-organization specifically organic is the fact that it involves a circular causality between the parts and the whole: on the one hand, the parts reciprocally produce each other and the resulting whole, and on the other hand, in so doing they are also determined by the (future of the) whole. What is thereby essential is the *structural, cohesive unity* that holds among the interdependent parts – a unity that is essentially 'contingent' in the sense that it is not necessitated by physical laws.[48] If we ask what makes self-organization specifically *purposive*, Kant points to the fact that the produced material components *are more than the mere matter of the system*: the material parts also generate its *self-constraining, future-directed structure* or *form*. In other words: living organization individuates not just living matter (cells, tissues, organs, etc.) but also *organic, self-regulating structure*. For Kant, this 'self-preserving' structure is not that of a mechanism, because mechanical features of a system cannot be truly directed towards a (future) purpose.[49] Whereas mechanical laws are essentially blind to purpose, organisms are generated by laws that are intrinsically purposive. Organic structure thus depends on the formative power, which purposively causes the reciprocal determination between the organic whole and its parts.

To clarify this philosophical conception of self-organization, let us briefly compare it with the theory of autopoiesis developed by the Chilean biologists Humberto Maturana and Francisco Varela in the early 1970s, which is a theory of cellular organization that is quite close to the Kantian view. In his book on the principles of biological autonomy, Varela defines autopoiesis as follows:

> An autopoietic system is organized (defined as a unity) as a network of processes of production (transformation and destruction) of components that produces the components that (1) through their interactions and transformations continuously regenerate and realize the network of processes (relations) that produce them; and (2) constitute it (the machine) as a concrete unity in the space in which they exist by specifying the topological domain of its realization as such a network.[50]

For both Kant and Maturana and Varela, self-organizing autopoietic systems can only be thought in terms of a reciprocal determination between the parts and the whole. The crucial idea is that explaining self-organization or autopoiesis must refer not simply to specific physical components of a system and their properties, but rather to the *reciprocal relations* that obtain between physical components to produce a certain effect. An autopoietic system should be described by a *relational topology* rather than the dynamical laws governing its material components. Like Kant, Maturana and Varela focus on the capacities of *self-production* and *self-maintenance* of a system, connecting these capacities to the specific organization of the relations between the components. Autopoiesis consists in a recursive *generative* process that produces the components of a system, and the global network of relations between the components establishes a *self-maintaining* dynamics, which constitutes the system as an operational unit.

Much like Kant, Maturana and Varela also put strong emphasis on the idea that the constitutive mereological organization of biological systems realizes a distinctive regime of causation, which is capable not only of generating and maintaining the components that contribute to the functioning of the whole system, but capable also of promoting its *autonomous* interaction with the environment. Maturana and Varela argue that this relational topology organizes a living system as an *autonomous* system, because autopoiesis produces a physical boundary (e.g. a membrane) between the system and its environment, protecting it from destructive external influences. Unlike other natural self-organizing systems, such as dissipative structures, which are spontaneous and mostly fully determined by external boundary conditions, autopoietic systems vastly contribute to determine their own conditions of existence.

As mentioned in the previous sections, it is my contention that Kant's reconsideration of the power of judgment in the third *Critique* may be understood as an attempt to construct just such a generative principle of self-organizing causality on the level of the cognitive faculties themselves.[51] To see how such a generative causality may be at work in both Kant's and Deleuze's faculty doctrines, the next chapter will consider how both thinkers link a *conatus* to the mind's cognitive powers, which designates a spontaneous internal striving towards *self-activity* and *individuation*. But before turning back to Kant's and Deleuze's faculty doctrines, I wish to indicate two different ways of thinking about self-organization in the wake of Kant, and which one of these Deleuze adopts in his transcendental philosophy.

The ontological aporia of self-organization

Kant's conception of organic structure opens up a deep ontological aporia: if the self-organizing structure of an organism is not that of a physical mechanism, but the effect of a purposive causality, then what is the ontological status of self-organization? If the *external* physical appearance of an organic system is governed by an *internal* organizing principle purposively producing structural connections between the material parts, then what is the ontological status of this internal principle?

To understand the difficulty we are facing, we can compare Kant's concept of organic structure with that of linguistic structure, which faces the same ontological aporia.[52] Linguistic structuralism begins with the assumption of the fundamental, constitutive existence of structures that are purely *ideal* and not material. Linguistic structures are abstract forms of organization that are *irreducible* to certain material components in interaction. For example, *phonemes* are considered as constitutive elements of linguistic signifiers, which are incorporeal elements, since the signifier itself is incorporeal. Structuralists such as Saussure and Hjelmslev emphasized the ontological autonomy of the phoneme as an ideal 'form of expression' that is 'embodied' in the material 'substance of expression' but that is not reducible to it. As such, there is a reciprocal dependence between the *phonetic form* and the *phonetic substance*: the phoneme is an abstract structure or organizational form that has a psychological reality and becomes attached or encoded in the physical audio-acoustic flux.

Rejecting empiricist reductionism, structuralism thus posits the ontological primacy of *non-material* structures, which are constitutive of meaning. The crucial founding idea of structuralism is that structure is the ideal form of organization of a material (phonic) substance, and as such structure is itself not a sensible phenomenon. It is essentially invisible, although its substantial realization and its meaning effects are observable and may be the object of certain rigorous empirical experiments. As such, each structure is a purely theoretical object and not a fact. In Deleuze's famous phrasing, structure is at once real and ideal: '*real without being actual, ideal without being abstract*', a '*pure virtuality of coexistence that pre-exists beings*'.[53] A structure 'incarnates' itself in its substrate, it 'expresses' itself in it, but it never actualizes itself *as such*. Instead, the sensible expression of a structure is always essentially a negation of its ideal, formal being.

Clearly, given their ideal, non-phenomenal status, structures are *ontologically* ambiguous. As Petitot has pointed out, although it is an ideal *eidos*, a structure cannot be detached from the substance in which it actualizes itself.[54] It is therefore both a *structuring* principle and a *structured* substance. In this regard, Petitot notes, two different ontological approaches are possible: either one adopts a *realist* point of view, and one takes ideal structures to be *given* or one takes a *nominalist* point of view, and one considers them as merely theoretically posited.[55] As Petitot points out, the 'great' structuralists of the twentieth century, Deleuze included, were realists in this regard: Saussure, Jakobson, Lévi-Strauss, Tesnière, Hjelmslev, Piaget, Chomsky, Greimas, Thom and Petitot himself.

We confront the same ontological aporia facing self-organization. Kant argued that although it refers to an empirical phenomenon, the concept of a purposive organic structure is only a 'noumenal' Idea and not a determinant concept or category. Attributing organic structure to organisms is not to be taken literally in the way we attribute physical properties to them, such as mass or acceleration. But then is self-organization *real*, in the same way that the wings of a bird are real? Clearly, for Kant, referring to circular causation or reciprocal determination in self-organization does not *explain* organic structure by referring to a physical mechanism.

Indeed, the circular causality, which Kant ascribes to self-organization, explicitly does not refer to physical mechanism. It explains organic structure in terms of a biological purpose, and it links that purpose to concrete structural conditions in reality (morphogenesis, self-regulation, plasticity, etc.). For Kant, this entails that we cannot view organic structure ontologically in the same way as physical causal mechanisms. Ultimately, Kant's position thus consists in two complementary principles, one mechanistic and one holistic: (1) given the *a priori* structure of possible experience, we cannot cognize any objective teleology in nature and objectively speaking, nature is necessarily mechanical; (2) nonetheless, a mechanistic explanation of self-organization would always remain *incomplete* to the extent that it would not explain the *contingency* of the organic structure of the organism, which eschews the laws of physics and geometry and can only be approached reflectively.

Given the advances in biology (neo-Darwinism as the synthesis of Darwinian evolutionary theory and molecular genetics) on the one hand, and the theory of dissipative structures in non-equilibrium thermodynamics (explaining how order can emerge just from the non-equilibrium dynamics of complex systems) on the other hand, one may be inclined to read Kant's stance as a temporary heuristic, and to assume that a fully mechanistic explanation of self-organization is possible.[56] I believe this is not Kant's position, and in fact it would be misguided to think that organismic teleology has been dispensed within science.

Neo-Darwinism proposes a reductionist approach to organisms which grounds scientific objectivity only in efficient causation and reduces all organismal dynamics to the physico-chemical level. It assumes that there is nothing to be explained other than the way in which the genome controls or causes the form and the development of an organism at the phenotype level. Neo-Darwinism agrees that the singularity of life consists in the manifestation of a functional, organizational structure or form that actualizes a certain internal (genetic) project or program. But it considers an organism's structural organization to be causally reducible to the primary structure of genes and proteins, and all else to be a matter of thermodynamic processes of self-organization and the external finality of evolutionary adaptation and selection.

Both the original Kantian and the contemporary autopoietic approach in biology start from another, reverse possibility: namely that there are irreducible structures of nested correlated interactions, that is, organizations, that are central to understanding why an organism's biochemical details are as they are, genomes included. On this view, organization or structure is just as fundamental to understanding life as the biochemistry: organisms are not just genetically controlled systems, but *also* self-organizing structures, or wholes organized by a system of internal relations. In the Kantian position, self-organization provides a source of activity by which the parts of an organic whole (i.e. its cells, its tissues, its organs, etc.) bear their own organizational constraints, in addition to those constraints that are imposed by the genome or by the selective action of the environment.

As the biologists Gerry Webster and Brian Goodwin have shown, this idea is also at the heart of the structuralist conception of the organism, which originated in the work of Cuvier and Geoffroy, and which strongly influenced Deleuze.[57] The central idea of structuralism in biology is that the relational structure of organisms is fundamental and points to the existence of internal constraints on morphogenesis and form (Kant's inner purposiveness). According to this view, organisms are not merely genetically controlled systems, and neo-Darwinism lacks a robust notion of the agency of the organism itself, that is, of internally generated constraints.

The organizational and structuralist approaches in biology and linguistics show that instead of taking a reductionist approach to Kant's holistic maxim of purposiveness, one can also take a *realist* approach to it: in this case, one takes a *neo-Aristotelian* approach to the concept of self-organization and one expands fundamental ontology to include organismic purposiveness.[58] This approach entails (1) that we follow Kant's maxim that the concept of natural purposes is *indispensable* to scientific explanation (and hence it cannot be *replaced* or *dispensed* by it) and (2) that purposive self-organization is to be conceived ontologically, as a distinct level of causation, operating in addition to physico-chemical laws and generated by the reciprocal determination between material structures of an integrated system. If we adopt this position, the biological and cognitive domains are conceivable as domains which generate themselves and within which general and systematic generative processes are at work. In the following chapters, I aim to show how Deleuze's philosophy of individuation develops this neo-Aristotelian option.

2

Conatus – power – faculty

There is something in us which has the power to think; but it does not thereby follow that it is always in action. Real powers are never simple possibilities. They have always tendency [conatus] and action.

— Gottfried W. Leibniz[1]

Leibniz's force ontology

Among Kant's and Deleuze's philosophical masters, Leibniz was certainly the most Aristotelian. Refuting Descartes's view of the essence (i.e., 'substance') of matter as extension, Leibniz returned to Aristotle's view that matter is essentially dynamism, or movement. Moreover, Leibniz also revived Aristotle's view that the dynamism of entities should be understood in terms of more primordial tendencies and forces, which are intrinsic and ultimately most essential to matter. In what has been aptly called Leibniz's 'force ontology', the metaphysical ground floor does not consist of substances that *possess* force, but rather, we just find forces.[2] Indeed, for Leibniz, all substances derive their unity from a fundamental or foundational force, and in this sense forces are not *properties* of substances but rather *constituents* of them. That is to say, for Leibniz, the essence or 'substance' of all entities is constituted by a number of internal forces, which actualize themselves in the actions of the entity. This conception of force is rooted in Aristotle's definition of movement as a transition of potentiality (*dunamis*) to actuality (*energeia*). Leibniz deeply meditated on this Aristotelian view of movement as a *transition*, and drew from it the idea that the *dynamical* is primary with regard to the *static*. Indeed, in Leibniz's force ontology, there is a metaphysical priority of potentiality over actuality: at the most fundamental level, all entities consist of a set of constitutive dynamical *forces* that are *potential* rather than *actual*.

To understand how Leibniz's force ontology adopts (and transforms) this Aristotelian terminology, a good starting point is the following passage from the *New Essays on Human Understanding*. The terminology, which Leibniz introduces in this passage, is implicit not only in many of his other key texts, but also plays a foundational role in Kant's and Deleuze's faculty doctrines. The passage begins with establishing a distinction between power and act:

> If 'power' [*puissance*] corresponds to the Latin *potentia*, it is contrasted with 'act,' and the transition from power into act is 'change.' That is what Aristotle means by the word 'movement,' when he says that movement is the act – or perhaps the actualizing – of that which has the power to be. Power in general, then, can be described as the possibility of change. But since change – or the actualization of that possibility – is action in one subject and passion in another, there will be two powers, one active and one passive. The active power can be called 'faculty' [*faculté*] and perhaps the passive one might be called 'capacity' or 'receptivity' [*capacité ou receptivité*].³

In this passage, Leibniz still remains close to the Scholastic interpretations of Aristotle. He tells us an entity's acts derive from the actualization of its powers (*potentia*), and for an entity to possess a power means it is possible for a given entity to change in certain ways. In this regard, powers can be either active or passive, since change always involves both an agent and a patient. For example, a fish has the active power of metabolizing algae and insects, while algae and insects have the passive power of being metabolized by fish. Leibniz calls an active power a 'faculty' and a passive power a 'capacity' or 'receptivity'. Now, in the second part of this passage, some important nuances are made:

> It is true that active power is sometimes understood in a fuller sense, in which it comprises not just a mere faculty but also an *endeavor* [*tendence*]; and that is how I take it in my theorizing about dynamics. One could reserve the word "force" for that. Force would divide into "entelechy" and "effort"; for although Aristotle takes "entelechy" so generally that it comprises all action and all effort, it seems to me more suitable to apply it to *primary acting forces*, and "effort" to *derivative* ones. There is, furthermore, another particular kind of passive power, which carries more reality with it: it is a power which matter has, for matter has not only mobility (i.e. the capacity for or receptivity to movement) but also *resistance*, which includes both impenetrability and inertia. When an entelechy – i.e. a primary or substantial endeavour – is accompanied by perception, it is a soul.⁴

In this section, Leibniz introduces a crucial distinction between simple faculty and something stronger and fuller, which he calls 'force', 'endeavour' or 'entelechy' and which he associates with active power. Although he does not explicitly say it here, it is this connection between active power and endeavour or force, which Leibniz is most interested in. In fact, as we will see, Leibniz says that simple faculties are not genuine powers at all. Rather, all genuine powers require an active force or an endeavour, so as to pass into actual acts. As he puts it in a different passage of the *New Essays*: 'True powers are never simple possibilities; there is always endeavour, and action.'[5] Endeavour, which he also calls *conatus*, can in turn take the form of either a primitive acting force (*entelechy*) or a derivative acting force (*effort*). Opposed to this fundamental active force that is characteristic of the *soul*, Leibniz also distinguishes a fundamental passive power that is characteristic of *matter*, and that designates the overwhelming tendency of material systems towards inertia, impenetrability and extensive movement.

Among the different terms Leibniz uses to refer to the *active forces* of the soul ('force' (*vis*), 'power' (*potential*), 'entelechy', 'disposition', 'faculty', 'endeavour', 'effort' and 'striving'), it is the relation between *endeavour* (*conatus*), *power* and *faculty* that is most important in the context of Kant's and Deleuze's faculty doctrines. To understand these doctrines better, it will help to look at Leibniz's conception of the relation between power, faculty and *conatus* or active force. I believe that focusing on this relation makes it possible to gain a deeper understanding of the fundamental contrasts between Kant's and Deleuze's transcendental philosophies. In fact, as I hope to show in this chapter, much turns on Kant's and Deleuze's divergent interpretations of this Leibnizian concept of the *conatus*.

In his *Lectures on Metaphysics*, Kant develops an intricate reading of Leibniz's force ontology, establishing a relation between (a) the mental powers, (b) the acts that are causally individuated by the mental powers, which are representations and (c) a *conatus* that is the causal potential of the powers in the sense that the *conatus* is a spontaneous, generative striving towards *self-activity* (and hence towards representation) that is inherent to each living power. Although Kant makes several critical amendments to the Leibnizian conception of the *conatus* as a self-unifying force of the soul, his understanding of mental causation remains intrinsically tied to this metaphysical notion of the *conatus*: it is always a mental power that causes a mental act to act, and every causal act of a mental power continuously arises from its conative striving towards self-activity. As such, the spontaneity of all unifying, synthetic acts ascribed to the transcendental apperception ("I think") is for Kant a *product* of an underlying *conatus*, a primordial predisposition of the mind to seek and find logical structure and order.

To see how Deleuze in turn adopts the distinction between *conatus*, power and faculty, we will take a step back and ask: what does it mean to embody the faculties in the stream of life? For Kant and Leibniz, the conative force, which animates the spontaneous striving of the mental powers, belongs ultimately to the human *soul* or *spirit*. For Deleuze, however, who adopts a resolutely Spinozist and Nietzschean reading of Leibniz's force ontology, the mind's conative striving has its roots in a primordial unconscious conative striving of the *body*. Indeed, for Deleuze, all conscious cognition, feeling and desire are genetically and ontologically animated by the energy of an *unconscious will to power*. Deleuze will call the fundamental active force, which actualizes itself in particular mental acts, a 'virtuality'. For him, as for Aristotle and Leibniz, this virtuality is – despite its lack of actuality – a positive, existing force that belongs to the essence of both life and consciousness. But Deleuze will find in Spinoza and Nietzsche an important naturalist amendment to Leibniz's force ontology: 'a devaluation of consciousness in relation to thought: a discovery of the unconscious, of an *unconscious of thought* just as profound as *the unknown of the body*'.[6]

The conatus in Kant's faculty doctrine

Faculty, power and conatus

According to the standard interpretation of Kant's faculty–power distinction, the powers (*Kräfte*) are the actualization of the faculties (*Vermögen*):

> Although sometimes Kant seems to use the expressions "Vermögen" and "Kraft" interchangeably, as when he characterizes the Urteilskraft or Einbildungskraft as "Vermögen" (e.g. 5:179; 7:264), they stand for two aspects of causal connections that are clearly distinguished by Kant. Whereas the *Vermögen* consists of the mere *possibility* of an "act," the *Kraft* consists of its actualization by a determining ground.[7]

This way of distinguishing the faculties from the powers can be traced back to Leibniz, Wolff and Crusius. For them already, the distinction between a faculty's mere possibility and a power's act concerns the idea of *self-activity*: a power is driven by a continuous striving or *conatus* to act, while a faculty consists in the mere possibility of acting.[8] This means that the concept of power is intrinsically tied to the concept of mental causation: it is always a power that causes a mental act to act, unless something external resists its internal striving (for example another power).[9] As Kant puts it in the first *Critique*, 'power' (*Kraft*) is 'the causality of a substance'.¹⁰ A faculty, on the contrary, does not entail this connection to causality and self-activity. A faculty never causes an act to act but it is merely the *possibility* of an act.

In the *Lectures on Metaphysics,* Kant adopts this distinction by calling a faculty a power whose act remains obstructed by the conflict with another power: 'This insufficient power is called a faculty'.¹¹ Kant also calls faculties 'dead' powers, whereas powers that are not obstructed in their self-activity are 'living' powers:

> *Faculty and power* must be distinguished. In the case of a faculty we have in mind the possibility of an act. It does not contain the sufficient ground of the act, which is the power, but rather it contains the mere possibility of the latter. Each power is either *living* [*lebendig*], in case it acts (and therefore is both internally and externally sufficient, being the ground of the effectuation of the cauβati or accidentis), or she is *dead* [*todt*], in case it is internally sufficient but externally insufficient or in case no act occurs because then an external cause must be there contravening it; e.g. each body has a power to fall, although this does not occur when another opposite power resists it; insofar as there is no resistance, all powers are therefore alive. The conatus or striving is actually the determination of a faculty ad actum. This should transform the faculty of dead powers into living powers, and means accordingly the insufficiency of a dead power, since the latter is dead only by a resistance, and something is in a state of striving only because something else is resisting it.¹²

The difficulty one faces upon interpreting this passage is to understand how Kant delineates at once faculty, power and *conatus*. At certain points in the text, *conatus* and faculty seem to say the same. However, as Stefan Heßbrüggen-Walter has pointed out, the faculties may themselves not be interpreted as having a *conatus* towards self-realization. Rather, the faculties should be understood as a Leibnizian '*nuda potentia*': a mere possibility.¹³ Unlike the *conatus*, a faculty is nothing but a possibility of acting, which needs an *external* excitation or stimulus to be transferred into action. As Leibniz writes:

> Active force [*vis activa*] differs from the mere power familiar to the Schools, for the (…) faculty of the Scholastics is nothing but an approximate possibility of acting, which needs an external excitation or stimulus, as it were, to be transferred into action.¹⁴

A faculty is a potentiality and not a *conatus* in the sense that it requires an external cause to activate itself. By contrast, the central defining trait of the *conatus* is that its striving always involves a certain act and does not arise from an external stimulus. Its active striving does not require an external stimulus or cause to produce an actual act. Leibniz writes:

> But active force [*vis activa*] contains a certain act or *entelecheia* and is thus midway between the faculty of acting and the act itself and involves a conatus.[15]

We find the same emphasis in the following passage from a 1694 draft of his essay 'New System':

> By "force" or "potency" I do not mean a power or a mere faculty, which is only a bare possibility for action and which, being itself dead as it were, never produces an action without being excited from outside; instead I mean *something midway between power and action*, something which involves an effort, an act, an entelechy – for force passes into action by itself so long as nothing prevents it. That is why I consider it to be what constitutes substance, since it is the principle of action, which is its characteristic feature.[16]

Leibniz emphasizes that the *conatus* does not receive the force of acting from another power, but rather it contains *within itself* a pre-existent striving or causal force of action. The similitude between faculty and *conatus* comes from the fact that both designate a *capacity*. But the *conatus*, unlike the faculty, is not a dead inactive capacity that has not yet come into play or existence. To the contrary, the *conatus* of the active force is always active, it is actively striving, and this activity does not rely on prior external circumstances: it is a restless impulse towards self-activity that is essentially self-propulsive.[17]

But Kant also delineates the *conatus* from the living or active power: the striving is what transforms the faculty of a dead power into a living power. The *conatus* is then a certain kind of act and nevertheless not 'yet' the activity of a power in its real accomplishment. Rather, it is a *tending towards*, a *striving for* self-activity. Paraphrasing Leibniz, we should say the *conatus* is 'midway' between the faculty of acting and the act itself: it is neither the mere possibility, nor the actual process. It is exactly to the extent that the *conatus* strives towards the accomplishment of a power's living self-activity and to the extent that it itself contains the necessary causal forces to accomplish this, that one may say that the power already contains this self-activity, still before it unfolds. It is in this sense that the *conatus* of the power may also not be confused with the dynamic activities of the power: the striving is not 'yet' an action.

Summarizing, the *conatus* of a power is *more* than the mere possibility to act (a potentiality in the sense of Leibniz's "*nuda potentia*") and also *less* than the carrying out of an act. The striving of a power is an active, living drive, an existing effort towards self-activity. This striving must be distinguished from a mere possibility ('*nuda potentia*' or '*facultas*'), which depends upon an external stimulus, an external causality, to pass into action. This striving must also be distinguished, however, from the power's actions themselves, precisely because it designates the *impulse or tendency* towards the act – a tendency that 'already' contains the very principle of the act from within. Within Kant's faculty doctrine, the concept of a *conatus* thus means a striving that is inherent in every living mental power. Each living act of a mental power continuously arises from this *conatus* towards self-activity.

Conatus and individuation

In his interpretation of the Leibnizian *vis activa* in *The Metaphysical Foundations of Logic*, Heidegger calls the *conatus* a 'drive' (*Drang, Trieb*) that must be distinguished at once from a mere disposition (a faculty) and from an actual process (an active power).[18] In Heidegger's view, the essential function of the drive or active force is the individuation of a monad's 'unity': the drive is 'unity-conferring'.[19] For Leibniz, the essence of the monad or soul is its indivisible unity, which cannot be compared to the composition of parts in material aggregates. More precisely, the essence of the monad consists in its striving to unify itself. And insofar as it unifies itself, the monad individuates itself. We may say therefore that a monad's individuation is structurally dependent on the *conative* essence of the monad as active force or drive.

If we ask how the active force unifies, and how it is individuated in the unification, we find that the active force unifies as a 'foregrasping grip'.[20] The *conative* character of the monad's striving entails that it is continuously *anticipating* its own unity, its own individuation: the active force is continuously *'reaching out'* towards its own unity, *'gripping in advance'*, or 'pre-hensive' (*re-präsentierend*).[21] If the *vis activa* strives for self-unification or individuation, this striving must thus also be a striving for *prehension* or *apprehension* (*perceptio*).[22] This means that the monad is continuously driven to unify the 'manifold' of dispersing 'perceptions' and 'appetitions' which it contains.[23] The active force unifies with a glance towards unity, always from within a certain point of view. Because monads are not isolated from the world, each presents the world from a viewpoint and 'this unifying presentation of the universe in each individuation is precisely what concerns each monad in its being, its drive'.[24] Heidegger notes 'the deepest metaphysical motive for the monad's characteristic prehension [*Vorstellungscharakter*] is the ontologically unifying function' of the *conatus* or *vis activa*: the monad has prehensions and eventually apprehensions and apperceptions *in function* of its striving for self-unification or individuation.

He adds: 'Prehension [*vor-stellen*] is to be understood here quite broadly, structurally, and not as a particular faculty of the soul'.[25]

Finally, we should see what connects a monad's *conatus* to its perceptions, apprehensions and apperceptions. In Leibniz's view, this is an '*appetitus*', which drives each individual monad towards representations. The *appetitus* is the way in which the *conatus* drives the monad from one representation to another. In Leibniz's view, this *appetitus* manifests itself as a fundamental '*uneasiness*' or '*Unruhe*' ('*inquiétude*') at the bottom of the soul. What is peculiar – and *structural* in Heidegger's sense above – about this *uneasiness* or *Unruhe* is that it manifests itself in a confused and almost unconscious ('imperceptible') manner: 'these are confused stimuli, so that we often do not know what we lack'.[26] With inclinations, emotions and passions, on the other hand, we know what we want because these are related to a particular object. Hope, fear, joy, shame, anger, envy, etc. are all emotional states that arise when the soul thinks of a determinate action, object, person, etc. This is different with the *uneasiness* that structurally animates the soul: *uneasiness* is not itself an emotion, a passion or a simple pleasure or displeasure, but rather *it is always present within them*. As Leibniz writes, 'there is disquiet even in joy'.[27] Indeed, 'Aversion, fear, anger, envy, shame, … all have their [disquiet] too'.[28] Strictly speaking, there is uneasiness or *Unruhe* implicit in *all the states of the soul*: all emotions, passions but also imaginations, volitions and cognitions implicitly contain an *uneasiness*, which animates them. This is why Leibniz agrees with Locke's saying that 'The chief if not only spur to human industry and action is uneasiness'.[29]

The conatus in Kant's faculty doctrine

Leibniz's characterization of the monad as composed of a manifold of perceptions, apprehensions and apperceptions, and of a structural, self-unifying force, which continuously strives to integrate these into a unified whole, was highly influential on Kant's conception of the spontaneity by which the cognitive powers produce representations, and synthesize them. One could easily show that although Kant rejects the traditional (Leibnizian) concept of the soul as a substance endowed with an original spontaneity (*vis activa primitiva*), his understanding of mental causation remains intrinsically tied to this metaphysical, Leibnizian notion of the *conatus*. I will not pursue this tedious task here and digress into an overly long exegesis of Kant's faculty doctrine.[30] Instead, one brief remark will suffice for our purposes here.

In the first *Critique*, the *conatus* that is associated with the spontaneity of the faculty of apperception (understanding) may, as Béatrice Longuenesse has shown, be conceived as a 'discursive *conatus*' towards cognitive representations.[31] This discursive *conatus* is a spontaneous cognitive tendency, an inborn disposition, to reflect on what is given in sensibility so as to discern some *logical form* in it: how do things relate to each other in the orders of space and time? Are things similar or even identical? Are they connected by causal relations? This primal disposition to reflect is according to Kant what essentially defines us as human beings: a spontaneous tendency of the mind to identify logical form or structure in the welter of experiences. It is this reflective predisposition, which makes possible the universal, logical forms by which we think the world. It grounds our cognitive relation to the world as a representational relation that has an objective meaning: by virtue of reflection, we can analyse concrete, particular sensible experiences in terms of abstract, universal representations. With this Kantian framework in mind, let us see now how Deleuze takes up the Leibnizian distinction between *conatus*, power and faculty.

Spinoza's force ontology

Dynamism reconsidered

In his first book on Spinoza, Deleuze finds in both Leibniz and Spinoza a common dynamist project:

> Their philosophies constitute two aspects of a new "naturalism." This new naturalism provides the true thrust of the anti-Cartesian reaction. In very fine pages, Ferdinand Alquié has shown how Descartes dominated the first half of the seventeenth century by succeeding in the venture of a mathematical mechanical science, whose first effect was to devaluate Nature by taking away from it any virtuality or potentiality, any immanent power, any inherent being. (…) With the anti-Cartesian reaction, it is a matter of re-establishing the claims of a Nature endowed with forces or power.[32]

Returning to Aristotle's view of the organizing force or entelechy of matter, Leibniz assumed a continuous hierarchy of animation from the simplest to the most complex monads. The essence of this new dynamist metaphysics of nature, Deleuze writes, concerns the Spinozist and Leibnizian concept of the *conatus*. Just as Leibniz conceives the essence or 'substance' of nature in terms of the dynamism of constitutive active and passive forces, Spinoza also conceives the essence of all entities in terms of a *conatus* that ultimately derives from nature's all-encompassing productive power. However, there is an important contrast between the Leibnizian and Spinozist conceptions of the *conatus*. Both philosophical systems involve questions which are very close but whose answers nonetheless diverge strongly. This is clear in Leibniz's condemnation of Spinoza's philosophy as a 'monstrous doctrine' that confounds the divine with created beings and takes physical objects to be part of the divine.[33] Moreover, in contrast with Leibniz's teleological animism, Spinoza's monism of body and mind admits only one, material kind of force and thus leaves no room for the existence of spiritual, finalist forces, which Leibniz's philosophy emphasized so greatly. As Deleuze writes:

> As opposed to that of Leibniz, Spinoza's dynamism and "essentialism" deliberately excludes all finality. Spinoza's theory of *conatus* has no other function than to present dynamism for what it is by stripping it of any finalist significance.[34]

The body as a model

As is well known, Deleuze's reading of Spinoza starts from the following passage in the *Ethics*, which he calls Spinoza's 'war cry' against traditional metaphysics:

> For indeed, no one has yet determined what the body can do, that is, experience has not yet taught anyone what the body can do from the laws of nature alone, insofar as Nature is only considered to be corporeal, and what the body can do only if it is determined by the mind. For no one has yet come to know the structure of the body so accurately that he could explain all its functions – not to mention that many things are observed in the lower animals which far surpass human ingenuity, and that sleepwalkers do a great many things in their sleep which they would not dare to awake. This shows well enough that the body itself, simply from the laws of its own nature, can do many things which its mind wonders at.[35]

Shortly after this passage, Spinoza writes that we speak of consciousness, the mind, the soul, the power of the soul over the body, etc.; we chatter away about these things, but we do not even know what bodies can do. Deleuze adds that for Spinoza, by contrast, 'As long as we speak of a power of the soul over the body we are not really thinking in terms of power or force.'[36] In traditional philosophical conceptions of the body, the body is considered as inferior and obedient to the superior commands of the mind. This is of course evident in Kant: at least in principle, reason has the capacity to become master over all the bodily inclinations striving against it through the mere idea of a moral law governing the individual's will and hence, at least in principle, his or her acts, too. Spinoza starts from a criticism of precisely this traditional conception of the body – a criticism which is equally central to Nietzsche's philosophy:

> Spinoza opened up a new path for the sciences and philosophy: he said we do not even know what a body *can do*, we talk about consciousness and spirit and chatter about all that, but we do not know what a body is capable of, what forces belong to it or what they are preparing for. Nietzsche knew that the hour had come: "We are in the phase of modesty of consciousness." To remind consciousness of its necessary modesty is to take it for what it is: a symptom, nothing but the symptom of a deeper transformation and of activities of entirely non-spiritual forces.[37]

Unlike Leibniz and Kant, then, Spinoza and Nietzsche take the internal dynamism of *bodily forces* as their philosophical point of departure: to really think in terms of force and power, that is, to develop a robust force ontology, one must consider it in relation to the body, and free the body from its traditional subordination to the mind. As Deleuze puts this central point:

> The question, "What can a body do?" must be taken as a model. *This model implies no devaluation of thought in relation to extension, but solely a devaluation of consciousness with regard to thought.*[38]

Conatus, power and affectivity

Leibniz's view of the conatus already contains a link between a force's striving for power and the affirmation of an entity's being itself – two themes also at the heart of Spinoza's (and Nietzsche's) thinking. It is certainly Leibniz's merit to have reintroduced a dynamist approach to the mind by conceiving it in terms of an Aristotelian entelechy or potential force, which strives to actualize itself in particular acts and which despite its lack of actuality is a positive, existing force (and not a mere inexistent possibility). If, however, Deleuze opts for a *Spinozist* interpretation of the *conatus*, it is because Spinoza understands the human being monistically as a single process, a single striving for self-preservation and self-enhancement that can be described under two modalities, bodily and mentally, but both expressing one single underlying dynamic of self-maintenance and self-furthering.

Although Spinoza's rethinking of the *conatus* breaks with the Aristotelian/Leibnizian philosophy of final causes, he nevertheless retained much of Aristotle's dichotomy of activity versus passivity. Aristotle believed that striving for an optimal dynamic state of human flourishing, which he designated as 'activity', was the essential characteristic of human nature. He famously developed an ethical model in which every natural thing and living species has a natural activity, proper to itself, that defines it and whose proper functioning defines its truest flourishing. For Aristotle, all natural creatures have to be understood as aiming at such a dynamic steady state through the defining activities that characterize them as natural kinds. With his notion of the *conatus*, Spinoza inscribes himself in this Aristotelian notion of flourishing, which he also conceives in terms of 'activity' in contrast to 'passivity'. But while Aristotle ultimately identified this activity with rational/theoretical thinking, Spinoza identifies it with a state of *desire* that spans both body and mind and is expressed affectively in various feelings or emotions. This means it is the emotions which register the varying state of a creature's *conatus* as its 'activity' or agency is strengthened or weakened.

What is particularly original about Spinoza's account is the way in which he conceives of this relation between the *conatus* and affective feeling. For Spinoza holds that our emotions can themselves be in either an *active* or a *passive* state.[39] Initially, human beings have predominantly passive affections insofar as their emotions – the way they feel – are entirely determined or caused by factors *external* to them. Affections become *active* to the extent that one reaches a rational self-understanding of the causes of one's emotions. That is to say, the emotions become active by virtue of progressively reflecting and ordering the causes that diminish or enhance one's *conatus*. In this sense, active affections express the individual's own striving for power instead of being determined by external forces. By contrast, passive emotions result from a reactive, passive submission to external circumstances and to unreflective attitudes, which form the cognitive dimension of the emotions. As such, passive affectivity entails the real danger of external causes to dominate the mind's feeling and thinking states. This is why Spinoza calls passive affectivity a state of servitude or slavery.

Active affectivity is the way in which an individual actively reflects on the causes of its feelings, investigating one's own causal constitution within the nested hierarchy of other natural, striving beings. The ethical question of human flourishing is thus for Spinoza a question of active and *free* feelings as opposed to passive and *servile* feelings. That is to say, one is to render both body and mind *active*, through the active transformation of one's affective feelings or emotions. This activation of body and mind through the activation of emotion is the form in which we truly become conscious of ourselves, through what Spinoza called intuitive knowledge. To Spinoza, this knowledge obtained through intuition is what allows us to truly take possession of our *conatus* and to experience active joys that form true virtue. If, as noted, active feelings are *free* it is because in the active transformation of our feelings *we ourselves* become the causes of our own affects.[40] This is to Spinoza *virtuous*, for this active transformation of emotion is what allows our body to gain access to its power of acting, and our mind to its power of thinking, which is its own way of acting. From this perspective, there is a great 'ethical difference' between simply seeking positive, empowering encounters *through mere chance* and truly striving to understand and organize the affective encounters with bodies that empower one's *conatus*.[41] Since a body's conative perseverance and power of acting relies on its affections, the crucial ethical question is how an individual is interpreting his or her *conatus*, and which affections he or she is really seeking or avoiding: is one, at bottom, actively seeking joy or sadness?

Insofar as one is actively striving to understand and organize one's affections, and to seek out whatever increases one's power, one's striving may for Spinoza be entitled *good, rational, strong and virtuous*.[42] Indeed, to Spinoza there is no other ethical virtue besides *power*. Its opposite is not evil but rather powerlessness and enslavement. An individual is called *bad, servile, foolish or weak*, 'who lives haphazardly, who is content to undergo the effects of his encounters, but wails and accuses every time the effect undergone does not agree with him and reveals his own impotence'.[43]

For Deleuze, who finds here a Nietzschean theme in Spinoza that will also deeply shape his own philosophy, Spinoza's force ontology is thus ultimately a philosophy of 'life': a philosophy that denounces all that separates us from life, all the imaginary opinions, clichés, values and norms that are turned against life *by separating the individual from its power to act*.[44] The point of such a naturalist philosophy of life, which equivocates virtue with power, is of course not to promote moral relativism or immoralism. The fundamental problem, which drives it, is that of the *singularity of the individual*, which is *dispossessed* of its capacity to be affected, its power to act and its power to think. As Deleuze writes:

> How can one keep from destroying oneself through guilt, and others through resentment, spreading one's own powerlessness and enslavement everywhere, one's own sickness, indigestions, and poisons? In the end, one is unable even to encounter oneself.[45]

In such a philosophy of life, *thinking* must be understood as a dynamic *activity* that has intrinsic ties to one's flourishing or well-being, such that its well- or malfunctioning must be accounted for not solely in terms of rational consistency or *truth* but also in the homeodynamic terms that were long reserved for the body alone. For with Spinoza, the energetic self-maintenance and optimization of the living body, its *conatus*, has come to be included into our desire for mental order and enhancement – the *conatus* of the mind. That is to say, Spinoza's *conatus* is neither a mere organic mechanism of static homeostasis nor a purely human or spiritual striving for rational consistency and order. Instead, it is a self-optimizing principle that directs the diverse affections of both body and mind. More precisely, the *conatus* of the mind accounts for both its order and coherence as well as its vital endeavour to grasp and integrate the logic of its own constitutive causes. To see how this Spinozist reworking of the *conatus* plays out in Deleuze's faculty doctrine, we should now address one final influence on Deleuze's conative understanding of the mind.

Nietzsche's force ontology

The monadology revisited

Nietzsche's doctrine of the will to power is deeply connected to both Spinoza's conception of the *conatus* and Leibniz's concept of active force or *vis activa*.[46] We will begin by considering here Nietzsche's relation to Leibniz.

In the middle of the nineteenth century, the emergence of thermodynamics and its principle of the conservation of energy brought with it a philosophical resurgence of Leibniz's force ontology, which deeply influenced Nietzsche (mainly via the work of the physicists Roger Josip Bošković and Julius Robert Mayer). Although he shared Spinoza's critique of Leibniz's finalism, Leibniz's metaphysical approach to force clearly appealed to Nietzsche. Indeed, Nietzsche agreed with Leibniz that all natural events must be conceived not merely in terms of the causality of external pressure and collisions, but rather in terms of the immanent, endogenous causality of forces, whose organization is most fundamental. In this context, an interesting textual reference to Leibniz can be found in the third volume of Karl Schlechta's edition of Nietzsche's *Werke in drei Bänden*, where one finds Nietzsche's original annotations, which were used for the posthumous publication of *The Will to Power*. In these notes from the 1880s, Nietzsche discusses his doctrine of the will to power as a 'monadological' theory. His central idea is that the world is composed of a number of 'centres of force', and all beings or 'forces' are nothing but pure 'power' in the Aristotelian sense of *potential* or *dynamis*. The relation between Leibniz and Nietzsche can be compared based on the following characteristics of Nietzsche's doctrine of the will to power:

First, for Nietzsche, every force is an active, endogenous and immanent striving for the actualization of certain quanta of power. Secondly, in this striving for actualization, every force seeks hindrances and resistances, which it can confront and overcome. Thirdly, all movement and change in nature must be understood in terms of the overwhelming conflict between force-organizations. Fourth, what is at stake in the confrontation between forces is both the conservation and the increase of power. Fifth, the existence of force organizations with relative unity, stability and duration relies on the fact that all quanta of will to power can at all times fully actualize their force, because forces only subsist insofar as they are actualized.

Clearly, the first point is in full agreement with Leibniz: every force is an endogenous causal striving towards self-actualization. In the second point, however, Nietzsche breaks with Leibniz's finalism: he does not conceive forces in terms of Aristotelian entelechies, whose goal, perfection and essence have been programmed into them. Also, with regard to the third and fifth point, Nietzsche does not take resort to a divine pre-established harmony to explain the organization, order and unity that can be discerned in the activities and interactions among forces. As far as the relational character of his force ontology is concerned, Nietzsche emphasizes that all centres of force are dependent on the conflict with resisting external forces. Thus, while he fully endorses Leibniz's conception of an essentially endogenous, immanent force, he also emphasizes that these forces can only actualize themselves *in and through* their conflicting relations with other forces – an idea that is lacking in Leibniz's finalist doctrine. In this way, that which has 'value' for each centre of force – namely the conservation and increase of power – is fundamentally dependent on the contextual relation to other centres of force.

Conservation and evolution

As is well known, the will to power is conceived by Nietzsche in terms of both a conservation dynamics and a creative dynamics. But how should we interpret the relation between these two dimensions of the will to power? Is the will to power first and foremost a striving for conservation, and secondarily a striving for growth, or vice versa? In other words, does growth happen in function of conservation? Or does conservation happen in function of growth?[47] In this regard, Nietzsche's well-known answer is unambiguous:

> Physiologists should think twice before positioning the drive for self-preservation as the cardinal drive of an organic being. Above all, a living thing wants to *discharge* its strength – life itself is will to power: self-preservation is only one of the indirect and most frequent *consequences* of this. – In short, here as elsewhere, watch out for *superfluous* teleological principles! – Such as the drive for preservation (which we owe to Spinoza's inconsistency –).[48]

This and other critical references to Spinoza have often been discussed by commentators. It is well-known from Nietzsche's *Nachlass* that he understood Spinoza's *conatus* in terms of *both* the conservation or self-preservation and the increase of power, which makes statements such as the above puzzling. All that matters for our endeavour, however, is to understand *why* Nietzsche prioritizes growth over conservation. For Nietzsche, this question is crucial because if growth is but a function of conservation, then growth would never exceed that which is necessary for conservation. In other words, the will to power would then in effect be but a reactive will towards adaptation and assimilation – the kind of will implicit in Darwin's idea of a struggle for existence. Although Nietzsche certainly did not trivialize the idea of conflict and struggle, he strongly disagreed with the idea that these would be primarily concerned with conservation. If there is any energetic impetus at the heart of life, it is an impetus towards maximal discharge of strength: "It can be shown most clearly that every living thing does everything it can not to preserve itself but to become *more*."[49] For Nietzsche, this means life wills not being but becoming, not *self-preservation* but *growth*, not merely *conservation* of energy but to *accumulate* force. To Deleuze, this places Nietzsche closer to Spinoza than he himself tended to grant.

Like Spinoza, Nietzsche fundamentally diverges from Leibniz in his conception of the *conatus*. In the doctrine of the will to power, it appears as an impulse that has not *one* but *two* fundamental modalities: one active/original and one reactive/derivative. Being the original vital impetus that animates all life, the will to power can express itself in the highest of human pursuits, such as art, philosophy or knowledge. However, it is Nietzsche's view that among our many intellectual perceptions and thoughts, we nonetheless tend towards those that are *not* in tune with our vital drives. Nietzsche argues that most of human psychic life is regulated by a drive for conservation and assimilation. This results in the view that our psychic life is mostly animated by a *nihilistic* drive that *suppresses* the universal drive to live. Indeed, by emptying the *conatus* of its Leibnizian finalism, Nietzsche finds in it a fundamentally nihilist undertone. This is, undoubtedly, his most important contribution to our conative understanding of the mind.

As Deleuze has shown, the nihilism of the *conatus* as an active force consists essentially in its *negating, suppressing* character.[50] The 'conservative' tendency of the will to power consists in a kind of *counter-will* that regulates and controls the universal drive to live in human beings. It expresses itself in *resentment* (the spirit of *revenge*), which Deleuze understands not merely as a psychological trait, mood or tone, but rather *as a transcendental structure of thought itself*. As Deleuze puts it, '*Ressentiment* is not part of psychology but the whole of our psychology, without knowing it, is a part of *ressentiment*.'[51] '*Ressentiment*, bad conscience and nihilism are not psychological traits but the foundation of the humanity of man.'[52] In Nietzsche's own wording, 'As soon as man began thinking he introduced the bacillus of revenge into things.'[53] Deleuze presents this nihilistic drive of thought as the reactive force of an intelligence that *depreciates* and even *accuses* life. It opposes thought and knowledge to life and judges the latter as something inferior, erroneous or even blameworthy. Accordingly, it also turns the will itself into something inferior or bad, something to be denied and suppressed: 'There is no philosopher who, discovering the essence of will, has not groaned at his own discovery and, like the timid fortuneteller, has not immediately seen bad omens for the future and the source of all evils of the past.'[54]

Just as the nihilistic will is a fundamental drive, which animates psychic life in its variety of feelings, imaginations and thoughts, so also the active, creative will to power is a primitive drive, which animates the whole of psychic life. In its most primordial form, however, will to power manifests itself as an *affective* feeling of power, a primitive affective form from which all the other feelings derive. As Nietzsche writes:

> My theory would be: that the will to power is the primitive form of affect, that all other affects are only developments of it; that it is notably enlightening to posit *power* in place of individual "happiness" (after which every living thing is supposed to be striving): "there is a striving for power, for an increase in power"; – pleasure is only a symptom of the feeling of power attained (…); that all driving force is will to power, that there is no other physical, dynamic or psychic force except this.[55]

For Nietzsche, as for Spinoza and Deleuze, sensibility is thus primarily a capacity of being affected that is correlated to either an *active* or a *reactive conatus* (will to power), which commands or animates each individuating exercise of thought. This commanding drive can take on either a reactive, passive or nihilistic modality, or an active, creative modality. With these Nietzschean ideas in hand, we can now finally see how the *conatus* plays a foundational role in Deleuze's doctrine of faculties.

The conatus in Deleuze's faculty doctrine

We have seen that for Kant, thought is the spontaneous and universal exercise of an innate faculty of apperception, which is driven by a discursive *conatus* to continuously subject sensible representations to conceptual abstract rules. This ceaseless effort of the faculty of apperception must rely, according to Kant, on a number of universal and timeless logical rules and categories, which together articulate in a purely formal manner the essential structure of all judgment or thought. These rules are logical 'laws' of thought, by virtue of which the thinker overcomes the contingent features of his or her empirical consciousness and attains insight in the necessity of the rules determining his or her thought. Today, we would call these structural elements that are relevant to truth-preserving inference the 'form' of thought, which is expressed in the formal language of a logical calculus.

We have also seen that for Deleuze, Kant's illusion was his assumption that he could attain a definitive formulation of the essential structures of thought as such. Kant's philosophy is situated in what Deleuze calls a philosophy of 'common sense', which takes it for granted that all judgment or all thought possesses a fixed logical form, a form that Kant believes he has articulated in his table of the logical forms of judgment and his correlated table of categories. However, for Deleuze, this cannot be true: as demonstrated by the history of logic and mathematics, the *a priori* structures of thought can evolve and change. This has two important consequences.

First, thought itself is irreducible to both a purely formal logic and a transcendental logic of truth, which reduces judgment (i.e. thought) to a predicative function. Certainly, as Kant has shown, the conceptual 'rules' by means of which true judgments constitute the objects of thought are founded in conceptual predication. But to reduce thought to the instantiation and predication of conceptual rules is to miss the fact that systems of logic and mathematics are themselves open to dynamic evolutions. Thus, there must be a genetic, creative dimension of thought, which is concerned precisely with this dynamic evolution and production of new structures of thought. In Deleuze's philosophy, this genetic dimension of thought is the act of *learning* and it is in relation to this act that his conception of the *conatus* should be seen.

Second, if pure thought is irreducible to the realms of logical signification and predication, there must also be an extra-conceptual, ideal realm of thought, within which learning takes place. Deleuze conceives this as an ideal realm of *sense*, which is concerned with the interpretation of *problems* and their ideal conditions. In Chapter 5, we will examine this distinct, creative dimension of learning and its conative striving for psychic individuation. For now, it will suffice to keep in mind the consequences of Deleuze's Spinozist and Nietzschean conception of the *conatus*.

On Deleuze's account, all human behaviour and thought express a constant *conative* striving to preserve and enhance one's power of acting (*potentia agendi*) and one's power of thinking (*potentia cogitandi*). But this fundamental *conatus* is not reducible to a striving of the human understanding towards logical, rational order. To conceive the *conatus* in terms of bodily forces means the cognitive faculties are rooted in dark affective registers rather than purely conceptual structures. Thought always emerges from an unconscious register of nihilistic or creative affects, which animate it, and which the thinker must learn to adequately interpret, evaluate and organize.

3

The metaphysics of individuation

The universe endures. The more we study the nature of time, the more we shall comprehend that duration means invention, the creation of new forms, the continual elaboration of the absolutely new.

— Henri Bergson[1]

The main conjecture

Deleuze's philosophy develops a metaphysical framework for describing generative processes of individuation that constitute natural systems at different levels of organization: physical, biological, psychic and societal. This metaphysics of individuation is based on the following central conjecture: *there is a continuous creation of unforeseeable novelty, which seems to be going on in the universe*. This metaphysical conjecture entails two distinct theses. First, it entails that there is an ontological priority of generative processes of individuation with regard to constituted individuals. Deleuze's metaphysics installs a veritable *ontological difference* between generative, dynamic processes of individuation, on the one hand, and individuals considered as static products or outcomes of such constitutive processes. Secondly, the conjecture entails the thesis that individuation cannot be the result of *a fixed totality of possibilities*; instead, individuation must be *the continual creation of new possibilities*. This thesis entails that generative processes of individuation do not simply realize existing possibilities, but rather they generate new realities that did not subsist beforehand even logically or abstractly. In other words, individuation brings forth something unforeseeable and new, such that it does not simply enact timeless, pre-existing possibilities, but rather it involves the creation of new, unseen possibilities.

Deleuze adopts this metaphysical conjecture from Henri Bergson and Gilbert Simondon, who first adopted it faced with paradoxes that arise when we picture the totality of *biological* and *mental* possibilities as fixed. On our currently dominant (meta-)physical view of the universe, we obtain a reality whose successive states are in theory calculable in advance, like the images placed side by side along a cinematographic film, prior to its unrolling. Ever since the rise of classical dynamics and the mechanistic philosophy of nature that accompanied it, any indeterminacy in nature was relegated to the subjective, factual limits of our finite knowledge, whereas the whole of nature was considered absolutely and principally deterministic in itself. As is well known, this is the crux of Laplace's famous thought experiment: given the pertinent observables and parameters of all the particles in the universe (momentum, position, energy, etc.), an 'infinite intelligence' could, using the laws of nature, deduce the entire future and past of the universe. Although today many scientists have given up hard determinism for unpredictable chaos and quantum randomness, the resulting picture of nature is no less deterministic. In today's predominant 'block universe' framework, becoming or dynamism is not seen as a real feature of the world. Instead, nature appears as a static block universe in which all events are laid out in advance. The way that things move around in this block universe – whether it is particles, waves and/or something else – obeys a *fixed* set of *timeless* mathematical possibilities.[2] This leads to an astounding Parmenidean view in which the physical world simply is and nothing changes or becomes. Just like personal freedom and agency, time itself makes no sense in this framework – it appears just as another static dimension on which events can be plotted. A paradox then arises as the contradiction between, on the one hand, this static image of a deterministic, timeless and changeless nature, and on the other hand, the pervasive *open-ended variation* which the living world exhibits, and our immediate sense of *agency*, our capacity to influence the future as we shape our lives. Bergson puts the paradox, which he assigns as the starting point of his philosophical reflections, this way:

> Suppress the conscious and the living (…), you obtain in fact a universe whose successive states are in theory calculable in advance, like the images placed side by side along the cinematographic film, prior to its unrolling. Why, then, the unrolling? Why does reality unfurl? Why is it not spread out? What good is time?[3]

In his process metaphysics, Bergson adopted exactly the opposite view: *there is becoming but not being*. His metaphysics introduced time or 'duration' as an *active* process in nature, something that exists and that *acts* in the universe. Its action is not simply the fact of hindering everything from being given all at once. Rather, it is a vehicle of indetermination, creation and choice: the existence of time would prove that there is an objective indetermination of material, living and mental processes, a real generative activity of the present that rules out its identification with the past. Indeed, time or duration would be the constitutive indetermination of material processes itself. The main metaphysical challenge, which a Bergsonian philosophy of individuation thus faces, is to show how we can understand the reality of biological and mental possibilities as evolving in an organic, non-arbitrary way. How can one dismiss the Platonist idea of an eternal, fixed totality of possibilities for the whole of nature as an erroneous fiction, and instead provide a rigorous development of the idea of newly created biological and mental possibilities? It is this question, which this chapter will address. Bergson, Simondon and Deleuze all realized that if possibility-creation were *only* a matter of time or duration, the generative, creative agency they ascribed to individuation would always remain ill-understood. Concepts such as duration and individuation would then inevitably remain burdened with the speculative inadequacies of a spiritualist or vitalist philosophy of nature. To ground their dynamical philosophy of nature empirically, these process philosophers turned to thermodynamics, the science of energy transformations. As we will see, they propose to account for the creative becoming of living and mental processes based on an energetic and thermodynamic basis.

The dynamics of individuation

Let us begin by clarifying the notion of individuation. Individuation occurs when the properties of a physical, biological or psychic system allow it to take on a more ordered, structured state through the dissipation of energy (entropy production), some of which goes into the formation of the new structure. Structure here refers to the spontaneous development of spatial and temporal organization in physical, biological and psychic systems. In Simondon's philosophy, individuation happens when a material system with particular singular or critical points enters in contact with a metastable source of potential energy, which leads to the 'transduction' of a particular form or structure. By transduction, Simondon means a physical, biological, mental or social process through which the domain in question becomes more *structured* and *organized*. He gives the example of crystallization, whereby non-living chemicals can become more organized when they freeze and solidify into crystals.[4] The crystal starts from a tiny germ, which increases and extends a certain structure within a supersaturated liquor. The crystalline germ functions as a 'singularity', whereas the supersaturated liquor has a potential energy that can become transduced to form progressive crystalline structures. For Simondon, it is important to note that the individuating process of form-taking cannot be conceived simply as the imposition of a pure form onto a brute matter. First of all, it is necessary that raw matter itself already contain certain properties that allow it to become more structured.[5] Secondly, the organization of the form does not require just a raw matter but also, and essentially, the dissipation of potential energy. By contrast, in non-individuating conservative systems, particles would bounce back to their original potential energies, and there would be no individuation of structure.[6]

Hylomorphism, particles and process

To see why it is important to note that structure emerges from matter through energy dissipation, one should recall that a long philosophical tradition considered form, structure and relation to be more basic than matter, energy and substance. This traditional focus on the priority of structure and form dates back to the Pythagoreans, Plato and Aristotle, and led to a *hylomorphic* metaphysics of individuation. Simondon analyses hylomorphism as a technological way of thinking about individuation, which represents a particular entity as consisting of a predetermined form (*morphè* or *eidos*), which is realized materially (*hyle*). When we think about human-made machines, we intuitively consider the structural organization as a formal essence, which imposes itself upon the matter it is implemented in. Likewise, a hylomorphic approach to the individuation of living systems or mental states sees formal organization as an abstract principle of individuation, which precedes the genesis of the actual individual. From Descartes up to cybernetics, the modern variant of the hylomorphic idea is that living or mental systems are essentially like technological artefacts in that they are to be defined in terms of their functional organization or form, and not by their particular material realization.[7]

In contemporary terms, hylomorphism can be seen as an anti-reductionist, functionalist way of thinking about life or mind. It is typically motivated by the central guiding idea that the individuation of living or mental systems cannot be explained *either* by reducing life or mind to its material substrate *or* by invoking some non-material substance or substrate (vitalism). Hylomorphic approaches to individuation instead seek explanation in the form or functional organization of matter. In the twentieth century, such approaches emerged in the wake of the birth of information theory, approximately around 1948, when Claude Shannon published his first paper on this subject. In this theory, information is considered to trigger material (inter-)actions and energy, and information itself is contained not in material objects themselves but rather in their differences, that is, in their relations. In this sense, information theory returned to the priority of structure, form and relation over matter, substance and energy. In molecular biology, this idea had a major influence, leading to the view that genetic information structures the flow of free energy and materials.[8]

Likewise, the computational foundations of cognitive science were largely cast in terms of information networks and control systems. Computationalism distinguishes two distinct explanatory levels of cognitive systems above the physical (or neurophysiological) level: a symbol-processing or syntactic level and a representational or semantic level. The syntactic level is traditionally conceived as an internal formal coding language (*morphe*) that manipulates materially implemented symbols (*hyle*). In a hylomorphic vein, computationalism posits identifiable cognitive forms or structures that are distinguishable from the system's physical processing. It assumes that, as in computer science, symbolic representations are as far as their formal structure and informational contents are concerned independent of their implementation in physical-biological substrata.[9] Indeed, the natural causality in which information processing is implicated is considered to be a strictly *formal* and *syntactic* one. It is this idea that I understand here as hylomorphic: the idea that to explain the individuation of cognitive states, the form or functional organization is essential and the material implementation is accidental.

The opposite of hylomorphism is what Simondon calls *substantialism*. On this approach, which Simondon traces back to the Ancient Greek atomists, individuation is the effect not of a predetermined form but of pre-given atomic individuals. Today, substantialism would correspond to a reductionist physicalist approach to individuation. In the philosophy of mind, one can find such an approach in the work of Jaegwon Kim, which famously refutes the prospects of non-reductionist functionalist or emergentist approaches. In its contemporary guise, substantialism holds that 'all is particles' and accordingly all causal power is resident in that basic physical substance or particle-level – thereby refuting the kind of emergentist 'downward causation', which organizational or functionalist approaches may invoke.

How does Simondon position his own, energetic theory of individuation vis-à-vis substantialism and hylomorphism? According to Simondon, substantialism is both physically and metaphysically wrong. It assumes that particles participate *in* individuation and organization, but they do not themselves *have* individuation or organization.[10] Simondon, by contrast, argues that all individuals – particles included – emerge from pre-individual processes of individuation. The important rejoinder of this claim is that at the most fundamental level, nature simply does not consist of particles.[11] Instead, the most fundamental level consists of 'pre-individual' processes of individuation and organization: 'the first reality is pre-individual and is richer than the individual understood as the result of individuation.'[12] His starting point for this claim is quantum physics: on his reading, the formation of elementary particles starts from primary continuum operators.[13] Today, contemporary process metaphysicians who criticize substance metaphysics tend to invoke a similar line of argument. Notably, Mark Bickhard has argued (against Kim) that a pure particle metaphysics would have serious coherence problems because 'our best contemporary physics argues that there are no particles'.[14] Instead, according to Bickhard, what appears as particle interactions are quantized oscillatory field processes, and these are fundamentally processes, which are inherently organized.

What is missing from hylomorphism, according to Simondon, is a *genetic* account of individuation, which acknowledges the *energetic conditions* of its material realization. In his view, hylomorphism only retains two aspects of individuation, namely the initial brute matter and the structure or form as a materially realized end result.[15] As such, it lacks a detailed recognition of the actual process that connects these two extremes of matter and form together, namely the process of individuation itself. Crucially, with this lack comes a neglect of the fundamentally energetic conditions of 'metastable equilibrium' in which individuation occurs.[16] For Simondon, one should consider this energetic condition as 'a middle and intermediate zone between form and matter'.[17] This intermediate zone is that of the pre-individual singularities that are the initiators of the operation of individuation, and of an exchange between energy and structure.[18]

Applied to biological individuation, this intermediate zone would imply generative, metastable dynamics that *precede* the self-maintaining, homeostatic dynamics of a living system.[19] Preceding the passage to functional life, which they organize, these metastable dynamics of individuation constitute what Simondon calls 'a sort of intermediate static life between inorganic reality and functional life properly speaking'.[20] For Simondon, as for Deleuze, this idea is crucial. If we ask: *where does the individuating dynamism of the individual reside?* The answer is the dynamics of organization *precede* the passage to functional life, as if individuation were a kind of *intermediate* order of life, between unorganized matter and life fully organized. This is why Deleuze will call the creative dynamics of individuation a power of *inorganic life* that is distinct from any individual organism as a functional unity.

However, as noted, the creative dynamism of individuation is not just a feature of *life*. The increase in diversity and complexity in living, phenotypic forms is but one aspect of the more encompassing power of individuation: a universal power of organizing matter, which spans many different levels of physical, biological and psychic organization. In Deleuze's Spinozist terms, we should say that individuating dynamics are a *natura naturans*, which stands to individual entities as a *natura naturata*.

Simondon's criticism of hylomorphism should not be taken as a complete rejection, however. Simondon's metaphysics of individuation shares with hylomorphism the fundamental idea that living or psychic systems cannot be reduced to their physical substrate: in living or psychic systems, individuation is constrained by the form or functional organization of matter. Simondon's criticism concerns the abstract hylomorphic duality between matter and form. In his view, hylomorphic dualism should be replaced by a genetic, energetic approach that can account for the dynamical emergence of structure and form. Individuation is then a dynamical process of structuration or 'form-taking' that should be described in terms of potential energy and time.

Structure and metastability

Turning to the thermodynamic study of energy transformations, Simondon observes that individuating dynamics are governed by potentials, which are local entropy functions. This suggests the appearance of structure and organization in a physical, biological or psychic system results from a dynamical evolution that is governed by a potential, which acts as a local source of information. Simondon defines this potential state of energy, which governs individuation, as a 'metastable equilibrium' that is distinct from stable equilibrium and from instability.[21] Stable equilibrium excludes individuation because it corresponds with the lowest level of potential energy possible. A stable equilibrium is achieved in a system when all possible transformations have occurred and no propulsive force remains. As Simondon puts it, 'all potentials have been actualized, and systems that have succumbed to their lowest energetic levels cannot transform again.'[22] Metastability, in Simondon's understanding, is a universal aspect of matter and its organization – from molecular arrangements and chemical reactions to the neural dynamics underlying perception and language use. 'In order to define metastability,' he writes, 'it is necessary to introduce the notion of the potential energy residing in a given system, the notion of order and that of an increase in entropy.'[23]

However, the idea that an increase in order and an increase in entropy would go hand in hand seems strange in light of the second law of thermodynamics. This states that free energy tends to progressively degrade and that in any isolated system, organization degrades and disorder and entropy increase until a final state of equilibrium is reached.[24] Entropy then becomes 'an indicator of evolution', expressing the existence of an objective 'arrow of time': 'for each isolated system, the future is the direction in which entropy increases.'[25] In other words, the second law dictates that systems naturally tend towards their lowest accessible state of potential energy and maximal entropy. Metastable equilibrium is no exception to this global tendency of entropic dissipation. However, it can constitute *local* regions of organization and order despite an increase in *global* entropy – and this is precisely what happens in individuation. Metastable conditions thus do not reduce or counter the production of entropy globally, which is impossible. Rather, metastable conditions generate and maintain order and organization by locally 'struggling' against entropy.[26] While thermodynamic forces push all systems to equilibrium, vital systems are capable of resisting this push by metabolically exploiting their environment to maintain a metastable, far from equilibrium configuration. In this sense, Simondon adopts Wiener's term of 'negative entropy' or 'negentropy' to define metastability.[27] Importantly, according to Simondon, these non-equilibrium, metastable conditions of individuation present an exception to the absolute determinacy of nature. In non-equilibrium conditions, living systems are said to create a certain degree of energy '*indetermination*', which corresponds to an objective indeterminacy in natural, material processes.[28] Simondon's basic idea is that for each physical, biological, or psychic system, there are both determined conditions of state and indeterminate margins of becoming, which exclude any linear and continuous relation between causes and effects. It follows that we live in an ordered world of cause and effect, but also in a creative world of individuations, which *create the possibilities of becoming* of new forms and new structures. Individuation is *self-generating* or *self-producing* in the sense that nothing external to it *causes* its growth. Like Bergson before him and Deleuze after him, Simondon sought in this world of individuation a new, non-mechanistic conception of nature: a world not of static, deterministic cause and effect, but a world of indetermination, potentiality and novelty.[29]

Now, having examined the energetic conditions of individuation, we should turn to more properly philosophical matters, namely the idea of an *ontological reality* that is inherent to individuation. For Deleuze, if things are said to individuate, it is less in themselves than in relation to the Whole of the universe in which they participate. It is to this ontological characterization that we now turn.

Ontological duration

Spinoza revisited

Individuation in Deleuze is unthinkable without the Bergsonian idea of a coexistence of many different degrees of duration, which are inferior or superior to the duration of human consciousness. But duration is not a simple term in Bergson's thought, and rather has undergone several transformations. In his first book, *Time and Free Will*, duration was conceived as a psychological 'fact of consciousness' that stands in contrast to external things, which do not endure in themselves. In *Matter and Memory*, however, Bergson introduced the idea of a duration that is immanent not just to consciousness, but to the reality of all living and even non-living things. As a result, the concept of duration was de-psychologized and attained a much broader, ontological meaning. As Deleuze writes, 'Psychological duration should only be a clearly determined case, an opening onto an ontological duration.'[30] This affirmation of an ontological reality that is inherent to duration itself entails that duration is not 'in' things, but things are 'in' duration. That is to say, all things coexist as degrees of 'tension' and 'extension' in one encompassing ontological duration.[31] It is this ontological conception of duration that will interest us here.

Simplifying a lot, we can say there exists one universal duration, which consists of two fundamental *tendencies*. On the one hand, there is a tendency towards *extension, expansion* and *dissipation* which is expressed in solid, extended (inert and living) matter. On the other hand, there is a tendency towards *tension* and *contraction*, which is expressed in *memory* and *organization*. In the Spinozist terminology we have been using we can say duration is a *natura naturans* (the actively creating nature generating things), which expresses itself in *natura naturata* in different degrees of tension and extension. *Natura naturata* is then the passively generated nature which is the result of the tendencies of extension and tension performed by *natura naturans*. As Bergson puts it, we should imagine many different 'rhythms' which, slower or faster, determine the degree of tension or relaxation of different beings and thereby 'fix their respective places in the scale of being'.[32]

But how is this cosmic reality of duration different from the material universe, you may ask? How can all things be said to consist of different degrees of tension *and* extension? Indeed, how can there be a reality of matter that is distinct from its extension in space?

To say that matter endures and is 'in' duration means it is composed of the distinct tendencies of 'extension' and 'tension'. Bergson explains the tendency of extension as one of 'solidification', which is responsible for the solidity of extended material things. Secondly, this expansive tendency is also responsible for the fact that elements in space exist alongside or *exterior* to each other: 'externality is the distinguishing mark of things which occupy space'.[33] In spatial manifolds, there is no interdependence but only external independent existence. This brings with it the property of being quantifiable: since elements exist exterior to each other, they are countable and behave, Bergson suggests, like numbers, which are set side by side. Finally, Bergson adds to this extensive, expansive tendency a *thermodynamic* interpretation, which holds that all physical changes have a tendency to degrade utilizable energy.[34] Prior to its solidified extension, matter in duration is to Bergson a pure flux of energy. The extensive, solidifying tendency of duration is then one with the entropic tendency of material systems to degrade potential energy and dissipate it as heat.

By contrast, to say there is a contrary tendency of *tension* or *contraction* in matter means firstly that there must be a tendency allowing its parts to be in a state of reciprocal implication and interpenetration. This is of course a tendency of organization. It then comes as no surprise that Bergson explicates this tendency of tension or contraction as a tendency to *retain* dissipation and to *save it up*, harvesting available energy and then using it for various purposes.[35] This tendency to 'accumulate' energy with a view to an 'effective discharge' is precisely the movement of tension in duration, which counters the entropic tendency of extended matter. I will return to this idea below.

But, as noted, aside from organization the tendency of tension also refers to the action of *memory*. Tension would imply therefore also something like a *memory* of matter in duration. This does not mean, of course, that inert matter is a proto-consciousness that would have psychological recollections. Bergson uses the concept of memory in an enlarged, non-psychological sense: 'the conservation *and* accumulation of the past in the present'.[36] In this broader sense, memory simply means that the past has an *active* role in the present dynamics of a material system. This can be understood without invoking any kind of conscious, psychological reality. Take, for instance, a biological system, which is organized around singular points that induce qualitative, irreversible transformations. Without the memory that constitutes its duration, the individuation of this material system would always be instantaneous, happening from moment to moment. The idea that individuation *endures* means that these singular points *continue to influence* the present and future dynamics of the system.

In living systems, tensions of duration constitute an *unconscious* duration, a properly biological and physiological time, which organizes the organism and its cognitive functions. In this way, the importance of duration for understanding biological individuation concerns the idea of an *active, organizing* function of a properly biological temporality within processes of individuation.

Philosophically, I will link this unconscious function of memory or duration to the energetic function of *metabolism*: both are concerned with a conservation and accumulation of 'something' past into the present.[37] As such, they both allow for the past to have an *active*, organizing role in the present dynamics of a material system. As we will see, this correlation between memory and metabolism will allow for a deepened understanding of the way in which vital and psychic individuation can be thought in terms of autonomous centres of indetermination and genuine novelty creation.

Memory and metabolism in vital individuation

Given this expansion of the notion of memory, we can conceive of an ontological plurality of degrees of durations inferior and superior to that of the human condition. Every degree of duration would correspond to a different degree of contracting the past (tension) and expanding towards the future (extension). At the lowest level of duration would stand inert material systems, which have no memory or metabolism.[38] Without these, there is only expansion of matter and time, without tension or contraction of the past. Accordingly, there is no reciprocal penetration of moments in time, characteristic of duration, but only the externality and juxtaposition of moments characteristic of spatial, discrete manifolds. The function of memory is to contract or bind together successive moments of the duration of things. At the lowest, material degree of duration, however, there is no tension, no memory, and the conditions of physical individuation therefore remain qualitatively identical to matter and energy itself. Accordingly, lifeless material systems are defined by a strict equivalence between a received movement (action) and an executed movement (reaction): any action or energy received is immediately released or dissipated in an equivalent reaction.

With increasing degrees of memory, however, we get an increasing degree in which a system's future developments are affected by its past – and not merely by its present. In living systems, memory is a power of contracting, conserving and accumulating the past in the present. Furthermore, in *Matter and Memory*, Bergson suggests this degree of duration correlates to the living being's metabolism, which is a power of conserving and accumulating the potential energy that the particular system needs to sustain its organization.[39] One might say that memory is to the mind what metabolism is to the body: a power of conservation and accumulation, which organizes the future.

Combined, memory and metabolism together engraft onto the determinism of physical forces a certain degree of *indetermination*. Whereas inert matter is defined by a deterministic action-reaction equivalence, memory and metabolism establish an interval between the two. As such, they constitute what Bergson famously called the organism as a 'centre of indetermination'.[40] Of course, like all natural bodies, this organic centre is exposed to the action of external causes, which threaten to disintegrate it. But by virtue of both memory and metabolism, organisms 'struggle' and 'absorb' some part of this action. Memory and metabolism suspend the immediacy of an instantaneous action-reaction cycle by the gradual conservation and accumulation of energy and by conserving and accumulating the effects of past events into the present. As Bergson writes, 'our action will dispose of the future in the exact proportion in which our perception, enlarged by memory, has contracted the past.'[41] But, again, it is crucial to see this action of memory cannot be reduced to a strictly *psychological* function. In Bergson's enlarged usage of the term, memory is fundamentally interwoven with metabolism:

> If there are actions that are really *free*, or at least partly indeterminate, they can only belong to beings able to fix, at long intervals, that becoming to which their own becoming clings, able to solidify it into distinct moments, *and so to condense matter and, by assimilating it, to digest it into movements of reaction which will pass through the meshes of natural necessity*.[42]

It is by virtue of the conserving and accumulating power of *both* memory and metabolism that living systems can 'free' themselves from the particular actions, which flow from matter. Memory is a power of conserving the past at intervals of variable length, and of solidifying the past into distinct moments, which organize the future. But no living creature is pure memory or pure mind; it is always embodied and geared towards action. Metabolism is the corporeal condition for memory to determine action: it condenses, assimilates and digests matter and energy, thereby creating the energetic indetermination that memory acts upon when shaping our bodily movements. Without memory, metabolism would be blind indetermination. Without metabolism, memory would be mere virtuality – out of this world.

Individuation ascending

The more systems have the capacity of conservation and accumulation, the more they are said to 'ascend' in duration; the less they do so, the more they 'descend' in duration.[43] In fact, we should say the universe itself, as an enduring Whole or an ontological duration, consists of two opposite tendencies of ascent and descent, which express themselves in material, living and psychic systems. The descent in duration is the deterministic movement of inert matter in extensive space. The ascent in duration, by contrast, corresponds to an 'inner work of ripening or creating' indetermination and imposes itself on the tendency of descent, which is inseparable from it.[44]

In *Creative Evolution*, Bergson explicates the tendency of descent in terms of the second law of thermodynamics: the law of the degradation of energy. Bergson calls this 'the most metaphysical of the laws of physics' because it points out the direction in which the natural world is going.[45] By proclaiming that energy becomes increasingly unavailable to perform work, the second law depicts a gradual breaking-down of physical order as energy becomes diffused in nature. In Clausius's original proposal, the concept of entropy (or thermodynamic disorder) was a measure of the degree of energetic dispersal or dissipation and, consequently, its unavailability to do work.[46] From this point of view, Bergson notes, it would seem that a world like our solar system is continuously exhausting something of the mutability it contains: in the beginning it had the maximum of possible utilization of energy, but this mutability diminishes unceasingly.[47]

However, as Bergson rightly emphasizes, this usage of the notions of energy and entropy concerns *physical* order and disorder and attaches energy to extended particles. Once we turn to the realm of living bodies, however, we find 'an effort to re-mount the incline that matter descends'.[48] That is to say, to continue to survive, living systems must somehow circumvent the inherent tendency of material processes to dissipate energy and become increasingly entropic over time. In other words, organisms must somehow be able to resist the cosmic determinism of the second law. As is well known, this observation led Erwin Schrödinger – in his famous 1945 book, *What Is Life?* – to argue that organisms must somehow 'extract order' from their environment.[49] However, living creatures do not violate the second law, because they 'pay' for their increased order ('negentropy') by producing an equivalent amount of entropy in the environment.

Bergson's famous idea of a vital 'effort' – an '*élan vital*' – to counter entropy is similar to Schrödinger's in that it too is incapable of '*stopping*' the entropic course of material changes downwards, but nonetheless 'it succeeds in *retarding* it'.[50] From an energetic point of view, living systems testify to a fundamental effort to *retain* dissipation and to *save it up*, harvesting available energy and then using it for various purposes. This metabolic tendency to 'accumulate' energy with a view to an 'effective discharge' is precisely the movement of ascent in duration, which imposes itself on the entropic tendency of descent. Bergson defines the metabolic tendency of life as a 'creative action', which consists in (1) 'an effort to accumulate energy' and (2) 'an elastic canalization of this energy in variable and indeterminable directions, at the end of which are free acts'.[51] *Both* tendencies are always present in living systems and lead us to an image of vital individuation as '*a reality which is making itself in a reality which is unmaking itself*'.[52]

From the two energetic tendencies of ascent and descent, there results a particular '*modus vivendi*', which is *organization*. Of course, there is not one single *modus vivendi*, but rather a wide variety of levels of organization. Any individual level of organization arises from the conflicting confrontation between the movements of entropic descent and metabolic ascent. As Bergson writes: 'Matter divides actually what was but potentially manifold; and, in this sense, individuation is in part the work of matter, in part the result of life's own inclination.'[53]

Thus, vital individuation would find its origin in the metabolic capacity of life to accumulate potential energy. This capacity is one with the *creative impetus* of life, because it essentially consists in a 'striving' to introduce into matter and energy 'the largest amount of indetermination and liberty'.[54] The more complex a type of metabolism, the stronger its capacity to generate a degree of energy indetermination, and the more it ascends in duration. That is, by retarding the dissipation of energy and by accumulating its possible utilization, metabolism creates a zone of indetermination – not only of *energy*, but also of *time*. The ways in which accumulated energy will be released are in no way pre-inscribed in some register of life. Instead, each metabolic degree of energy indetermination opens up an unseen space of possibility for new forms and new actions to emerge. In this sense, metabolism is the energetic motor driving the continuous creation of new possibilities in life and mind. Metabolism creates the indetermination of energy and time, which memory may act upon. It is as though metabolism contracts matter and potential energy into its duration, creating a zone of indetermination, and memory in turn contracts this energetic indetermination into its duration, merging the autonomy of life with that of mind.

Complexity and differentiation

The world as an egg

From the physical to the biological on to the psychic, individuation moves from simple, undifferentiated systems towards increasingly complex, differentiated systems. Contrary to what one might expect, greater homogeneity and symmetry in nature do not imply greater order or greater structure. On the contrary, homogeneity and symmetry imply disorder and structureless uniformity, whereas order, structure and form imply asymmetry and differentiation. Physical disorder is more symmetrical than physical order, which is asymmetrical and differentiated. This is clear in the example of crystal formation.[55] At elevated temperature, the molecules composing water vapour will move freely, without mutual correlation. When temperature is lowered, the vapour transforms into a liquid water drop. Now, the molecules keep a mean distance between each other with correlated motion. When we lower the temperature further beyond the freezing point of water, ice crystals are formed with a fixed molecular order. If this ice crystal were again melted down into a uniform pool of liquid and ultimately heated back up into a gas, its form and structure would be gradually lost – but it would increasingly gain in symmetry. Thus, the individuation of form and structure is not the emergence of *symmetry* out of disorder, but rather the gradual differentiation of the symmetry of disorder into the *asymmetry* of the order, form and structure we find in nature.[56]

If we ask ourselves, as the first Greek philosophers did, what was the origin and first cause of all existing things, then we should imagine an original matter that is in an initial state of complete homogeneity and symmetry – a disordered *apeiron*. As material, living and ultimately psychic forms and structures individuate, this initial state of symmetry and homogeneity becomes increasingly *differentiated* and thereby becomes asymmetrical and heterogeneous. Deleuze captures this cosmic process of individuation and differentiation metaphorically by saying that 'the world is an egg'.[57] Indeed, Deleuze argues that the way in which an individual develops and grows out of an embryonic egg provides us with a genuine model for the way in which individuation proceeds by differentiation and symmetry breaking. Let us therefore consider this paradigmatic example closer.

Differentiation in embryogenesis

All living individuals begin their life as a fertilized egg or zygote, which contains the full complement of genes required to construct the multicellular individual. Early embryonic development, during which the multicellular organism is formed, is a series of self-dividing, differentiating and symmetry-breaking events, which start from an initial, highly symmetrical spheroidal egg and which arrive at a fully shaped body with a much lower degree of symmetry.[58] At the beginning of embryogenesis, a mother cell self-divides into two daughter cells, which each contain a copy of the mother's nuclear DNA and half its cytoplasmic contents. At this stage, the daughter cells are genetically identical to the original mother cell and to each other. But continued cell division does not lead to more and more identical cells. On the contrary, it produces a highly *asymmetrical* organism with asymmetries between left and right, front and back, top and bottom, etc.[59] Although each cell of the organism (except for the egg and sperm and their precursors) contains an identical set of genes, this set of identical genetic instructions produces different types of specialized cells. It is one of the central aims of embryology to explain how genetically identical cells can generate the highly differentiated, asymmetrical and specialized cell types that make up the body.

Cell *differentiation* results in cells with vastly different appearances and functional modifications: red blood cells capable of soaking up and disbursing oxygen, bone and cartilage cells surrounded by solid matrices, electrically excitable neurons with extended processes up to a meter long, etc.[60] Although the specialized cell types of an organism are still genetically identical, they differ in *which* genes they are capable of expressing, that is, which segments of their DNA are 'open' and can be transcribed in protein synthesis.[61]

What interests Deleuze in the process of cell differentiation is, first of all, the fact that embryogenesis is highly relationally determined. It is a well-known fact of embryology that a cell from one tissue can be transplanted into another tissue and become a totally different cell type. The particular type of cell it then becomes is determined not by certain intrinsic properties but rather by *relational* properties: its position along certain morphogenetic gradients. The notion of a morphogen gradient is a very important one in developmental biology, because it explains how cells in the growing embryo can interact over long distances by exchanging transcription factors.[62] Morphogens are signalling molecules that organize a spatial field of surrounding cells into patterns. They form a gradient of concentration emanating from a localized source, and determine the arrangement of cells according to the different concentrations of the morphogen 'perceived' by the cells. This notion of a morphogen gradient is closely linked to the idea of *positional information*, which is central in the tradition of structuralist biology (Waddington, Goodwin & Webster, etc.).[63]

The equipotentiality of the embryo is a remarkable characteristic of the beginning period of development, in which there is an equivalence of parts, prior to their differentiation. In Deleuze's terminology, undifferentiated cells are primarily a 'virtual matter' to be organized: prior to any determination or differentiation, they have no clearly assigned properties or functions.[64] It is only through coupling or reciprocal determination that this developmental potency or virtuality is increasingly narrowed and ultimately becomes differentiated, resulting in specific cell types with vastly different appearances and functions.

A second element, which Deleuze emphasizes in the example of embryogenesis, is that this coupling or reciprocal determination between cells must be understood from a *biophysical* point of view: namely in terms of the intensive individuating field in which morphogenetic potentials or gradients constrain the interactions of the multiple cellular components. The cell nucleus and genes would designate only the virtual matter to be organized – 'in other words, the differential relations which constitute the pre-individual field to be actualized.[65] But cellular differentiation, Deleuze notes, is induced only on the basis of the intensive, morphogenetic gradients. In line with contemporary approaches to embryogenesis in terms of dynamical systems theory, Deleuze writes the dynamical interactions between multiple related components can be conceived in terms of coupled differential equations, which would represent the changes taking place.[66]

The conceptual lesson, which Deleuze wants us to draw from this paradigmatic example, is this: independently of the particular biochemical mechanisms involved in embryogenesis, morphogenesis and individuation in general seem to be governed by a general dynamical scheme of pattern formation, which runs through nature at different levels of organization. One always begins with a system of virtual, determinable elements (in our example totipotent cells) corresponding to a system with full symmetry. Then, differentiation is caused by gradual intensive changes in the system, which reach a certain *critical* or *singular point*, and which lead to an abrupt symmetry breaking in the system's global state (in our example morphogen gradients). At all levels of nature, differentiation is a process of reciprocal determination between the components of a complex, self-organizing system, which leads to the individuation of new forms and structures in conditions of metastable equilibrium (in our example, the specific cell *types* with their vastly different appearances and functional modifications). In the following chapters, we will see how Deleuze applies this metaphysics of individuation to *psychic* systems. But before doing so, we must consider one last important, overarching thought.

Ontological difference

There is an important idea of an ontological difference, which runs through this metaphysics of individuation.[67] This is the ontological difference between *individuation* and *organization,* that is, between generative processes of individuation and individual structures as static results of such processes. Structures refer to actual entities and to the actual spatio-temporal organization between the actual components that make up an entity. For example, in a living organism, the cells, cell membranes, organelles, tissues and organs are actual structures, which constitute spatio-temporal, functional relations between different components of the system. Individuation, on the other hand, does not refer to such a set of *actual* structures or spatio-temporal relations that make up a system. Instead, individuation refers to *possible* ('virtual') structures, which may generate new functions and new spatio-temporal organizations, thereby constituting new actual entities. Whereas *structure* refers to processes of self-maintenance and regulation, *individuation* refers to processes of evolution, adaptation and development.

The focal point of the notion of an ontological difference is Deleuze's conception of individuation as belonging to a power of *inorganic life* that must be distinguished from any particular *function, structure* or *organization* of the individual organism itself. In fact, there is no more fundamental opposition running through Deleuze's philosophy than that between *inorganic life* and *organization.* Whereas organization belongs to the *actual* organism with its individuated forms and structures, inorganic life is the *virtual* power of individuation, belonging to ontological duration. Deleuze formulates this ontological difference as follows:

> Life as *movement* alienates itself in the material *form* that it creates; by actualizing itself, by differentiating itself, it loses 'contact with the rest of itself.' Every species

is thus an arrest of movement; it could be said that the living being turns on itself and *closes itself*.⁶⁸

Although inorganic life is inherent to the movement of individuation, it is never 'given' in any individual cell, tissue, organ or whole organism.⁶⁹ We must go even further and say that as a virtual movement, inorganic life is never empirically given. As a fundamental element of ontological duration, inorganic life is at once *real* and *virtual* – but never *actual* (or *merely possible*). Invoking Spinoza's concept of the divine, Deleuze writes that inorganic life is like a '*natura naturans*', which expresses itself in particular organisms as '*natura naturata*'.⁷⁰ The difficulty in adequately grasping this metaphysical distinction lies in grasping inorganic life as 'something' that is at once *real* and *virtual* – but not *actual*. It is *real* in that it drives the movement of individuation, which generates individual forms and structures. But is *virtual* in that it consists of a variable degree of *potentiality* and *indetermination* – and therefore functions as a veritable principle of creation.

We should therefore consider two aspects of living and psychic organization. On the one hand, there is the ordinary homeostatic organization that corresponds to the normal life and self-maintenance of the organism or the psychic system. This mode of functioning presupposes a limited range of possible changes in the structure of the system. Bergson and Deleuze characterize this as a self-enclosed mode of functioning, which averts itself from 'effort' and tends towards 'convenience'.⁷¹ An organism can indeed become so self-absorbed in a static functioning that it obstructs itself from developing forward. On the other hand, there is an open-ended mode of individuation that is creative in the strongest sense, since it shifts the whole *range* of possible changes and behaviours in the system's structure – indeed it changes this structure itself. Individuation is then a positive source of novel differentiations: the actual organizations and structures, which have been formed, are re-organized based on the system's lingering potential for energy indetermination. Whereas organisms can always *enclose* the creative movement of inorganic life, the opposite occurs in processes of individuation: individuation always *liberates* a power of inorganic life, which individual organisms and human beings confine. As Deleuze and Guattari write with regard to the creative becoming of duration:

> This streaming, spiraling, zigzagging, snaking, feverish line of variation liberates a power of life that human beings had rectified and organisms had confined, and which matter now expresses as the trait, flow, or impulse traversing it. (…) In short, the life in question is inorganic, germinal, and intensive, a powerful life without organs, a Body that is all the more alive for having no organs.⁷²

4

From transcendental to dynamical structuralism

The crucial notion of singularity, taken literally, seems to belong to al the domains in which there is structure.

— Gilles Deleuze[1]

The structuralist turn

In his early, programmatic essay 'How do we recognize structuralism?' (1967) Deleuze presents a confrontation between structuralism and transcendental philosophy with the aim of demonstrating how structuralism transforms transcendental philosophy, and how a new transcendental structuralism becomes compatible with contemporary ideas in topology and dynamical systems theory concerning self-organization, singularities, structural stability, complexity, etc. Concerning the first point, the key novelty of structuralism is the idea that the constitution of sense and meaning in language does not presuppose an ideal, transcendental subject. Instead, language becomes the transcendental condition of possibility for both meaning and subjectivity. Unlike Kant and Husserl, who argued language presupposes a transcendental subject or ego, structuralists conceived language as a structural, symbolic/ideal realm that does not belong to the order of consciousness or subjectivity but that instead contains its conditions of possibility. Linguistic structure was therefore defined as a transcendental field *without* a subject that generates both meaning and subjectivity.

Deleuze's second key idea in this essay is that the foundations of structuralism are not only transcendental but also *topological*, and not *logical*.[2] Indeed, Deleuze speaks of a 'transcendental topology', which grounds empirical psychology and conceives the psychic element of symbolic structure in terms of a topological, spatial order of proximities defined by differential relations of emergence.

As he writes, 'empirical psychology is not only founded, but determined by a transcendental topology'.[3] Symbolic structure would emerge in a topological space, divided into regions (places) by a system of energetic differences and singularities. These intensive differences between the elements of a structure are not external relations between pre-existing identities, but rather generative relations of reciprocal determination. Generatively, symbolic structure becomes organized by the unfolding of singularities, which differentiate and organize it into a properly structural space.

The purpose of this chapter is to evaluate these two goals of Deleuze's transcendental structuralism: how does structuralism transform transcendental philosophy, and how should the foundations of structuralism be modelled topologically and dynamically? To address the first question, we will consider some key convergences and divergences between structuralism and transcendental philosophy concerning the autonomy of cognition, the constituency of structure, the principle of reciprocal dependency relations and the relation between language and subjectivity.

To address the second question, we will turn to Jean Petitot's *dynamical* structuralism, which has meticulously developed Deleuze's proposal of a topological foundation. Dynamical structuralism proposes an alternative to both traditional structuralism and classical functionalist computationalism, which both entail a strict dualism between the symbolic and physical levels, the relation between both being a matter of mere implementation. Instead of simply positing symbolic cognitive architectures in which cognition takes place, dynamical structuralism proposes to conceive symbolic structures as emerging from their material substrate base. Insofar as every symbolic structure is a system of reciprocal dependency relations, which links up different parts within a whole, every structure is modelled as a system of qualitative discontinuities emerging from the underlying substrate. But dynamical structuralism is nonetheless still a true functionalism because it considers emergent structures to have properties, which are to a large extent autonomous from the specific physical properties of their underlying substrata. Also, it fully endorses the important computationalist claim that high-level cognitive processes have properties (generativity, compositionality, systematicity, inferential coherence), which can only be modelled by constituent syntactic and semantic structures.[4]

The key issue here concerns the naturalization of transcendental, constituent structure: either one conceives the foundations of structuralism and functionalism in a purely *logicist* manner, thereby adopting a resolutely dualist stance and leaving the naturalization of structure wanting, or one conceives these foundations in a *dynamical* and *topological* manner, thereby naturalizing constituent structure in physical, morphological and ultimately symbolic terms. To see what such a dynamical functionalism entails, we will consider two of its key applications to categorical (speech) perception and visual perception.

In this light, the key theoretical innovation of Deleuze's proposal for a transcendental structuralism will appear as a *morphodynamic* approach to structure, which transforms the central structuralist principle of reciprocal determination into a morphogenetic process of psychic individuation, which generates ideal/symbolic structure. Indeed, in Deleuze's transcendental philosophy, the transcendental itself becomes a morphodynamic field of ideal/symbolic structure, which precedes the emergence of subjectivity.

Transcendental philosophy and structuralism

The autonomy of cognition

Structuralism shares with transcendental philosophy an exclusive concern for the autonomy of cognition, language and meaning. Both transcendental philosophers and structuralists claim that the phenomena of meaning and language have *a priori foundations* over and above physiological, psychological and cultural-historical conditions. For both, the faculty of language is psychic not in the psychological but only in the transcendental sense: the speaking subject processes linguistic information according to an *a priori* universal, constitutive system of formal, syntactical constraints that condition the assignment of semantic meaning to phonetic sequences. From a transcendental perspective, syntax is a *constituent structure*, which is akin to the constitutive function of the logical forms of judgment in constraining thought. Just as transcendental philosophy conceives the realm of meaning in terms of its own logical laws that are irreducible to physical reality and subjective psychological acts, so structuralists analyse our psychological linguistic experience as a sum of *sense effects* from the structural realm of language onto the psychological realm of experience.[5]

In cognitive science, the structuralist principle of constituent structure in *language* has been extended by computationalism to the *whole* of cognition. What computationalists such as Jerry Fodor and Zenon Pylyshyn call the 'systematic' and 'compositional' structure of *thought* exactly recapitulates the traditional structuralist argument for constituent structure in sentences.[6] For them, the constituent structure underlying our faculty of language is a paradigm of systematic/compositional cognition, but this constituent structure is not limited to language alone and rather appears as a thoroughly pervasive feature of human and infrahuman mentation. It postulates that *all* cognition relies on symbolic constituent structure, which belongs to a so-called language of thought that has the structure of a formal language (with symbols, expressions, inferential rules, etc.).

The transcendental ideality of constituent structure

Like transcendental philosophy, structuralism also rejects empiricist reductionism and posits the ontological primacy of ideal structures, which are constitutive of meaning. Structuralism begins when one assumes the constitutive existence of structures that are purely *ideal* and not material (or imaginary). As such, linguistic structures are abstract forms of psychic organization that are irreducible to certain interacting material components. The founding idea of structuralism is that structure is the ideal form of organization of a material substance, and as such structure is not a sensible phenomenon. It is essentially invisible, although its substantial realization and its meaning effects are observable and may be the object of certain rigorous empirical experiments. As such, structure is a theoretical object and not a fact. In Deleuze's famous phrasing, structure is at once real and ideal: '*real without being actual, ideal without being abstract*', a 'pure virtuality of coexistence that pre-exists beings'.[7] As an organizational principle, structure 'incarnates' itself in its substrate, it 'expresses' itself in it, but it never actualizes itself *as such*. Instead, the sensible expression of a structure is always essentially a negation of its ideal, formal being.

To understand this abstract idea, one can compare it to the Kantian conception of a pure intuition of space. As we have already seen, for Kant, our sense of three-dimensional space is not *derived* from the senses, but rather *produced* by the (unconscious) mind as an *a priori* framework within which sensorial input can become organized. Space as pure intuition is an ideal or virtual structure, which the mind projects onto the physical world, and which is 'filled' and 'realized' by means of actual sensorial input. In Kant's terms, space is an *a priori* 'form of intuition' through which raw sense data are first 'given', and can subsequently be processed or 'synthesized'. But this ideal form is not itself *derived* from sensory experience: spatial cognition is not an abstraction from the relations between objects or stimulus configurations, as empiricists would hold. On the contrary, cognitive processing or 'synthesis' of sensory information is only possible based on the mental generation of a pre-existing spatial framework.

Like spatial cognition, linguistic structure can be understood as a virtual frame that we project onto the physical world (i.e. the audio-acoustic flux of spoken sound). Deleuze gives the example of the phoneme. Phonemes play an essential role in the perception of sound sequences as *linguistic* sound sequences. They allow us to perceive the continuous audio-acoustic flux of sound sequences as a *sound structure* that consists of discrete interconnected parts, or units. The central idea is that speech perception is especially sensitive to qualitative discontinuities in the flux of sound sequences, which serve as cues of differences in meaning. For example, upon comparing 'bat' and 'pat', a qualitative discontinuity is perceived by virtue of the phonemes /p/ and /b/. Here, the phonemes p and b function as cues, which highlight an elementary categorical discontinuity, or what Deleuze calls a singularity. Thus, the phonemes are not perceived along a continuum but rather as discrete categories. As such, the perception of phonemes transforms the continuum of audio-acoustic sounds into a discrete, categorized structure.

But in what sense should the phoneme be a pure *virtuality* and not simply a well-defined speech sound? Here, we have to see that a phoneme can never be identified with one physical constant. Rather, there is a physical continuum of variations, which are all identified in perception as belonging to the phoneme. There is, in short, a marked lack of correspondence between sound and perceived phoneme. The phoneme is an abstract *type* that is instantiated in actual speech by concrete *tokens*. For this reason, many structuralist linguists such as Roman Jakobson and Nikolaj Trubetzkoy considered the phoneme not as a physical, audio-acoustic property but rather as a psychological or mental reality (X). As Petitot emphasized in his early work, this leads to a 'foundational aporia' underlying linguistics: how can an acoustic, phonetic flux of a physical nature become the perceptual basis of a phonological code of a strictly linguistic nature, governed by differential relations?[8] This aporia concerns the relation between the physical-phonetic and the symbolic-structural dimensions of language.

As abstract linguistic types, phonemes are not defined by intrinsic physical properties but by a network of differences and reciprocal dependency relations. Since Saussure and Jakobson, phonemes have been understood as purely *relational* entities, rather than substantial ones. As Petitot puts it, they are eidetic 'Gestalten' depending upon a purely *formal* level of reality.[9] In this sense, the phoneme is essentially 'double-faced':

1. On the *phonological* side, it is a structural, linguistic category that is traditionally believed to be of an algebraic-combinatorial, computational kind: identity of position, relational unity, difference, discrimination, reciprocal determination, etc.
2. On the *phonetic* side, it is a psychophysical or neuropsychological, audio-acoustic category: spectral forms, deformation of these forms, control by acoustic cues, invariance/variability, categorization, boundaries, etc.

Structuralists such as Saussure and Hjelmslev emphasized the ontological autonomy of the phoneme as an ideal 'form of expression' that is 'embodied' in the material 'substance of expression' but that is not reducible to it. As such, there is a reciprocal dependence between the *phonetic form* and the *phonetic substance*. In the Kantian sense, phonemes function like categories that determine our phonetic perception. Thus, if Deleuze calls the phoneme an exemplary case of a 'pure virtuality', this must be understood in the sense that it is an abstract structure or organizational form that has a cognitive reality and becomes attached or encoded in the physical audio-acoustic flux.

The central principle of structuralist linguistics asserts that only the *form* of expression is *significant*, and not the substance of expression. Signs, that is, linguistic functions, relate forms of expression to forms of content. As such, the effects produced by meaningful substances can be studied only by abstracting forms from them. Now, if we want to understand how form or structure itself can be meaningful, we must turn to a third concept marking a deep convergence between structuralism and transcendental philosophy: the concept of reciprocal dependency relations, which constitute meaningful form in an autonomous dimension of sense and meaning.

Reciprocal dependency relations

One of the most fundamental concepts of structuralism is that of a relation of reciprocal determination. This category informs the very idea, proposed by Saussure, of a *primacy* of relations to their terms. Saussure's main contribution to linguistics lies in conceiving linguistic units not as substantial ones but as purely relational ones. In a linguistic structure, the value or identity of a particular linguistic unit, such as a phoneme, is purely 'positional'.[10] The sounds of language become phonemes when they are reciprocally opposed to one another. This means a linguistic structure is not a system of relations between predefined terms. As regarding their value, the terms of the structure do not have any autonomous existence. They can be defined only by their *reciprocal determination* within a self-organizing whole. Similarly, words in natural language never possess meaning by themselves but only insofar as they are opposed to other words within the lexical structure of a language. Ever since Saussure, the category of reciprocal determination has been fundamental to structuralism, and as we will see, it plays a central role in Deleuze's structuralism as well.[11] Indeed, the category of reciprocal determination entails the structuralist principle according to which difference is prior to identity, so important to Deleuze.

Transcendental philosophy easily aligns with this core feature of structuralism, which is the idea of relations without substantial *relata*. One might even say that one of its first substantial philosophical developments appeared in Kant's treatment of biological self-organization in terms of reciprocal dependency relations. Likewise, Husserl's Third Logical Investigation ('On the theory of wholes and parts') is one of the key philosophical developments of the mereological relations between a whole and its parts. In his analysis of structural relations of dependencies, Husserl argued that such relations should be conceived as metaphysical connections that are not merely applicable to linguistics (i.e. to linguistic contents and their expression) but rather applicable *a priori* to many spheres of objects. His paradigmatic example is that of the dependency relation between qualities (e.g. the colour red) and extension: the redness of a particular thing cannot exist independently from spatial extension and, vice versa, extension itself is also necessarily colored.[12] The same holds for the relation between intensity and quality: both are reciprocally dependent upon one another. Eliminate quality and one eliminates intensity, and vice versa. For Husserl, these kinds of reciprocal dependency relations are not merely empirical – instead, they have an *a priori* necessity, grounded in pure essence. That is to say, the necessity of dependency relations 'stands for an ideal or *a priori* necessity rooted in the essences of things'.[13]

A Kantian unconscious

That being said, we should now consider a significant divergence between structuralism and transcendental philosophy. The greatest difficulties for the concept of a transcendental subjectivity come from the study of language. For instance, one of the fundamental problems, which animated Husserl's phenomenology, concerns the relation between *insight* and *expression*. Husserl considers insight to be purely ideal and to be identically repeatable within consciousness. In order to *share* insight, it must be dressed in the physical form of an expression (e.g. the spoken word or the written sign). An expression then allows a reader or listener to 'see' a meaning, which as an ideal entity is itself irreducible to the expression (and to any psychological event grasping the meaning).[14]

In *The Origin of Geometry* (1936), Husserl sketches this relation between insight and expression as follows. Imagining how a highly abstract discipline such as geometry may have emerged, he believes this must have taken place in an originary visionary intuition within the consciousness of a particular individual, which might be seen as the originary geometer. He or she 'saw' the geometric truth as an ideal given that was immediately present (*selbst-da*) and self-evident. Although this moment of discovery was psychologically localizable within the mental space of this proto-geometer, the geometric insight as such is not psychological in nature. Indeed, geometric existence is not psychic existence. For example, the Pythagorean theorem does not exist as something personal within the personal sphere of consciousness but rather it exists as an 'ideal objectivity' (*ideale Gegenständlichkeit*) that is there for everyone to 'see'.[15] For Husserl, geometric insight has not a *real*, psychological but an *irreal*, purely ideal status. This means it is (a) supra-temporal, (b) infinitely repeatable and (c) valid *a priori* for any other rational subject.[16] In order to transcend the intra-personal psychic origin and to attain an *intersubjective* objectivity, the insight must then be linguistically expressed. Important in this regard is Husserl's view that insight in and of itself *already* has an ideal objectivity to it, *prior to* and *independent of* all expression. Expression is rather a secondary and even accidental matter. It merely transmits what will forever remain identically the same – in the original language of Euclid and in all its translations. As Husserl emphasizes, 'the idealities of geometrical words, sentences, theories – considered purely as linguistic structures – are not the idealities that make up what is expressed and brought to validity as truth in geometry; the latter are ideal geometrical objects, states of affairs, etc.'[17]

It is these assumptions on the relation between insight and linguistic expression, which have been questioned by structuralism: can we posit a subjective sphere of pure insight and pure interiority, which would precede language, or is such subjectivity itself constituted by language? In the *Logical Investigations*, Husserl himself already pointed out that the ego is not only an instance of thought or of consciousness, but also of speaking. In speaking, the ego *signifies itself*, which leads to a remarkable doubling between the signifying ego and the signified ego. In this context, the Libanese linguist Émile Benveniste explicitly argued that the ego *emerges within the signifying act*. As such, language would be a transcendental condition of possibility for subjectivity: 'It is only in and through language that the human being constitutes itself as a *subject*; because only language grounds in reality, in *its* reality, the concept of the "ego."'[18] Around the same time, the transcendental was conceived by Jean Hyppolite – Deleuze's first philosophical master – as a transcendental field *without* a subject, a field that is neither of the order of consciousness nor of the ego, but instead would contain the conditions of possibility of subjectivity, meaning and consciousness.

Along these lines, Paul Ricoeur famously called structuralism a 'transcendentalism without a subject' or a 'Kantianism without a transcendental subject'.[19] As Ricoeur points out, structuralism is concerned with 'a categorial system without any reference to a thinking subject'.[20] It posits a preconscious categorizing activity that concerns our unconscious *competences* in understanding and expressing language. The object of structuralist linguistics is the preconscious rules and categories of language, that is, the laws, which the competent linguistic subject has an implicit, unreflective knowledge of. As Ricoeur puts it, structuralist linguistics invokes therefore a 'Kantian unconscious' rather than a Freudian one, since it is concerned not with the energetics of instincts, drives and desire, but rather with a preconscious categorization of auditory sound fluxes into phonemes, words and sentences according to the structural laws of language.[21]

Transcendental structuralism: Key principles

Traditionally, the *origin of structure* was left open, and its naturalistic understanding was often considered to be illusory. Consequently, structure was considered to be a *transcendent* instance within which the differential reciprocal relations are established, which determine the meaning of signs and which principally exclude the question of the 'origin' of meaning. The main principle of structuralist linguistics asserts that all meaning is generated exclusively by reciprocal determinations in the autonomous, transcendent dimension of structure. Of course, meaning needs always to be realized concretely in the psychological immanence of speech acts. But nonetheless, the key idea of structuralism is that the reciprocal relations between linguistic elements such as phonemes, letters, words, etc. cannot be reduced to the immanence of psychological processes and pertains exclusively to disembodied, purely ideal signifying relations in the autonomous, ideal domain of structure. It asserts that for the order of meaning, *causality is structural and formal before being physical and material.*

Although Deleuze subscribes to this central structuralist principle, his proposal for a transcendental structuralism is one of the first critiques of the traditional conception of meaning in structuralism. For Deleuze, meaning cannot be seen as completely *detached* from its psychic and physical realization; by contrast, meaningful forms and structures *emerge* from dynamical processes of matter. His proposal claimed that the structural concept of form must be replaced by a genetic concept of structure or form, as an emergent self-organization. Deleuze proposed that symbolic structures should be modelled *topologically* (i.e. geometrically) and that the mathematical concept of *singularities* could be used to explain the *emergence* of the structural values in symbolic structures. As he put it:

> The crucial notion of singularity, taken literally, seems to belong to all the domains in which there is structure. (…) Every structure presents the following two aspects: a system of differential relations according to which the symbolic elements determine themselves reciprocally, and a system of singularities corresponding to these relations and tracing the [topological] space of the structure. (…) It is not a matter of mathematical metaphors. In each domain, one must find elements, relationships and [singular] points.[22]

In this regard, it is possible to see in Deleuze's proposal a key forerunner to the more recent debate in the cognitive sciences between dynamical systems approaches to cognition and classical functionalist approaches. Classical functionalism, for example in Fodor and Pylyshyn's foundational work, entails a strict separation between the symbolic and physical levels – the relation between the physical and the symbolic being one of mere implementation or realization, as in classical structuralism. Deleuze's topological approach to structuralism, however, sought to overcome this dualism by providing an emergentist approach.[23] On this view, every symbolic structure is epistemically reducible to a system of singularities or qualitative discontinuities emerging from an underlying physical (e.g. neural) substrate of morphodynamical, generative mechanisms. As Petitot argued, 'structures are essentially dependent on *critical phenomena,* i.e., on phenomena of symmetry breaking which induce qualitative discontinuities (heterogeneities) in the substrates (…). Discrete structures emerge via qualitative discontinuities.'[24] In his seminal *Morphogenesis of Meaning* (1985), Petitot pointed to Deleuze's early topological proposal as one of the key philosophical inspirations underlying his application of René Thom's Catastrophe Theory (proposed in the 1970s) to cognitive semiolinguistics.[25]

However, just like Petitot's dynamical structuralism, Deleuze's transcendental structuralism is at the same time still a true functionalism, because emergent structures have properties, which are to a large extent independent of the specific physical properties of their underlying substrata. In this sense, transcendental structuralism and dynamical structuralism share with traditional functionalism the refusal of ontological reductionism or reductionist physicalism (defending only a 'softer' epistemological reductionism), and recognize the immaterial content of mental acts.[26] As such, both transcendental and dynamical structuralism can be seen as a variant of 'dynamical functionalism.'[27]

Simplifying a lot, we may summarize Deleuze's proposal in the following three key points.

The topological *a priori*

Deleuze's proposal starts with a monist-naturalist assumption, which is to say that both mind and life share fundamental organizational principles, and the organizational principles distinctive of mind are an enriched version of those fundamental to life. Like contemporary proponents of the enactive approach in cognitive science, Deleuze argues that the natural continuity between life and mind justifies approaching the emergence of structure and meaning in terms of morphogenesis.[28] Structure and meaningful form emerge then like dynamical forms do in embryogenetic development, namely as morphodynamically self-organized and self-regulating structures or wholes. Now, insofar as every natural being has a form, one must imagine a space in which this form unfolds itself. Deleuze proposes to conceive this primary space as a continuous space that becomes categorized or discretized by a system of discontinuities or singularities. *Structural* space is divided into regions (places) by a system of differences, and for the elements in this space, the differences are not external relations between pre-existing identities but rather generative relations.[29]

Genetically, the generative relations between regions in structural space are obtained from the unfolding of singularities, whose unfolding organizes the structure of the space. These singularities are intensive discontinuities within the substratum space. This means ultimately that a meaningful form or structure must be defined as a system of intensive discontinuities or singularities that unfold within an underlying substratum space. However, as Petitot notes, the singularities themselves are not signifiable: 'their inscription in the signifiable (expression and representation) reformulates them as lack, as lacuna'.[30]

Petitot proposes a connection between this conception of singularity to Thom's concept of 'catastrophe', which opens up a rigorous understanding of how the general and primitive phenomenon of *discontinuity* can give rise to structures. We will consider this application below.

Differential structure

Secondly, a structure becomes properly organized only by virtue of the principle of reciprocal determination. Deleuze proposes to conceive the principle of reciprocal determination in terms of Leibnizian differential calculus. Following the work of Jules Vuillemin and Hoëne Wronski, he proposes that differential calculus may function as a universal algebra of pure thought: a *mathesis universalis* of the Cogito. The general idea is that in *all* the different domains of thought – mathematics, literature, physics, philosophy, culture, etc. – the psychic individuation of new concepts and ideas involves one universal genetic mechanism taking place in structural, intensive space. The shift to differential calculus is meant to formalize this mechanism as an *a priori* principle of *reciprocal determination*, which is at work in the emergence of all new meaningful form or structure. In this sense, Deleuze's transcendental structuralism extends the idea of constituent structure from language to the whole of thought – a classical *functionalist* move. Deleuze then defines three phases in the emergence of a structure:

1. First, there are undetermined differential elements (dx, dy), which corresponds to a principle of determinability;
2. Secondly, differential elements become determinable (dy/dx), which corresponds to the principle of reciprocal determination;
3. Finally, the determined (the values of dy/dx) corresponds to a principle of complete determination.

From this perspective, we can already see a meaningful form or structure is for Deleuze a system of differential relations between reciprocally determined elements. Moreover, one might add that reciprocal dependency relations have in Deleuze's transcendental structuralism the same cognitive function as the schematism in Kant's philosophy: they allow for an *internalization* of sensory information, which stands for a process of *virtualization*. As in Kant's philosophy, this is a process that *detaches* lived experience from the sensorial here and now and places it under a horizon of logical time. Moreover, by virtue of the principle of reciprocal determination, virtualized elements acquire a cognitive function or value that is completely detached from their intrinsic properties. However, for Deleuze unlike Kant, this process of virtualization is not organized in terms of generic-particular relations, but in terms of singular-ordinary relations.

Virtual multiplicity

Deleuze maintains that the process of reciprocal and complete determination belongs to a differential unconscious of pure thought: an unconscious of pure reason. The primary model for this differential unconscious is Bernhard Riemann's mathematical concept of multiplicity. In this context, Deleuze emphasizes that the concept of multiplicity may not be interpreted as a simple set or collection of elements that are united in some way. In the Riemannian sense, a multiplicity is a collection of elements, which are not merely united but also *organized* and *connected* in a continuous manner. A multiplicity is an *organized connection* that is defined by the *relations* between its elements rather than by those elements themselves. Deleuze then specifies the three conditions, which together allow us to define the process in which a structure emerges in the differential unconscious as a multiplicity:

1. Virtual indetermination: the elements of the multiplicity must have neither sensible form nor conceptual signification, nor, therefore, any assignable function. They are, however, inseparable from an 'incorporeal' potential or a 'virtuality'.
2. Reciprocal determination: the differential elements are determined through the process of reciprocal determination, which forms reciprocal relations that allow no independence of the elements to subsist. Such reciprocal relations are non-empirical, non-localizable ideal connections, which determine the ideal multiplicity globally.
3. Actualization/incarnation: the differential connections or relations of a multiplicity must become actualized in diverse spatio-temporal relations, at the same time as its ideal elements are actually incarnated in a manifold of terms and forms.

Together, these elements allow Deleuze to define structure as an internal multiplicity: 'a system of multiple, non-localizable connections between differential elements which is incarnated in real relations and actual terms'.[31] But what exactly does the concept of multiplicity add to the concept of reciprocal determination? The important issue here is how we understand the organizational function of reciprocal determination. We already noted that a multiplicity can only be defined in terms of its connections between its elements, that is, in terms of the relations established by reciprocal determination. Now, the concept of multiplicity brings with it the important idea of *genesis* or *individuation*: in a multiplicity, there are only elements with a particular function, value or signification insofar as the latter *emerges* from the connections between elements. Thus, the process of reciprocal determination is *generative*. It *actualizes* values by means of relations between elements that are in themselves merely undetermined and *virtual*. As such, the generative process of reciprocal determination is always a process of *qualification*.

Once we understand that the emergence of a structure entails (1) a qualification of a virtual multiplicity, which is (2) driven by a genetic process of reciprocal determination, we should also see that the structure's determination happens by means of a principle that is *intrinsic* to the system. The connections between its virtual elements are not *external* relations between pre-existing identities, but *constitutive, generative* relations of reciprocal determination *within* the system. Thus, the determination of a symbolic structure happens by means of a creative, organizational process that is *immanent* to its ideal-virtual structure. According to Deleuze, this is ultimately the fundamental property of structures: they dispose of a genetic, self-constructive principle of reciprocal determination that is characteristic only of ideal (also called symbolic or virtual) structures and not of the empirical real, the imaginary or even the conceptual.

Thus, conceiving reciprocal determination as a process taking place in a virtual multiplicity allows Deleuze to develop its genetic, constructive, individuating nature: reciprocal determination is an ideal event taking place within a virtual structure that is in the process of being actualized and incarnated.

The example of linguistic structure

Let us consider at this point Deleuze's example of the phoneme in linguistic structure.[32] In the discussed formal terminology, linguistic structure can be regarded as a virtual system of reciprocal connections between 'phonemes' which is incarnated in the actual terms and relations of diverse languages. From a phonological point of view, a linguistic structure indeed has the mentioned properties of a differential structure:

1. The presence of differential ideal elements (phonemes) which are *extracted* from the continuous sonorous flux.
2. The existence of differential relations (distinctive features) which *reciprocally determine* these elements.
3. Finally, the *ideal value* or *signification* of singular points assumed by the phonemes in that reciprocal determination.

From this point of view, linguistic meaning can be regarded as an *ideal* system of reciprocal connections between phonemes (1 & 2), which becomes *incarnated* (3) in the actual terms and relations of diverse natural languages. The process of reciprocal determination thus makes possible speech perception and actual speech as a faculty.

How does this proposal differ from classical structuralism? In structuralist linguistics, the structural connections between phonemes, lexemes, words, etc. form the crux of syntax. These connections are immaterial, disembodied or as Deleuze has it, 'incorporeal'. Traditionally, structuralist linguistics understands the relational structure as a logical-combinatorial description of the relevant forms. However, in Deleuze's topological approach, the reciprocal and complete determinations of a structure occupy particular *places* in a structure, which are defined by *a dynamic process* of reciprocal determination that is continuous and *energetic*, making use of relative forces linking the determinations. Deleuze introduced the mathematical concept of singularities to conceive the generating potentials, which underlie the reciprocal and complete determination of structure. In other words, for Deleuze, structures become *dynamical entities* that are regulated and controlled in so-called possibility spaces or phase spaces. This brings us to the dynamical structuralism of Jean Petitot, which has meticulously developed these theoretical ideas underlying Deleuze's proposal.

Naturalizing constituent structure: Dynamical structuralism

Petitot's dynamical structuralism is an attempt to ground cognitive phenomena such as language and perception – studied in semiotics, linguistics, phenomenology of perception, etc. – in the mathematics of René Thom's Catastrophe Theory. One of its central theoretical ideas is that cognitive structures can be modelled at the macro-level by the topology of an 'attractor' of an underlying micro-dynamics. Syntactic and semantic constituent structures should then be considered as *emergent phenomena*, analogous to the processes we find in physics under the name of *critical phenomena* and thermodynamic phenomena of *phase transitions*. This constitutes a key innovation compared to traditional structuralist linguistics: structures should be understood in terms of their emergence from underlying dynamical mechanisms.

Secondly, a key idea underlying dynamical structuralism is that the syntactic and semantic constituent structures of *language* should be understood in relation to constituent structures of *perception*. Just like underlying dynamical mechanisms, so the structures of perception impose certain universal constraints on the grammatical structures of language.[33] In line with Ray Jackendoff, Petitot proposes there is one single level of mental representation – 'conceptual representation' – at which linguistic, sensory and motor information are integrated.[34] Although this hypothesis remains compatible with the framework of computationalism, it introduces the idea that perceptual structures constrain semantic structures, and these in turn constrain syntax. Conceptual structure first transforms the *physical* world into a *projected* morphological world – the *phenomenal, sensory* world as *qualitatively* structured and phenomenologically organized – and into *semantic* structures, which in turn *constrain* the syntactic structures of natural languages. Thus, the perceptual level is more primitive than the semantic level: the latter is grounded on the former, not the other way around. This claim should be understood in an evolutionary sense: phylogenetically speaking, perceptual structures are deeper than linguistic structures. As a result of evolutionary adaptation, the perceptions and actions of an organism are fine-tuned to the qualitative structure of its environment (forms, qualities, etc.): this qualitative structure has become intrinsically meaningful to the organism. It is this perceptual/morphological structure, which in turn constrains linguistic structure. As Petitot puts it, 'The idea is that the *spatio-temporal a priori* is deeper than the symbolic *a priori*: the human visual system is inherited from a very long natural evolution, while ideography and writing are extremely recent cultural acquisitions.'[35]

Constituent structure in categorical perception

One of Petitot's first proposals was a catastrophist reworking of Roman Jakobson's structural phonology via the concept of 'categorical perception'. Given Deleuze's mentioned focus on the notion of the phoneme, we will briefly consider this case.

Categorical perception is a remarkable phenomenon: although the acoustic-phonetic input of language is a variable continuum of sound, the perception of speech sounds is discrete, discontinuous and categorical. In speech, the acoustic-phonetic flux of individual sounds may *vary* substantially but listeners typically perceive them unambiguously as canonical sound *types*. For example, when presented with intermediate varieties between /b/ and /p/, listeners perceive each sound as either a distinct /b/ or /p/, and not an intermediate sound.[36] In other words, there is no 'intra-categorical' discrimination: listeners do not distinguish between two adjacent sounds unless they belong to two different categories. Contrary to what happens in continuous perception, categorical perception depends on an *identification* of categories, which turns the audio-acoustic continuum into a discrete structure that can be used to support a phonological, linguistic code. Indeed, by virtue of categorical perception, phonemes become *encoded* in the audio-acoustic flux.[37] And it is only the phonemes and their differences, which are linguistically pertinent – *not the phonetic sounds as such*.

This is clear when we compare English and Thai: in English, there is only one boundary separating /d/ and /t/; in Thai, however, there are two boundaries separating /d/ from /t/ and /t/ from /th/. These boundaries vary from language to language. Take the following divergence between English and Japanese. In English, the phonemes /r/ and /l/ differentiate the words *rock* and *lock*. However, in Japanese, these phonemes are used interchangeably and do not alter the meaning of a word. Accordingly, Japanese people find it difficult to hear the distinction between the American English /r/ and /l/ sounds. The reason is that both tend to be *categorically perceived* as a Japanese /r/.[38]

Cross-linguistic experiments on preverbal children have demonstrated that young infants can discern even slight acoustic changes at the boundaries between phonetic categories, and that they can do this even for phonemes in languages they have never experienced. At the end of the first year, however, infants can no longer discriminate phonetic changes, which they successfully recognized six months earlier. Finally, in adults this capacity of categorical perception has become much more restrained: adults have this ability only for phonetic units in the languages in which we are fluent. This is why, as noted, Japanese adults have difficulties to hear the distinction between the American English /r/ and /l/ sounds.

One of the key challenges of structuralist semio-linguistics is to understand the relation between the physical level of audio-acoustic sounds and the phonological level of linguistic forms (phonemes), which are encoded in the physical flux based on qualitative discontinuities and differential thresholds. How can one relate the essentially *continuous* nature of speech with the essentially *discontinuous* nature of speech perception and linguistic description? How can the audio-acoustic flux of sounds become encoded as instantiating the abstract, linguistically functional units or types, which are defined not by intrinsic (physical) properties but by a linguistic network of differential relations?

Tackling this question, Petitot's morphodynamic approach starts from two assumptions: (a) categorical perception functions as an *a priori* form of perception, projecting its eidetic types onto the physical continuum and (b) this *a priori* form is essentially a sensitivity to *discontinuity*.[39] The overarching idea is that the phoneme as a linguistic-relational form of expression *emerges* from the *dynamical organization* of the phonetic substance of expression. This implies assuming a morphodynamical mechanism 'X' that is neurophysiologically implemented and generates this expressive, phonemic morphology. Instead of first defining this generating mechanism explicitly and then deriving the observable discontinuities from it, the morphodynamic approach first describes the observable discontinuities geometrically and then derives from them a minimally complex generating dynamics.[40] This minimal, explicit dynamics is then conceived as a simplification of the real, implicit dynamics (X).

For Petitot, the morphogenesis of phonemes as abstract forms is structurally similar to the case of phase transitions in physics: the boundaries between categorical units would correspond to the existence of *critical points* – for example, the end point for the liquid/gas interface for water.[41] Categorical perception is modelled as an essentially *non-linear* process in relation to acoustic parameters. The idea is thus that categorical perception segments and categorizes the audio-acoustic continua *by virtue* of its sensitivity to qualitative discontinuities, thresholds or singularities. The *internal* cortical/perceptual state is controlled by the *external* audio-acoustic parameters. This neural/perceptual state remains stable (phonologically invariant) faced with much of the audio-acoustic flux, but it undergoes sudden variations ('*bifurcations*' or '*catastrophes*') when the external continuum reaches certain *critical* values. For Petitot, the main import of Thom's Catastrophist mathematical models concerns the analysis of these singularities and discontinuities, which emerge at the macro level from underlying micro-physical mechanisms. Their main purpose is to explain how observable morphologies, which dominate the phenomenologically experienced world (such as phonemes), can emerge from an underlying physics (in this case the neural substrate of speech perception). As such, the theoretical import of Catastrophe Theory is to introduce – by mathematical means – a new level of functional, cognitive architecture, which would function as an *a priori* condition of possibility for the implementation of syntactic processes into brain dynamics. The challenge for this approach is to show how it can also be aligned with an effective computational theory, which captures other fundamental levels of cognitive architecture. However, it should be noted that dynamical functionalism was certainly not conceived as antithetical to computationalism.

Constituent structure in visual perception

Turning to the phenomenology of visual perception, we can see how dynamical structuralism posits a *morphological* level of reality that is *intermediate between the physical and the symbolical*: 'it is of a physical (emergent) origin but without being material, it is formal but without being symbolic; it is *topologically and geometrically* formal and not *logically* formal.'[42] Accordingly, the external world would contain a morphological, qualitative dimension of information, which has a *physical* origin but nonetheless is *phenomenological* in nature and, as such, is intrinsically significative. As noted, it is this morphological, intrinsically meaningful dimension, which serves as the basis for the properly symbolic information processing at higher levels of cognition. Its structural constituency derives from a spatio-temporal *a priori* that is phylogenetically more originary than the symbolic *a priori* of higher cognition. Indeed, one of Petitot's key disagreements with classical computationalism concerns the idea that the morphological/phenomenological dimension cannot itself be derived from the syntactic-semantic: 'this is clearly impossible, since the intrinsically spatio-temporal and dynamical dimensions of the morphological *are not* of the formal order in the sense of the logico-symbolical.'[43] For Petitot, the classical computationalist approach is legitimate only in the context of a logical objectivism, a formal semantics and/or a phenomenological logic of essences. However, it is generally *incompatible* with naturalist approaches to cognition, since it offers no clue as to the existence of symbolic forms in nature. The morphodynamic approach, by contrast, assumes that all the constituent structures of mind, language and meaning are dynamical and geometric forms.[44] Of course, these must be symbolically translatable and treatable at higher levels of cognitive representation. But their *type of objectivity* can, for Petitot, not originally be that of symbolic objectivity. If the constituent structure or form of mind, language and meaning is to be *natural*, it cannot be strictly symbolical. To formalize, describe and explain constituent structure, one must pass from the logical to the topological.

How, then, does dynamical structuralism conceive of constituent structure at the spatio-temporal, morphological level? In this context, the paradigmatic case is the study of visual perception. Once again, the general problem is to understand how perceptual macrostructures and their morphodynamics can *emerge* from an underlying neural microlevel. The approach is again functionalist, meaning it attempts to formulate the cognitive architecture (the constituent structure) that is implemented in neural networks considered as functional units.

Taking his cue from David Marr's pioneering work in vision research, Petitot starts from the question how vision can reconstruct three-dimensional objects on the basis of two-dimensional retinal images. Computationalists such as Marr and Fodor treat this question by distinguishing two types of information processing. On the one hand, there are peripheral, 'modular' systems, which transform or 'transduce' peripheral neuronal information into a propositional form that is adequate to symbolic cognitive processing. These 'vertical' processes function in a 'bottom-up' manner, ascending from peripheries to the centre of the brain. For Fodor, whose terminology we are adopting, phoneme or face recognition, and perception more generally, are typical instances of modular or vertical processes. Although these bottom-up processes already analyse sensory information, they are informationally 'insensible' to higher-order cognitive knowledge, belief, etc.

On the other hand, computationalism posits 'central' or 'horizontal' cognitive processes, which are non-modular, non-specific, descending 'top-down' and interpretative (sensible to beliefs, memories, knowledge, etc.). Today, the wide popularity of top-down approaches to cognition – so-called 'predictive processing' and 'predictive coding' approaches – consider information processing in vision to be essentially concerned with top-down *predictions*, which are compared with lower-level representations to verify potential prediction errors.[45] Marr and Petitot, however, place a firm emphasis on bottom-up processing, casting perceptual synthesis as the serial extraction of visual information from primary physical information. Their approach lends itself very well to *natural* (rather than artificial) vision, because unlike top-down processes, bottom-up processes are governed by universal rules that are largely 'built' into the brain at birth by biological evolution. They allow different species to extract particular key elements of images in the physical world and project them onto objects. Such extracted elements include contours, colours, intersections and the crossings of lines and junctions, which animals use to discern objects, people and facial gestures, to ascertain their placement in space (perspective), etc. For example, if the neurons of the brain of a hungry frog allow it to catch an earthworm by jumping up and capturing it, it is because its neurons are biologically 'wired', by evolution, to be *sensitive* to a particular configuration of visual stimuli, a particular form or *Gestalt*: longitudinal movement of any elongated subject.[46] Similarly, the neurons of the brain of a cat allow it to catch a mouse by *anticipating* its future positions because the neurons are sensitive to the speed of the movement.

This *selective* response of the mammalian eye to information makes vision something profoundly different from simply recording the image of a scene or a person, like a camera would, pixel by pixel. The mammalian visual system *selects* and *discards* certain contours and lines with a specific orientation, which form the physiological building blocks for the neural elaboration of the image that will be consciously perceived. By means of this bottom-up processing, each human visual system extracts the same essential information from an environment. It is what enables animals to scan an open field and tree line for predators and prey, allows babies to recognize faces and it is why, after not having seen a friend for many years, we may instantly identify her in the midst of an anonymous crowd at the single sight of the facial expression characteristic of her smile.[47]

Petitot considers Marr's bottom-up approach to be a *neo-ecological* one, close to James Gibson's ecological theory of perception. Gibson posited that in an animal's *Umwelt* there exist qualitative and cognitively significant structures, which are objective without being strictly physical (they are morphological in Petitot's sense).[48] An animal's visual system would *choose*, *select* and *extract* particular morphological invariants and based on these, it would construct its inferences, anticipations and interpretations.

At the heart of Marr's computational theory of perception, we find three distinct levels of information processing. Marr based these proposed mechanisms on what is known about mammalian, and in particular, primate, vision. He distinguishes the following three stages:

1. The first level is that of the so-called 2D *primal sketch*. It makes explicit the *local* geometrical and morphological organization of the sensory signal. The first stage is concerned with detecting light intensity edges or what Marr calls 'zero-crossings' of the visual scene in order to represent it in a 'primal sketch'. A zero crossing is an intensive point where the value of a function changes its sign; it corresponds to a sudden change in intensity in the image. The primary processing of such zero crossings allows for segmentation processes that will support the intermediate and final (cognitive and inferential) stages, such as interpretation, recognition, understanding, etc. As Petitot emphasizes, the primal sketch essentially involves a local analysis of the sensory signal in terms of *qualitative discontinuities*: edges, ridges, blobs with a particular elongation and orientation, bars, etc.

2. The second level is that of the so-called 2 ½ D and is an *intermediate* level between the 2D and 3D levels. It is, for Marr, the essential level of the theory, calling it the 'pivotal point' of 'pure perception'. It is a *viewer-centred* and *globally* organized level, integrating several modular computations carried out on the primal sketch: contours of visible surfaces, textures, stereopsis, movement, shading effects, etc. It represents the external world as composed of visible surfaces filled with sensible qualities and moving in three dimensions. Petitot notes that this level is neither purely *sensory* (because surfaces are distal and not viewer-centred), nor purely *objective* (because the appearances are still subjective). Rather, it is concerned with interpreting certain 2D qualitative continuities as *apparent contours* of 3D objects. As such, he considers this level, along with Ray Jackendoff, as the level of *phenomenological appearance* or *phenomenal consciousness*.[49] In Petitot's terms, the 2 ½ D level is 'of a true *morphological* nature'.[50] This processing of contours is crucial, because it is what allows the transition from 2D to 3D perception in space-time.
3. The third level of '3D models', finally, is the *objective* level of real things and material volumes with their real properties. It is from this level that superior cognitive constituents of 'conceptual structure' (Jackendoff) operate, for example, the hierarchical decomposition of shapes into parts, the constitution of prototypes, etc. Jackendoff contends that consciousness lies in the 2 ½ D sketch and not in the 3D model, which corresponds to a higher cognitive level of the hierarchy that remains outside of our consciousness. Like many of our memories, anticipations and understanding, the 3D model would remain outside of conscious awareness yet it would heavily influence the final product of which we are conscious. It should be noted, however, that these contentions are purely psychological (independent from the actual characteristics of the neuronal implementation) and, in fact, no one really knows where the consciousness-determining neurons are located.

Following Marr and Jackendoff, Petitot considers perception to be, primarily, a *bottom-up* process that ascends from 2D → 2 ½ D → 3D → Conceptual Structure. This bottom-up process possesses top-down feedback mechanisms, which regulate it by means of anticipation, inferences, interpretations, etc. Top-down feedback moves from conceptual structure 'down' to the morphological level of

2 ½ D. As such, the 2 ½ D level would be the final level of bottom-up perceptual processing.

The distinction between three levels of perceptual information processing corresponds to the above-mentioned distinction between the physical, the morphological and the symbolical. In fact, Marr himself emphasized the importance of the 2 ½ D morphological level for higher levels of symbolic representation. He introduced the idea that the passage from the physical to the morphological involves primarily finding the light-intensity edges of the visual scene in order to represent these qualitative discontinuities in the primal sketch. The morphological structure of perception would derive primarily from a detection of zero-crossings, which analyses physical stimuli in terms of qualitative discontinuities of a physical (intensive) and geometrical nature, and which subsequently are processed as perceptual edges or borders. With regard to this morphological information processing, Marr writes:

> zero-crossing provides a natural way of moving from an analogue or continuous representation like the two-dimensional image intensity values I(x,y) to a discrete, symbolic representation.[51]

Accordingly, Petitot emphasizes that perceptual information processing becomes accessible to symbolic, higher-order cognitive processing only on the basis of this intermediate *morphological* structuration of physical stimuli. The essential idea is that morphological structure is situated at a cognitive level between the physical continuum and the symbolical discrete, and that all *natural* vision presupposes it. As Petitot writes:

> For natural systems (where the symbolical discrete cannot exist immediately), *qualitative morphological discontinuities provide, once they are made explicit, the condition of possibility for the constitution of a symbolical level. Insofar as they are objective singularities that are encoded in the physical signal, they carry information.*[52]

The morphological structure of perception begins with its raw intensity values, which are gradually transformed into a more symbolic, compact and robust representation of the world. But this conceptual structuration of vision is for Marr and Petitot *not essentially a top-down process*. On the contrary, it starts from a bottom-up processing of intensity variations, which become coded in primitive morphological signs or representations. This morphological processing, taking place in the 2D and 2 ½ D phases, does not have to be inferred (top-down) from *a priori* supplementary knowledge. It is largely constructed bottom-up, starting from what Marr calls 'the physics of the situation'. As Marr writes:

> The raw primal sketch is a very rich description of an image, since it contains virtually all the information in the zero-crossings from several channels. Its importance is that it is the first representation derived from an image whose primitives have a high probability of reflecting physical reality directly.[53]

If the first level of the 'primal sketch' is concerned with detecting local singularities or qualitative discontinuities, the second, 'pivotal' level of 'pure perception' is concerned with *integrating* the local morphological information obtained in 2D. Marr emphasizes this is an internal representation of objective physical reality that *precedes* the decomposition of the scene into 'objects'. As we will see in Chapter 6, this integrated, morphological level of pure perception – being still pre-conceptual and pre-objectifying – provides the cornerstone of Deleuze's aesthetics.

5

Psychic individuation

The psychic system

Following a topological model that runs through Deleuze's early philosophy and that is constitutive of our psychic and linguistic life, we must distinguish three dimensions of psychic systems that all interact with each other but nonetheless have their own consistency: height, surface and depth.

1. The height and depth belong to a primary organization.
2. The surface is a secondary organization that emerges from the primary order through a dynamical genesis and functions as a transcendental field, which generates ideal/symbolic structure.
3. The tertiary organization is the empirical subject-object field that is constituted through a static genesis, which derives from the secondary surface-organization.

The primary organization of psychic life concerns a pre-linguistic semiotic, which is fully determined by the actions and the passions of the body, and its unconscious energetic dynamics. Generally speaking, this primary organization constitutes the collection of mechanisms that control the significance (semiosis) of interoceptive and exteroceptive bodily stimuli. We have already seen that organisms *selectively attend* to certain stimuli, or aspects of stimulation, in preference to others. The primary organization of psychic life is concerned precisely with this selective attention to stimuli. Its central cognitive concern is the influence of *memory* on the perceptual and affective processing of sensory, interoceptive and exteroceptive information. At this primary level, memory is responsible for the formation of involuntary mechanisms that operate autonomously, outside of voluntary control and outside of conscious representation. These mechanisms organize the motivational energy of our bodily behaviour in the form of endogenously and exogenously *driven* behaviour.

The function of the secondary 'surface' organization is to generate *a zone of energy indetermination*, which can be used by *language* and *thought*. In the primary order, the sensorimotor agency of the body already draws upon an energy indetermination, which is generated by metabolism. But within the psychic system, a second zone of energy indetermination is required for the organization of the *constituent structures* of language and thought.[1] For Deleuze, the psychic surface organization exhibits the same basic operation as that enacted by the membrane of a cell: it disposes of an internally generated potential energy, which it uses to mediate its selective interactions with the environment. But whereas the cell membrane uses potential energy in function of its selective *actions*, the surface uses potential energy in function of *thought*. The surface organization is entirely dependent upon energy indetermination, which reorganizes perception, action and even the will. Indeed, Deleuze likens the creation of psychic energy indetermination to an indetermination of *will*, whereby *driven* perceptions and behaviours, derivative from the primary order, become suspended. In this indetermination of will, the psychic system regains a relation to *duration*, and with it, to the creative potential of psychic individuation.

By virtue of the transcendental surface, mental acts and states can relate, in different ways, not to physical stimuli, bodies or objects, but rather to peculiar ideal entities such as phonemes, verbs, concepts, states of affairs, propositions, etc. These ideal entities may be of a strictly linguistic nature (phonemes, verbs, etc.) or of a more complex, logical nature (concepts, states of affairs, propositions, etc.). The tertiary organization of psychic life concerns the organization of these ideal entities in three propositional modalities of thought. First, propositions can *denote* states of affairs, in virtue of which such judgments can be true or false. Here, propositions function as cognitive judgments. Secondly, propositions can *manifest* the subject, which speaks and expresses itself. Here, propositions manifest beliefs, desires, promises, etc. in the form of cognitive assertions, speech acts, etc. Lastly, propositions can *signify* conceptual implications by virtue of universal or general concepts (categories), which refer to other propositions. This propositional modality of thought concerns formal logic as a theory of signification. Together, these three dimensions of the tertiary organization form the representational realm of propositional thought. It is generally characterized by conscious intentionality and object representation. All three modalities of propositional thought are organized according to an overarching identity principle and a logic of recognition, which organizes conscious experience in terms of generic concepts and categories.

On a first approximation, the aim of Deleuze's topological model of psychic life can be seen as an attempt to provide a non-psychologistic genesis for this propositional realm of thought in a way that would not, as in the philosophy of Bolzano and Frege (and as in most subsequent analytic philosophy of language and logic), simply detach logic and meaning from the empirically existing, situated thought *in which* logical structure is somehow embedded. Such a transcendental genesis of thought should allow us to affirm the objective structures governing this realm (concepts, propositions, states of affairs, etc.), but also to demonstrate how these structures can emerge from a situated reality, and are subjected to an open-ended evolution. The great hypothesis of Frege's logicism was that mathematics is the development of the absolute laws of thought, which are *logical laws* existing outside of this physical world and independently of any cognitive subject. According to this Platonist hypothesis, the laws of thought (as they are developed in mathematics and logic) have no cognitive, historical or empirical genesis: they consist of concepts without conceivers. The limitation of such a hypothesis, however, is precisely that it cannot account for the fact that the laws of thought, like logic and mathematics itself, are never *definitive* and may evolve by the invention of new problems.

This leads Deleuze to isolate a *fourth* dimension of language and thought, which belongs to the transcendental surface: a dimension of *sense* and *non-sense*. Unlike truth, which is concerned with the correspondence between language and reality, and signification, which is concerned with conceptual implication, *sense* is a genetic and productive instance in thought, which is concerned with the evaluation of *problems* in terms of the *conditions* that are related to them, and with a perpetual, creative *redistribution* of problems and their respective conditions. Indeed, for Deleuze, the history of thought consists of the repetitive positing of different problems and of constraining these in terms of specific conditions.

This perpetual redistribution of problems and their conditions makes all the dimensions of propositional thought perpetually subject to change. Deleuze calls this the 'dialectical' movement or becoming of thought. That thought is *dialectical* means that it is essentially evolving, developing. Thought does not only have a static, timeless structure – the tertiary order with its fixed set of logical and mathematical laws – but rather it also has a dynamical, developing structure. Indeed, we do not have *any* completed science, philosophy or art of anything whatsoever, not even the most fundamental of sciences, such as physics, or the most abstract of sciences, such as geometry. There is, instead, an infinite dialectical development of thought through time. Thus, there lies in every static theory an infinite power to expand itself beyond its current limits.

For the purpose of my overall argument in this book, this infinitary and creative character of thought plays a crucial role. But what does this fourth, creative dimension of thought consist in? In this chapter, I will pursue this question by explicating it as a *sensitivity to singularity*, which implies a capacity of evaluating a given situation as a *singular* occasion that escapes propositional/conceptual thought. The leading question of Deleuze's dialectic is how cognitive processes are sensitive to a particular situation that constrains or forces thought to think something *singular* that cannot be reduced to an identified *token* of a pre-conceived, general *type*. Indeed, psychic individuation as a creative cognitive process should be understood in relation to the effects, which a singular situation exerts on our cognitive faculties. Psychic individuation results from the confrontation with a concrete, singular situation, which cannot be adequately grasped or recognized as being a particular token of a general type. Such situations *resist* representational/propositional thought, and call the thinker to adopt a different attitude, which is akin to an aesthetic/contemplative attitude: they suspend one's typical, dispositional reactions to a situation and make the situation appear as a remarkable, singular event.

Such singular situations cover a vast territory. Beautiful landscapes are irreducibly singular and unclassifiable, but love, people, illness or organisms, are no less so. Besides their 'typical', general, conceptual/standard components, these phenomena are irreducibly singular and individual. And it is precisely to that extent, that they confront us with problems, which call for a creative, autopoietic mode of thought. It is the mark of the true thinker to strip reality of its generality and to confront the irreducible singularity of the challenges it contains.

Primary order

Following Freud's quantitative approach of nervous energy in the *Entwurf einer Psychologie* (1895), Deleuze considers psychic life to manifest itself primarily as an intensive, dynamical field. According to this approach, all of the subject's sensorimotor, perceptive and cognitive faculties (perception, imagination, memory, language, etc.) result from a *dynamical organization* of such 'fields' in the nervous system and the brain. In Freud's *Entwurf*, the intensive field of psychic life is presented as a field of physical and chemical forces in which intensive differences produce excitations (*Erregungen*) and are reciprocally related by their differences (*Bahnung*). The first level of the unconscious or Id consists of local primary processes of excitations and their releases in pleasure. Like Freud, Deleuze thinks that the magnitude of an excitation and the frequency with which it is repeated are constitutive of the memory of the nervous system. This formation of a primordial memory is at the origin of all the other psychic processes.

The dynamical organization of psychic life constitutes an imaginary dimension that is primarily rooted in the mechanisms of biological regulation and obscure animal instincts, and that occurs entirely in function of *affectivity, perception* and *action*. As Petitot puts it in linguistic terms, one may say this imaginary is 'a substance without a content', a pure imaginary medium that is still entirely empty of semantic meaning or *thought*.[2] The term 'imaginary' should not be understood here to refer to the manipulation of fictional representations. It refers instead to a bodily, unconscious imaginary that is purely instinctual and affective, based on interoceptive and exteroceptive signals. The developmental stages of the primary order stand for the processes in which this bodily imaginary is gradually organized in function of the perceptions, affects (pleasure/displeasure) and autonomous actions of the organism, and in which it is *subjectivized*, that is, in which one becomes conscious of this imaginary experience of the flesh as a body one possesses and one identifies with. Psychotic delusion (particularly in schizophrenia) is considered by Deleuze to be an exemplar of a psychic regression to the first, unorganized stages of the primary order.

For our purposes in this chapter, we need not dwell on this primary organization of psychic life. What is more important is the difference between the secondary and tertiary organizations. To grasp what is at stake in the secondary order, however, it is necessary to first jump ahead, and consider the tertiary order of propositional thought.

The organization of propositional thought

What are propositions?

As noted, Deleuze distinguishes three fundamental dimensions of propositional thought: denotation, manifestation and signification. Denotation expresses the relation between a proposition and a 'state of affairs' ('Mars is smaller than Venus'), which it points to. Manifestation concerns the relation of the proposition not to external reality but to the subject, which expresses its assertions, beliefs, etc. in it. It expresses what we would call today 'propositional attitudes' or 'intentional states'. Signification, finally, concerns the complex web of conceptual relations that constitute the states of affairs that are expressed by propositions. For example, in the state of affairs 'the rose is red' we have a relation of inherence between the rose and the colour red. Based on a mastery of these kinds of conceptual relations, propositional thought has a capacity of propositional inference and can thereby determine whether or not statements about states of affairs are logical, based only on the wording of the statement. Below, we will see that Deleuze aims to provide not a logic of states of affairs but rather a logic of events. This will open up a situational and creative form of thought, which I will contrast to propositional thought. To approach this distinction, let us first take a closer look at the relation between propositions and propositional attitudes.

Propositional attitudes are mental states in which a thinker is related to a proposition – for example, the belief that the earth is flat or the hope that tomorrow will be sunny. Although some deny the actual existence of propositional attitudes, most agree they do exist and play a central organizational role in our everyday rationalizing, explaining and predicting of the world and ourselves. On Frege and Russell's classical view, propositional attitudes are psychological relations between subjects and propositions, which express the *content* of those attitudes. Their traditional view came with a very puzzling implication: propositions are in fact *distinct* from particular natural languages themselves. A proposition is an abstract extra-linguistic *bearer of meaning*, which a subject's propositional attitudes may relate to *through* different languages. There are several good arguments for this peculiar extra-linguistic nature of propositions. For one, different individuals may assert, believe, hope the same 'thoughts' in different languages, that is, be intentionally related to the same proposition ('I hope it won't rain tomorrow'). As the abstract meaning of sentences, propositions would be required to explain how different sentences in different languages can be synonymous. Moreover, as abstract meaning bearers, propositions can have a truth-value, that is, be true or untrue, and as such it is far from clear how they might be identified with mere linguistic statements. That is to say, if we take a sentence as correctly describing an external fact, we must suppose that its syntactic-semantic structure possesses an objective correlate, and that there is thus an objective structuration of the fact taking place in thought and being expressed in language. The problem is that such a cognitive structuration is neither of a physical nor of a strictly linguistic kind. Being neither physical nor linguistic, it subsists ideally as a logical articulation of the physical world.[3]

These kinds of puzzles concerning the peculiar meaning-bearing property of propositions have led some philosophers, notably Karl Popper, to defend a Platonist view, according to which propositions would belong to what Frege called the 'third realm' of objective thoughts, which is neither psychological nor physical. Here, one takes intentional attitudes or propositional attitudes to be the distinctive feature of true intelligence and true rationality: unlike physical states, mental states are rational in that they are capable of logically manipulating propositional attitudes related to propositional contents.

A second, fairly widespread view of propositions largely agrees with this Platonist picture, although it makes one fundamental amendment: having (propositional) content or meaning is just a matter of playing a specific functional role in a complex inferential/computational economy, and as such the propositional attitudes of organisms (relating to propositional content) can be explained by the inferential/computational and physical states of a brain or a computer. In other words, for any propositional attitude of an organism, there should be a corresponding computational state. As stated by Jerry Fodor, who proposed this idea as one of the bedrocks of the Computational Theory of Mind (CTM), this leads to the following view: the intentional relation to a proposition is actually a causal effect of an underlying computational process.[4] This does not contradict the classical idea that propositional attitudes relate to propositions. But it does entail that propositions only come in on the semantic level, which is constrained by an underlying syntactic level. Thus, CTM can make sense of the classical view that propositional attitudes are relations to propositions, as long as they are *mediated* relations to propositions, with underlying computations doing the mediating.[5]

In CTM, the key idea is that propositional contents arise from the intricate *relational* features of a network of mental representations. A cognitive system would be an inferential system, which uses formal, combinatorial rules (constrained by syntax) to process representations. From this inferential processing would emerge the proposition's meaning-bearing properties. One of the key consequences of CTM is that propositional or intentional attitudes are no longer to be conceived as purely *conscious* attitudes: it are *physical* states (e.g. brain states), which do the inferential processing.

Which one of these camps has more or less convincing arguments is not our concern. What is important to our Deleuzian context, however, is to note that both camps fundamentally agree that propositional thought is concerned with conceptualizing and classifying reality in terms of type-token relations. This idea is crucial if we are to grasp Deleuze's claims about the limits of propositional thought and his contrasting conception of psychic individuation.

Propositions, types and tokens

Turning to the dimension of predication, mental states can predicate things in the external world by virtue of relating not directly to concrete things (which is impossible for language, as opposed to perception), but rather by virtue of relating to the abstract meanings, which are expressed by propositions. In this context of predication, Deleuze conceives these abstract meanings in terms of Husserl's notion of the *noema* and Frege's notion of *sense*. Like Frege, Husserl embraced the view that propositional attitudes can predicate reality only by virtue of being correlated with an abstract meaning nucleus ('*sense*'). The crucial point here is to see that a propositional attitude does not do the work of predicating an object on its own, so to speak. Rather, the cognitive act can predicate objects in reality only by virtue of this abstract sense or noema that is correlated to the act. Let us briefly consider its function.

According to Husserl, the propositional job of the noema is to enable the mind to be directed at objects. To do this job, it must contain three components: a first one must select a particular external object, a second one must provide a description of that object under a partial aspect and a third component must add a description of further aspects, which the object should also exhibit. Like Fregean *Sinne*, these descriptions are 'predicates', which refer to atomic properties of objects and which are synthesized into more complex descriptions of complex objects (and ultimately into propositions). The final component of the noema anticipates or predicts which other possible descriptions might also apply to this same object, concerning, for example, currently invisible aspects of it (e.g. its backside). Much like Kant, Husserl conceives the function of the noema as a hierarchy of *rules*: the first predicate-senses prescribe what the object looks like, whereas the higher order predicate-senses prescribe what other predicates might apply. As Hubert Dreyfus has pointed out, this conception of the predicative function of the noema largely coincides not only with Frege's account but also with Fodor's computational theory of mental activity as the rule-governed processing of information.[6]

One key aspect of the remarkable convergence between Husserl, Frege and Fodor (and in this context also Deleuze) concerns the idea that the senses and propositions structuring mental representations and propositional attitudes are *types* and not *tokens*. That is to say, senses as such are content types that remain invariant across times and persons. Propositional or intentional attitudes are taken as relations between a psychological attitude and an *instantiated* token sense, which makes for the intentional content of the attitude. While senses *as such* are abstract, invariant *types*, their instantiations are taken to be real moments of *token* mental states.[7]

The interesting point for our purposes is that this distinction between sense as an ideal *type* and its instantiation in particular token acts of consciousness is based, according to Deleuze, on the traditional form of the conceptual, with its distinctions between generality and individual, possibility and actuality. The predicate-senses of any type of object provide a general set of rules governing *possible* other token instantiations of the object as being identical. That is to say, the general rules contained by predicate-senses exemplify predefined types. These noematic types have a *normative* status: they prescribe *a priori* all the necessary and possible properties that belong to a certain type of object, and may therefore be expected upon experiencing them *a posteriori*. In other words, the noematic sense anticipates and prescribes what *typically* and *generically* belongs to a certain region of objects. Husserl describes this in the *Cartesian Meditations* as follows:

> Any 'objective' object, *any object whatever* (even an immanent one), points to *a structure, within the transcendental ego, that is governed by a rule*. As something the ego objectivates, something of which he is conscious in any manner, the object indicates forthwith a universal rule governing *possible* other consciousnesses of it as identical – possible, as exemplifying essentially predelineated types.[8]

This means that propositional thought is fundamentally concerned with shaping our experience of the world as a *typified world*. The noematic sense, which propositional attitudes are directed at and which allows them to predicate objects in the world, contains rules describing all the properties that can be expected with certainty in exploring a certain *type* of objects. Moreover, the rule also prescribes 'predelineations' of properties that are not necessary but still possible features of a type of object.[9]

As Dreyfus has pointed out, this predictive function of propositional predicate-senses is strikingly similar to the kind of data-structures, which Marvin Minsky proposed for Artificial Intelligence. What Minsky called 'frames' were data structures for representing a stereotyped situation, like being in a certain kind of living room, or going to a child's birthday party. In frames, the top level was a developed version of what in Husserl's model were the properties in the representation that can be expected with certainty. Dreyfus describes the remarkable parallel as follows:

The task of AI thus converges with the task of transcendental phenomenology. Both must try to explicate the prototypes in various domains which determine the possible default assignments.[10]

Nativism, rule-following and the identity principle

This logicist/computational conception of propositional thought leads to a rationalist view of thinking in which the relation between the thinking subject and external reality is pre-fixed and certainly not a matter of creativity. On this rationalist view, what determines thought's purpose (correspondence or truth) is not a matter of creativity because it is determined by a fixed set of logico-mathematical rules and laws that are formally inherent to both reality and thought. This leads to a number of further assumptions about the nature of thought.

First, thought is understood as a natural, innate capacity. From Plato, Descartes and Kant up to Fodor's CTM, one assumes thought to be an innate faculty, or what Deleuze calls a '*Cogitatio natura universalis*'.[11] According to this view, thought has an affinity with the true; it *formally* possesses the true. Take Fodor's proposal of an innate Language of Thought (LOT). Fodor argues we have an inborn LOT, which is available as the formal vehicle of cognitive processes (e.g. rational inference, concept learning, perceiving, etc.). Unlike a talent for tennis, which may be inherited but which is not invariant across populations, all humans have an innate faculty of thought that is a veritable cognitive *instinct*, an innate drive towards logical inference.[12] At heart, the computational theory of mind is the idea that the mind is endogenously constrained to be an automatic formal inference system. As some have pointed out, this may explain why we can have automatic, largely unconscious strains of thought *without* any reflective, logical intent.[13] For example, in playing chess, we often follow rules of deductive inference without explicitly representing the rules. For CTM, however, these are no exceptions but rather the rule: thought is *inherently* formal. All thinking corresponds to formal, inferential manipulations of formal representations.

Secondly, the logicist conception of propositional thought comes with a key assumption about the nature of rationality, which defines it as rule-following. Even though the new-born thinker must still learn a natural language and all kinds of disciplines of thought (mathematics, logic, etc.), his or her innate faculty of thought predisposes her to formally process representations in accordance with inference rules that will constitute rational propositional attitudes. To rationally constitute one's propositional attitudes, such as beliefs, is essentially to bring a logical coherence among one's representations. This entails that thought is sensitive to the *logical form* or *structure* of representations – what CTM would call their syntax and vocabulary. That is, we can get a logical ordering of representations only if we are sensitive to their mutual relations in the first place (conjunction, opposition, etc.).[14] The general picture of a rational agent is here one of a computing system with access to a certain amount of data or information and a number of heuristic rules to draw inferences from these data. Rationality is thus inherently linked to rule-governed behaviour, where following the rules determines one's rationality. The thinker may not be able to *state* his or her reasons for doing so explicitly, but the mere *fact* that he or she follows the rules properly suffices to be rational. In fact, the very objectivity of the rules of thought (the fact that they invariably lead to truth) *implies* that they require no (or very little) interpretation on the thinker's part. Beyond deciding whether or not they are applicable in a given situation or inquiry, their application itself requires no interpretation. Thus, the rule-governed nature of thought implies no *active*, *creative* involvement on the thinker's part.

Finally, the rationalist contends that thought can only have the remarkable success it attests to if the *world* it is faced with actually possesses certain structural properties, which correspond to thought. If any given situation is to be apt for rational thinking, logical/conceptual rules must apply. According to Deleuze, this leads to an overarching identity principle, which governs propositional/representational thought: in any given situation, every act of thought entails a subordination of the particular to conceptual identity, conceptual analogy, conceptual oppositions and perceptual similarity. Applied to perception, for instance, this means one is always oriented by a search for identity, by trying to detect what in certain situations and objects is identical to pre-given concepts, and what obeys pre-given rules and laws. This implies, in turn, that everything that cannot be captured within the formal frame of identity *cannot be thought* and is deemed *irrelevant* to thought.

According to Deleuze, this identity principle grounds a model of thinking as *recognition*. Our rational thought is largely occupied by episodes of interpreting perceptual stimuli: recognizing facial expressions, identifying gestures, interpreting speech utterances, reading the results of a blood test, solving a problem of math provided by the teacher, etc. In all of these cases, thought applies a general method of 'recognition': it seeks to identify certain particular tokens in terms of general cognitive types, which it recognizes therein. Thus, recognizing 'sadness', identifying 'goodbye', interpreting 'farewell', reading off 'ApoB', solving a math problem ... all involve recognizing *in* a well-defined stimulus certain conceptual rules, which determine its meaning.

The transcendental illusion of propositional thought

Deleuze picks up the Kantian idea of inner illusion, internal to reason, to *characterize* this sketched propositional mode of thought. Kant has famously argued that our inferential exercise of reason has certain inevitable, structural illusory effects on our reasoning itself. Unlike empirical illusions, which can be adjusted by a corrected perception, *transcendental* illusions are structural and inevitable because they are tied to the constitutive structures of cognition itself. The transcendental illusion of propositional thought derives, for Deleuze, from the conceptual function of *recognition*: the more thought recognizes its concepts in objects, the more thought becomes 'filled with no more than an image of itself, one in which it recognizes itself the more it recognizes things'.[15] As a result, thought becomes driven by what Theodor Adorno has aptly called a 'compulsion to identify'.[16] For Adorno and Deleuze, representational thought is continuously driven by a cognitive instinct to transform every sensuous particular to be the *token* of some context-independent, immaterial *type*: exchange value, scientific law, law of reason, etc. The more thought recognizes its types in the material token world, the more this creates the illusory impression that reality itself is actually a predictable, logically ordered domain, which essentially obeys the subject's *a priori* laws. The world then appears as a Platonic world: every token-instance in reality is but an instantiation of a set of eternal, ideal types, which formally prescribe its behaviour.

But this rationalist world is in fact an illusory dream world. The mind itself is under a rationalist spell. It dreams it is in possession of a vast domain, which is governed by the laws of rational thought. Of course, the rational subject is equipped with a set of general concepts, rules and laws, which allow it to predict and control the course of *certain* events. But this knowledge leads to an illusory perspective: the world consists of some fixed totality of mind-independent objects and events, and thought can attain *one overarching complete* description and prediction of the way the world unfolds. As Hilary Putnam has pointed out, this is nothing less than a God's Eye point of view.[17] Adorno calls this a Platonic tendency inherent to rational thought, whereby it tends to *transcend its finite limits* and to assume an infinite, quasi-divine perspective.[18] As Adorno writes, the 'transcendental delusion' of the transcendental subject is that it is itself 'the Archimedean fixed point from which the world can be lifted out of its hinges'.[19]

In contrast to this, Deleuze posits the world as a 'chaosmos', which continuously produces unforeseeable novelty. The world we experience as stable, predictable and ordered is forever subjected to contingency and singularity. Indeed, as we have seen, the intensive pre-individual plane of Nature from which new physical, biological and psychic forms emerge is fundamentally tied to contingency and possibility creation. Take the emergence of the first eukaryotic, complex cells from the symbiotic relationship between two or more prokaryotic cells. Two billion years ago, nothing in the evolution of the biosphere determined this contingent event to happen; indeed, it was as contingent and unpredictable as an asteroid impact.[20] And yet the symbiosis of two or more prokaryotic cells produced an unprecedented space of possibilities for subsequent natural evolution: the evolution of flight, sight and human intelligence all derive from it. Or take, more recently, the emergence of global warming, which introduced a fundamental new observable to be taken into account for the future of the planet. Like the emergence of eukaryotes, the emergence of global warming is an irreducibly *singular* event, which fundamentally transforms the conditions of possibility of a particular system (in our examples, cellular life and the biosphere of the Earth).[21] These kinds of singular, creative dynamics fundamentally differ from dynamics whose conditions of possibility remain fixed (those in physics, for example, that are defined by universal equations).

This does not mean that the world is made up of pure chance and contingency, of course. Much in nature is determined by fixed laws and is therefore predictable. But the problem, for Deleuze, is that the conceptual-propositional nature of thought does not allow it to take into account the way in which properties of a contingent, *singular event* can co-determine processes of thought themselves. In other words: it is blind to the fact that in some situations, what is to be thought is crucially *dependent* on the unpredictable singularity of the event. On the propositional/computational level, cognitive inferences are driven by concepts and rules that are fundamentally *context invariant*. The rules determining propositional thought are by definition *not* context-dependent: the essential properties underlying *objects* are by definition properties that it *always* has, *whatever* the context. Therefore, the general rules and concepts that constitute objects on the level of propositional/conceptual thought are by definition *insensitive* to *singular, unique* context-depending properties of situations.[22] As such, propositional thought is blind to singularity, and cannot account for a thought that is determined by it.[23]

By its very nature, conceptual thought draws on general rules, laws and principles, which are valid from one situation to another and therefore capture their essential, shared properties. This means, as noted, that thought grasps situations as tokens for pre-identified types. But for Deleuze this also means that propositional thought is a highly *selective* metabolic filter in which input and output are never identical. Conceptual/propositional thought is a selective metabolic filter, which does not select for singularity and is, by definition, insensitive or blind to it. As Deleuze puts it:

> The elementary concepts of representation are the categories defined as the conditions of possible experience. These, however, are too general or too large for the real. The net is so loose that the largest fish pass through.[24]

Let me try to state the problem more clearly: when confronting particular situations, what we experience is not always conceivable in terms of a *type* that is instantiated by that situation. So let's take a particular situation, which *cannot* be identified as a token of a pre-identified type. How can we account for the singular effects, which such a singular situation has on thought? On Deleuze's view, the propositional organization of thought simply cannot.

Faced with this problem, the following answer may come to mind: one might appeal to something like the *Bayesian, predictive processing* model of the mind, according to which the mind would grapple with the unclassifiable situation by updating its predictions and by thereby making it into a *new* type.[25] Of course this is possible, but this would be to miss the point: oftentimes, there is something about a given situation that cannot be exhausted by its being a *token* of the type. So using it for an 'updating' of the types would completely *misapprehend* the situation. It would turn the singular (inherently unique and context-bound) into the particular (inherently subsumable under the general). Certain situations do not only resist conceptual classifications, but *they also call for a different mode of thought*. Their 'solution' is not to classify or objectify them. My claim here is not that one could not classify or conceptualize them altogether; my point is that their 'typification' does not *exhaust* them, and this calls for a different, additional mode of thought: a creative, constructive thought, which invents new, unprecedented possibilities on the level of thought itself.

Let me clarify, before pursuing, that what we have said does not deny, in the least, that the propositional organization of thought is a large part of our psychic life. I am not claiming that thought is not representational or propositional, or that we could do without. To the contrary, I believe rationalist philosophy is right in holding that representational/propositional thought is fundamental.

The point I am making is that this dimension of thought has its limits: it is fundamentally blind to singularity. As Deleuze writes:

> It is apparent that acts of recognition exist and occupy a large part of our daily life: this is a table, this is an apple, this is the piece of wax, Good morning Theaetetus. But who can believe that the destiny of thought is at stake in these acts, and that when we recognize, we are thinking?[26]

Psychic individuation

Towards another sensibility

For Deleuze, as for Adorno, the tenacity of an inevitable transcendental illusion that is inherent to thought can, strictly speaking, not be *dispelled*. Rather, it can only be *repressed* by bringing to life, *in intelligence itself*, another tendency (*conatus*), which is critical.[27] Against the typifying, representational tendency of thought one must bring to life, within thought, another, critical tendency. But where, precisely, does this second tendency come from? Only intuition can produce and activate it, because it rediscovers singularities beneath particularities and generalities, and conveys to intelligence the criteria that enable it to distinguish between the singular and the ordinary. Thus, the critical tendencies, which repress transcendental illusion, must necessarily be engendered from the order of the sensible.[28]

According to Deleuze, thought undergoes a qualitative shift, a veritable leap, in a contingent context, which it is unable to determine on its own. Faced with something singular and contingent, which cannot be anticipated and subsumed under preconceived types, thought enters into a co-dependent way of relating to its context. In such a materialistic moment, a material encounter has something like a *driving force*, which *forces* the intimacy of thought to leave the realm of its preconceived possibilities and to *realize* itself by adopting a different mode of sensibility: a sensibility to the singular.[29]

That which is encountered and cannot be recognized always belongs to the order of sensibility. Its primary characteristic is that it can *only* be sensed and grasped in a range of affective tones: wonder, fear, love, suffering. This is not the case in conceptual recognition: here, the sensible aligns with something that can also be recalled, imagined or conceived. In conceptual recognition, the sensible is grasped as an object, which may not only be sensed but also may be attainted (and classified) by other faculties. In a veritable *encounter*, by contrast, representational/propositional thought is fundamentally *suspended* and *blocked*. No matter what may be its affective tonality, the encounter therefore always has a *violent* character. It is experienced as a contingent *shock* that forces thought to abandon its natural *stupor* (its eternal, preconceived possibilities) and that *forces* it to think. This is the difference between a recognition and a real *encounter*.

When an effective encounter takes place, sensibility, or the faculty of being affected, is elevated (*Erhebung*) towards a *transcending* and properly sublime exercise in which it *transgresses* its pre-existing possibilities. What is sensed in such a limit experience in an immediate and unmediated manner is something that gives rise to *sensations* in the strict Deleuzian sense, namely: *intensive singularities*, which *present unmediated differences*. Eukaryotic cells, climate change, falling ill, discovering love … these are more than what our conceptual thought recognizes. They are also singular events, which can only be sensed as *different* and *new*. Within the re-presentational logic of recognition, by contrast, the intensive singularity of an event cannot be experienced *as* an intensity, which forces us to think. The merely *empirical* exercise of sensibility, which hangs together with that logic, always experiences intensive singularity as mediated by sensory *qualities* and conceptual *types*: 'this is love, this is climate change, this is a cell with a nucleus'. Intensive singularities are homogenized in the process of *perception*, which prepares them to be conceptually grasped. To enable the logic of recognition to function, it is crucial that all the different faculties envision the *same*, identical object and the exercise of each faculty remains *limited* to its contribution to the process of recognition. The object of the (neutralized) sensibility, memory, imagination and finally of thought is within representation *identical*.

Summarizing, the first qualitative shift, which thought undergoes in the face of a contingent *encounter*, is that sensibility grasps *singular difference*, which *forces* the intimacy of thought to leave the realm of its preconceived possibilities.[30]

Infinitary learning

For Deleuze, psychic individuation is the true element of *learning*. But learning is here not understood as subordinate to knowing: learning is not the mere method that leads to knowledge. In fact, in the propositional/representational model of thought, one gets a fundamental misconception of what learning *is*, because it reduces learning to the purpose of propositional/rationalistic thought, namely attaining knowledge/truth. In Deleuze's philosophy, learning is completely detached from the purpose of attaining knowledge and acquires two distinct meanings, which ultimately coincide. On the one hand, learning entails the exploration of a *problem* or Idea; on the other hand, it entails the sublime elevation of all the faculties to their transcending and truly transcendental exercise.[31]

First of all, learning means that one exerts constitutive acts in relation to the ideal objectivity of a problem. As Deleuze puts it, a contingent encounter, which can only be sensed, also 'moves the soul' or 'perplexes' it – in other words, 'forces it to pose a problem'.[32] Whereas learning entails *constructive* and *creative* acts in relation to a problem, knowledge always remains in the calm, ensuring element of conceptual rule following, which guarantees objective, correct outcomes (solutions) and which excludes creativity. One need only think of the difference between mathematicians working as administrators or businessmen and mathematicians inventing new theories.[33] The first are rational and intelligent, but they do not pose problems in the creative sense, which transcends preconceived possibilities and rule following. For Deleuze, learning is an a-conceptual exercise of thought, which consists in penetrating into the singular conditions of problems, which determine new Ideas. In representational thought, by contrast, learning is degraded to an empirical, inferior moment of knowledge-acquisition. Even the formidable learning process laid out in Hegel's *Phenomenology of Spirit* remains principally subordinated to the demands of the ideal form of knowledge as absolute knowledge.

Defined in terms of the exercise of the faculties, learning consists in the effort of thinking singularity (and difference) without subordinating it to conceptual generality (and identity). This comes down to a discordant accord of the faculties, whereby every faculty is constrained to interpret the *sense* of signs that present themselves as undetermined problems. Such signs are no freely formed intellectual constructions, but rather impose themselves as foreign elements that *cannot* yet *must* be thought. It is the reciprocal determination of such signs between the different faculties (sensibility, imagination, memory, language, etc.), which underlies the emergence of an Idea.

Initially, problematic signs shake thought to its foundations: familiar assumptions and beliefs lose their natural self-evidence, and the natural self-evidence of the familiar world loses its familiarity. Indeed, trying to make sense of a problem which does not yet make sense, and which has not yet received 'its' solution, provides us with a world that is strange. For the person learning how to swim, it may seem there is no gravitation (because floating largely cancels it out). The swimmer is submerged in a world with new, different forces to think about when moving forward – for example, water resistance. This discovery hits him or her like a flash of insight: the resistance of water is a property of the problem that is not ordinary but remarkable; it is a singularity that will contribute to determining the conditions of the problem, that is, to making sense of it.[34]

Deleuze uses this example of learning swimming to illustrate the central idea that learning, as opposed to conceptual thought, does not consist in following rules or instructions:

> We learn nothing from those who say: 'Do as I do'. Our only teachers are those who tell us to 'do with me', and are able to emit signs to be developed in heterogeneity rather than propose gestures for us to reproduce.[35]

With Deleuze, we should therefore say there are at least two kinds of learning. One could be called finite, the other infinitary. Finite learning is enacted for the purpose of attaining knowledge, whereas infinitary learning for the purpose of continuing to learn. If learning is for attaining knowledge, it comes to an end when knowledge is achieved. And as it is essential to finite learning that it should come to an end in knowledge, it is also evident that it must *follow certain rules*, a certain grammar, which *may not change in the course of learning* – else something else is learned. It is on this point that we find a clear distinction with Deleuzian infinitary learning: it is not essentially governed by instructions or rules, and in fact consists in *a constructive rule-making capacity*. This amounts to saying that no external limits can be imposed upon infinitary learning. And this is the sense in which it is infinitary: it is unbounded, unlimited, in its creative exercise. Finite learners think *within* boundaries, whereas infinitary learners think *with new* boundaries.

For Deleuze, true learning is to explore ordinary and singular points of a given situated context, which together form a 'problematic field' and in which, eventually, an Idea will emerge from the reciprocal determination of singular points. As he writes,

> In fact, the Idea is not the element of knowledge but that of an infinite 'learning', which is of a different nature than knowledge. For learning evolves entirely in the comprehension of problems as such, in the apprehension and condensation of singularities and in the composition of ideal events and bodies.[36]

This transition, from exploring obscure signs to 'having' an Idea, is a veritable 'phase transition' in thought, which shifts from an *undifferentiated* state of perplexity to a fully *differentiated*, structured state of ideation. As a process of psychic individuation, to have an Idea means to explore a heterogeneous differential/problematic field that is composed of ordinary and singular points, which may or may not give rise to integration. What comes out of this integration cannot be predetermined, since the problematic field is a veritable space of creation. Its individuating dynamics introduce the possibility of a change of the rules and laws of thought. As a genuinely autopoietic, that is, self-productive, process, it constructs new concepts (philosophy), new functions (science) and new affects and percepts (art).

Idea and individuation

In the previous chapters, we have seen that vital and psychic individuation have two key requirements: a metastable source of potential energy, which forms a degree of energy indetermination, and reciprocal dependency relations between the parts of the living or psychic system, which make use of that energy to generate and regulate those very parts themselves. To Deleuze, every biological and cognitive structure is a structurally self-generating and self-regulating system of reciprocal dependency relations between virtual positional values. But how, then, does this generative principle of reciprocal determination apply to the psychic individuation of Ideas?

As we have seen, on the level of *thought*, Deleuze distinguishes between two fundamental synthetic regimes of the mind, which constitute our encounters with things and situations in the world. On the one hand, there is a representational/propositional regime of synthesis, which is organized by the conceptual. On the other hand, there is a sub-representational/extra-propositional regime of synthesis, which is organized by the ideal. Ideas are distinct from concepts in two regards.

First of all, concepts are general/universal rules that subsume empirical particulars and singularities to lawful regularity. As such, they constitute our encounters with the world in terms of anticipated, pre-existent possibilities. Secondly, conceptual synthesis is essentially context-independent because conceptual rules provide logical possibilities that are by definition context-invariant. A thing's conceptual properties are ipso facto properties that it *always* has, *whatever* may be the context. As Kant showed in his theory of the schematism of concepts, a schematism is a system of general rules for the constitution of *things* into *objects*. The conceptual schemata structuring mental representations are *types*, which apply to things as tokens.

Ideas are opposed to concepts firstly because they are not organized in terms of the type-token distinction and leave behind the categories of generality and particularity. Secondly, unlike concepts, Ideas derive from our sensitivity to the singularity of an event and from a correlated *situated* way of thinking. Let us consider both points more closely.

The Idea is organized in terms of ordinary and remarkable singularities, which compose a problematic field that is in an initial state of indetermination. As its individuating principle, it is the mind's instinct for learning – its creative *conatus* – which strives to distinguish ordinary from remarkable singularities during the progressive determination of the problematic field. Indeed, with the notion of individuation, the Idea itself can be seen as a process of structuration and self-organization, which determines the singular conditions of a problematic field. Unlike the conceptual, the ideal disposes of a generative principle of reciprocal determination, which enacts a synthesis of differential relations between the singularities that make up the problematic field. Unlike conceptual synthesis, ideal synthesis constitutes Ideas not as *logical forms* of but rather as *topological* and *relational forms*. As an ideal structure, every Idea is a system of ideal relations that links up parts (singularities) of a problematic field within a whole. As such, every Idea is reducible to a self-organized ideal morphology, which itself is reducible to a system of singularities.

To Deleuze, the singularities composing a problematic field do not characterize what we know about a situation; they do not characterize something that may be subsumed under the general or the universal. They rather characterize the objectivity of what we do not know about a situation, *but this non-knowledge is not a negative or an insufficiency*.[37] On the contrary, singularities provide something *to be learned*, which corresponds to a fundamental dimension of the situation. Indeed, to Deleuze, what is undetermined in a problematic field is something that sustains thought as a living, creative process. It *imposes* itself upon the individual as an *imperative* to think and to act, that is to individuate itself, despite there being no clear solutions at hand.

When someone falls chronically ill, or when someone must choose between life-paths that appear equally risky or appealing … one encounters a concrete and singular situation that may be said to present an undetermined problem.[38] It is singular because no two individuals can live such a situation in an identical manner. As a situation it is undetermined because its problematic character is not straightforwardly clear. It is clearly 'problematic' in that it forces us to think and to act, but there is a plethora of implicit contextual factors that condition it and that require our questioning: Where? When? Why? How much? In what case? In such *context-bound* questioning our thought traverses the problematic field as a multiplicity, without overarching principles or rules to 'solve' it.

To determine the problematic field, one must organize the elements involved in the situation into a hierarchical structure with ordinary and remarkable singularities. But it is important to see that these characteristics are not intrinsic to the situation itself: they *derive* from the evaluating perspective, which organizes the situation by imposing a hierarchy (ordinary/remarkable) upon it. One cannot simply take the situation as a natural, objective fact, which can be analysed into simpler elements and is a matter of objective knowledge. The problematic field can be determined only *from the point of view of the observer tied to that field*, and not from an external, detached position.[39] One must first *select* and *compose* a multiplicity of contextual factors so as to obtain any determinable order or structure in the problematic field at all. And these factors are *a priori unbounded*. Not only does the present context and one's individual past contain a myriad of factors conditioning the situation, but the future may also continue to contribute factors to it. The problematic field is therefore open-ended, irreducibly perspectival and contextual. It is a construct. An unbounded, undetermined field that requires organizing. It is up to the thinker to compose this virtual field into something of a structure, and to act upon it.

Of course, one can also generalize and conceptualize such situations by abstracting away from their contextual singular aspects and by seeing them as universal or general types: illness, life-choices ... One can devise general, rational rules of conduct and follow their pre-determined guidance. Again, the point here is not to deny the possibility (or utility) of rational, conceptual thought, but to tease out its distinction with an intuitive mode of thought that *depends* on the embedding circumstances and is *constrained* to think creatively. For in abstract generalizing thought, these situations lose their *imperative* singular nature, they lose 'the claws of absolute necessity' by which they inflict a violence on thought and *force* one to think and/or act creatively.[40] One then returns to the calm, reassuring element of knowledge, the element of rule-following that excludes genuine creativity.

Situations of this 'undetermined' type are what I propose calling 'pathic' situations, in the sense that they imply something of a *crisis* that forces one into taking a particular affective *attitude*. It is this attitude, which we should now examine further, for it forms the central affective and volitional condition underlying psychic individuation.

6

Passibility

Not to exercise all the power at one's disposal is to endure the void. This is contrary to all the laws of nature. Grace alone can do it.

— Simone Weil[1]

Affectivity and individuation

For Deleuze, the link between thought and individuation is established in a field of intensity, which constitutes the sensibility of the thinking subject. But with this notion of sensibility, we are facing an interpretative difficulty: Deleuze conceives the sensation of intensity in a 'pure' state, independently from the qualities and extension with which it is always mixed in our conscious experience.[2] This approach to sensation entails a profound modification of the traditional transcendental conception of sensibility. For Kant and Husserl, human beings do not merely sense conditions relevant to their bodily functions, they also *perceive objects*. To do so, they must be able to locate things in external space: external space provides the formal condition of objectivity in perception, and the common representational framework for experience. For Kant and Husserl, it is only by virtue of the extensive form of intuition that intensive matter may *appear* to the subject in the form of representations that can be cognized, that is, that can be correlated to concepts and categories. In Kantian/Husserlian terms, the perceptual presentation (*Darstelllung*) of an extended, qualified object derives from underlying synthetic acts of apprehension (*Auffassung*), which process the intensive hyletic data of sensation (*Empfindung*). These syntheses of apprehension function as noetic, intentional acts, which 'form' the hyletic 'matter' taken up by the senses.

For Deleuze, by contrast, pure sensibility does not grasp qualified objects in spatial extension. In its pure state, sensation is strictly speaking not even *intentional* because it grasps neither an object nor even a representation. But how, then, can there still be *sensation* at the level of pure intensity – a sensation that cannot arise in representation?[3] We have already seen that the link between sensibility and psychic individuation entails a mode of *affectivity*, which 'moves the soul' and 'perplexes' it. Contingent encounters, which suspend representation, essentially touch us in a range of *affective* registers. But what does this affective movement of the soul consist in? And how does it form the very *ground* from which the mind (*Gemüt*) can elevate itself beyond its static, representational closure? In other words, what is the relation between affectivity and psychic individuation?

Grasping intensity for itself, independently from the qualities which cover it and the extensity in which it is distributed, it would seem that sensation is somehow cut off from the external world. If we follow this hypothesis, it would detect, with extraordinary acuteness, certain changes in its bodily interior, especially oscillations in the tension of its instinctual drives, and these modifications would become conscious as affective feelings. The internal body is not an object of perception and representation – unless it is externalized and presented to the classical senses (sight, hearing, touch, etc.). Rather, our inward sensation of the interoceptive, instinctual body forms a primordial, subjective presence underlying representation. In sensation, the subject appears to itself or discovers itself in and through an originary relation to the continuous pulsation of the life that animates its body from within. In this chapter, we will explore this aspect of sensation as it relates to the organic body and to the inorganic life, which is its instinct of individuation.

Although I will speak here, in line with my conative approach to the mind, in terms of instinct, it will be important to also single out the specifically *human* character of sensation as it pertains to psychic individuation. Unlike animals, who are captive to their environment and who must respond to unforeseen circumstances with a variety of actions, human beings transcend the formative cycle between an external event and the immediate necessity of a behavioural response. Human affectivity has the capacity to *suspend* one's actions and to take an affective *attitude* to events, which ranges from *openness* and *affirmation* to *negation* and pathological *closure*. As such, sensation is a responsive capacity that shapes a variable degree of freedom: it makes possible a detachment from one's ego and self-image, an open projection into the future, and allows for making choices.

In this chapter, we will examine what this distinct mode of sensation entails, and how it is constitutive of psychic individuation. How is it distinct from mere animal sensing and behaviour? And if indeed human beings do not relate to sensation as egological, reflective subjects relate to the objects of their representations, then how should we understand this distinct, pre-intentional dimension of subjectivity? We will find a solution to these questions in Deleuze's distinction between an *ontic* and an *ontological* dimension of the affective: being affected by *things* and being affected by *Being*. The affective dimension of psychic individuation is an ontological receptiveness, which calls the mind into its own pre-individual ground, namely Duration. The exaltation of being rooted in this dynamical ground isn't an ontic affect or emotion. This experience of inclusion is for Deleuze an ontological one, meaning that the mind is now opened onto *another Being* than the stable, ordered world of representation.

The pathic dimension of sensation

The pathic and the gnosic moments of sensation

At the beginning of the sixth chapter of his Bacon study, Deleuze devotes a note to an article of Henri Maldiney from 1966 on 'The Disclosure of the Aesthetic Dimension in the Phenomenology of Erwin Straus'. This article proposes, with Straus, a profound revaluation of the concept of sensation. Maldiney's aim, so we read in Deleuze's note, is 'to analyze sensation, or rather "sensing" [*le sentir*], not only insofar as it relates sensible qualities to an identifiable object (the figurative moment), but insofar as each quality constitutes a field that stands on its own [*valant pour lui-même*]'.[4] Maldiney has no more pressing concern than to insist that the affective life of the subject may not merely be thought in terms of the reflective, objectifying intentionality of consciousness:

> The subject-object polarity of a subject who objectifies the world, and who at the same time distinguishes itself from the world-object by a doubling internal to self-consciousness, is not deniable but it is secondary, and only possible starting from a more originary situation: that of sensing.[5]

Straus and Maldiney do not deny, of course, that many affective states are reflective and intentional. However, the central idea is that the affective life of the subject *precedes* the intentionality of representations and accordingly the study of affectivity should not (only) be based on the model of external, objectifying *perception*. Following Straus, Maldiney writes that every sensation contains both an affective, '*pathic*' moment and a representational, '*gnosic*' moment.[6] For both thinkers, the representational dimension concerns speculative and pragmatic functions of the subject, such as *perception* and *recognition*. Maldiney illustrates the distinction with the example of colour sensations:

> The immediate lyricism of a stained glass window or of a mosaic is independent of the object that is represented in it. The rosette of a cathedral induces in us by the play of color a bodily and spiritual movement that precedes every iconographical reading. The pathic moment of a color sensation is expressed in the musical and rhythmic dimension of colors.[7]

In the pathic dimension of experience, the subject is connected to the *how* of being with the world, rather than the *what* of the world and its objects. The pathic is a pre-intentional, pre-logical and pre-linguistic dimension of experience that is always inevitably *lost* in *perception*, which must be taken as a first level of a reductive and even repressive process of objectification that is governed by the conceptual. As Maldiney writes, 'With perception, which is the first level of objectification, we have already left sensation.'[8] The pathic is the *event* of being-with-the-world that *precedes* the correlation between subject and object and discerns no noetic-noematic intentional structure whatsoever.

A first point of access into this concept of the pathic is Husserl's well-known distinction between 'sensual moments' (*sensuelle hyle*) and 'sensible moments' (*sinnliche morfe*) within the field of unitary lived experiences of consciousness. Husserl maintains that the *hyletic* data are given as a raw material (*Stoff*) that is to be animated (*beseelt*) by a signifying (*sinngebende*) intentionality and directed to a thing-object. As he puts it in *Ideas I*: 'We find those sensuous moments overlaid by a stratum which, as it were, "animates," which *bestows sense* (…) – a stratum by which precisely the concrete intentive mental process arises from the *sensuous, which has in itself nothing pertaining to intentionality.*'[9] The *hyle* is a kind of formless content that has the potential to receive a form, and that is often not directly perceived in conscious acts. Husserl gives the following examples: 'color-data, touch-data and sound-data, and the like (…), sensuous pleasure, pain and tickle sensations, and so forth, and no doubt also sensuous moments belonging to the sphere of "drives."'[10]

Although the primary sensual moment has in itself nothing pertaining to intentionality, it implies for Straus and Maldiney 'a communication with the world beyond its constitution into an object'.[11] As Straus puts it, the pathic dimension entails the 'immediate communication, which we have with things based on their changing sensory presence'.[12] It is this 'communication with hyletic givens', *independently* from a conceptually mediated perception, which constitutes the pathic dimension of sensation[13]:

It is precisely this presence (and this *non-objective reality*), which forms the center of the phenomenological oeuvre of Erwin Straus. He has disclosed the communicative and signifying [*signifiante*] dimension prior to all objectification, on the level of the Sensing [*le Sentir*] itself. He begins where Husserl's intentional analysis ends, with this hyletic, which he has named without being able to edify it. Unlike the sensible data, which are constituted into qualities of things by the intentional noeses in relation to the object, the sensual data, which constitute the *hyle* are the *Empfindungen*, data which have in themselves nothing intentional. They serve merely as the matter for the first. Erwin Straus edifies a hyletic of a wholly different kind, which exposes in the Sensing itself, outside of each reference to an object, a non-intentional sense, for which the expression direction of sense [*Bedeutungsrichtung*], introduced by Ludwig Binswanger, would be appropriate. Straus' hyletic is a phenomenology of the αἴσθησις, of that αἴσθησις which aesthetics derives its name from, and which, according to Erwin Straus it can also derive its meaning from.[14]

But how might the sensual *hyle*, which we sense in sensation, possess an 'originary form that is irreducible to all the intentional noeses of objective perception'?[15] How does a pre-intentional sensation become '*full of sense* for the one who inhabits the world through it'?[16] As the cited passage from *Ideas I* suggests, the way in which hyletic data acquire a non-intentional sense is primarily related to the subject's bodily sphere of 'drives' (*Triebe*). For Husserl already, feelings, emotions, tendencies and drives had their origin in the pre-intentional sphere of sensations and their hyletic data. However, his analysis in *Ideas I* is dedicated to the application of intentional consciousness to this material dimension of sensation and thus still absorbs the analysis of affectivity within the analysis of the representation of an object. Erwin Straus gives hyletic sensations a completely different interpretation by considering them as *kinaesthetic* sensations, that is, as originary sensations of movement, which condition the sense of the senses.

The hyletic intentionality of the body

For Straus, the autonomous movement of an organism, as motivated by its vital tendencies, is a primordial foundation of the intentional process of the subjective constitution of the world. This means that for Straus the intentionality of human consciousness is ultimately grounded in the movement of the animal body. Tracing intentionality in organic movement implies in turn an examination of what *constitutes* movement: what kind of constitutive structure precedes the noetic-noematic structure of intentionality at the level of movement? And how may this primordial intentionality constitute the sense of hyletic data?

For Straus, the constitution of the meaning of things in the animal environment relies on a self-organizing connection between hyletic sensations and motivating kinaesthetic sensations. In the psychology of the late nineteenth century, kinaesthetic sensations were understood as proprioceptive, muscular sensations caused by the movement of a part of the body. Kinesthesia designates the specific capacity to sense the motion of a limb or a joint – a sense which is primarily influenced by muscle spindles and secondarily influenced by skin receptors and joint receptors. In phenomenological terminology, kinaesthetic sensations are themselves one class of hyletic sensations. Examples include the sensations of bodily movement involved with eye movements, hand movements, head movements, etc. Straus, however, conceives kinaesthetic sensations as a (pathic) way in which the corporeal subject *appears to itself*, or rather, feels itself as a carnal, 'flesh' (*Leib*) that stands in relation to its world.[17] Thus, kinaesthetic sensations are a special class of hyletic sensations in that they do not bring *external* things to presence as do hyletic data of sound, colour, touch, etc., but in that they function to *bring the subjective body (Leib) itself to presence in consciousness*. More crucially, the movement, which kinaesthetic sensations bring to awareness, is not the movement of external things, nor merely the movement of one's own limbs in space, but rather *the movement of the affected body that contains a certain power and disposition to act.* Insofar as they reveal inner sensed movements, kinesthesia manifests for Straus an intentionality of the body, in the sense of a felt disposition to orient itself towards something and to act. When, at Straus' time, the physiological psychologist spoke of kinaesthetic sensations, she spoke of the body as an isolated system. Yet, when considering kinesthesia as a self-affection of the *Leib*, Straus attributes to kinesthesia a singular mode of intentionality.[18] As a result, a new concept of intentional *act* must be accorded to the body, which is sensed in kinaesthetic sensations as a *sense of action*, or a *sense of movement*, and which is distinct from proprioception as the sensation of the movement of the limbs.[19] One must then say at once that kinesthesia are *non-intentional* hyletic data (in the sense that they do not present an object or a meaning), which direct the subject to its body not as an object but as a sensing body that is *intentionally* oriented towards its environment.

With Straus' interpretation of the pathic dimension of sensation we are now a step closer to uncovering the complex relation between affectivity and psychic individuation: in the pathic dimension of sensation, the corporeal subject *appears to itself,* or rather, feels itself as a carnal 'flesh' (*Leib*) that stands in relation to its world. For Straus, this kinaesthetic experience of the *Leib* is a reduction of the human ego towards the vital, autonomous functioning proper to the body.[20] Thus, when sensation is divested from representation, intensive hyletic data bring to awareness not only *external* things but also the movement of the affected body, which contains certain powers and instinctive dispositions to act. *It is as though the subject then appears to itself or discovers itself in and through an originary relation to the continuous pulsation of the life that animates its body from within.* Like Straus, Deleuze will also trace the pathic dimension of sensation in the bodily movement of life, which belongs to all living beings. But Deleuze also gives us a novel interpretation of the pathic, which is largely absent from Straus's work. Here, the work of Henri Maldiney provides us with a second key to uncovering the relation between affectivity and individuation.

The ontological interpretation of the affective

In Maldiney's interpretation of the affective, two ideas are central: first, there is the idea that pathic affectivity is a singularly human capacity of *non-action*, a capacity of pure *endurance,* which he calls 'possibility'; second, there is the important idea that pathic experience has an *ontological* dimension that must be distinguished from its *ontic-bodily/organic* dimension. As such, possibility entails for Maldiney both a *restraint on action* and a *disclosure or unveiling of Being.* Let us begin by turning to the idea of *non-action.*

Pathei-mathos

In Maldiney's philosophy, the pathic designates a human potential capacity to *restrain the exercise of action* and to *endure* an event. Maldiney explains this capacity in terms of Aeschylus's term *pathei-mathos,* which he translates as *learning from suffering.*[21] *Pathein* is a capacity not of doing (*poiein*) but of undergoing. However, this does not mean that *pathein* is a pure passivity. Rather, *there is also an active force involved in undergoing*: our receptivity can either be in an *inert, incapable* state, or it can be in an *active, capable* state. The potential capacity involved in possibility is strictly speaking *a capacity to endure.* As Maldiney writes: '"Passible" means "*capable* of undergoing, of bearing"; and this capacity implies an activity, immanent to the ordeal, which consists in opening up one's field of receptivity.'[22]

Following Heidegger, Maldiney considers this introduction of a restraint into the dynamic movement of life as a singular and essential human trait. The restraint exercised upon the dynamic potentialities of life opens up a distinctly human, existential dimension of *abstaining* from the usage of power. This is precisely what Maldiney calls *possibility*: the pure capacity of undergoing an event *without acting* on it. The only act is here that of passivity itself.

Drawing on Heidegger's 1929/30 winter course on the mode of being of living organisms – published as *die Grundbegriffe der Metaphysik* – Maldiney conceives the organic life of animals in terms of 'capacities' or 'drives' which are fundamentally self-regulating and self-conserving and which continuously strive towards their self-realization in an act.[23] As such, the organism's mode of being is essentially that of a set of drives, which continuously seek their unrestrained expression or actualization in movement and action. Like Heidegger, Maldiney takes this mode of organic being to be a 'poor' or deprived mode of the being-in-the-world of human *Dasein*. To be sure, however, for Maldiney human beings *also* tend to spend many days of their lives living in this existentially 'poor' manner. The Heideggerian term for this mode of being is '*Benommenheit*', which designates a closure upon oneself or a self-absorption.[24] Maldiney considers the essential, defining trait of this mode of being to be a continuous *striving for the dis-inhibition of drives*.[25] The organic mode of being is caught in a never-ending loop: its relation to an environment (*Umwelt*) is continuously dominated by a never-ending striving to dis-inhibit its drives and to actualize them. As such, the organic mode of being searches in its environment those things, which stimulate or trigger the actualization of its capacities or drives.

In contrast to the continuous monotony of organic being, human *existence* or *Dasein* is for Maldiney something essentially *discontinuous*: it is constituted by critical moments, which are experienced as disruptions of daily life. *Dasein* is constituted by a passible openness to critical *events*, which are essentially *rare*. As Maldiney explains in an interview: 'I mean that a human being does not exist each minute of its life. Most of the time, it is content to be or to live, but existence is something that is always decisive and critical.'[26]

Like animal life, human life is essentially marked by crises, which disturb the harmonious integration of a subject in its world. Following Viktor von Weizsäcker, Maldiney defines a crisis as an event that disrupts the fundamental relation (*Grundverhältnis*) between organism and environment and thereby *inhibits* the realization of an organism's vital capacities or drives.[27] In a crisis, the organism undergoes a brutal expulsion from its environment: it is dispossessed of its relation to the environment. In animal life, such a crisis must be met with a behavioural reorganization of the environment. By contrast, in human life, a totally different kind of response can be given in order to react to a crisis, a response that is diametrically opposed to the pressing urge or demand of new actions. Indeed, the radical *pathei-mathos* of Aeschylus is tantamount to learning how to *remain* in a state of crisis without fearing the disappearance of a firm practical world.[28] The method of this response is to *accept* the crisis, to be *present* to it and to find, so to speak, a *stay* within it: to let oneself be affected even by what can only be experienced as a decline of the familiar world.

Wu wei

To explain this singularly human response to crises, Maldiney often turns to Taoist philosophy, as represented in the *Zhuangzi* and the *Laozi*. In this Ancient Chinese tradition, one finds a spiritual ideal that is very akin to possibility, namely of *non-action*, as described by the concept *wu wei*. The term '*wei*' means both 'to act' and 'to consider as', and may be interpreted as 'to act from a perspective'.[29] Action is understood here in the broadest sense of active life, which pursues the realization of ends and in which even perception and imagination are forms of action. *Wu wei* means the negation of *wei* – literally 'non-action'.[30] It is in this sense of *wu wei* that Maldiney defines possibility as 'a receptivity of non-action'.[31] But 'non-action' does not mean doing nothing at all; it means *acting without deliberate intention or effort* – a spontaneous, unengaged activity that is *purely receptive*. As Maldiney puts it, *wei wu wei* is 'the acting in which there is no agency'.[32] What is essential is that the mind be emptied of external goals and evaluative judgments so as to be purely responsive to 'things the way they are'. In the *Zhuangzi*'s sense, non-action implies one's actions lack our typical concern with our own motives; it entails a mindless indifference to the process of evaluating one's desires and motives.[33]

In *Der Ursprung des Kunstwerkes* (1935–6), Heidegger has envisioned something analogous when conceiving the 'letting-happen of the advent of truth' (*Geschehenlassen der Ankunft von Wahrheit*).[34] As he clarifies the term 'letting-happen' (*Geschehenlassen*) in his *Addendum* from 1956, 'this "*letting*" is no passivity, but the highest doing in the sense of a "working" and "willing" that, in the present essay, is characterized as "existing man's ec-static letting-himself-into the unconcealedness of being."'[35] The subject of this 'highest doing' (*höchstes Tun*) is not the egological subject of representation and action but rather a pure receptivity that is *freed* from each form of self-absorption. As Heidegger puts it, 'in *letting*-happen there announces itself a joining-oneself and thus the like of a not-willing that grants freedom' (*ein Sichfügen und so gleichsam ein Nichtwollen, das freigibt*).³⁶ 'The resoluteness [*Ent-schlossenheit*] thought in *Sein und Zeit* is not the decided action of a subject, but the opening-up of *Dasein* out of its captivation by beings, to the openness of Being' (*die Eröffnung des Daseins aus der Befangenheit im Seienden zur Offenheit des Seins*).³⁷

In Maldiney's interpretation of *wu wei*, this exceptional state of pure receptivity entails that the relation between subject and world, inside and outside, is inverted. The external space which is opened up in passibility is not the 'oriented space' of my body's hyletic drive-intentionality and its corresponding *Umwelt*, nor is it the 'homogeneous space' of the objective world, which is constituted by the ego's intentionality.³⁸ In passibility, my surrounding environment 'is no longer opened up *starting from myself*.³⁹ Instead, *passibility seems to be emptied of the ego*: both the subject's bodily self-absorption (*Benommenheit*) and the ego's reflective intentionality are suspended. But in this sense, again, passibility is not a pure passivity: it entails an intense *capacity*, a *highest doing* as Heidegger calls it, and which Maldiney conceives as 'being capable of emptiness'.⁴⁰ As he puts it, 'In the order of action, non-action (*wu wei*) is the equivalent of Nothingness or Emptiness.'⁴¹ As he points out, Emptiness (*shu*) is in Taoist philosophy synonymous for Nothingness or *wu*.⁴² This means that *non-action* or passibility is *being capable* of *wu*, being capable of Nothingness. But in precisely what sense, then, is *passibility* related to the ontological ground of human existence? How does passibility bring this ontological ground of subjectivity to appearance?

Crisis and creation

If passibility brings the subject back to its deepest ontological ground, this entails for Maldiney the undoing of our usual *estrangement* from this ground, which Heidegger called our 'captivation by beings' (*Befangenheit im Seienden*).⁴³ Passibility has a revelatory, truth-constitutive effect in the sense that it *suspends an estrangement* from the conditions of existence, an estrangement which for Maldiney and Heidegger is part of daily human life.

The suspension of action and representation in passibility functions for Maldiney as a kind of phenomenological reduction or *epochè*. He does not have in mind, however, Husserl's method of suspending the 'natural attitude' in order to analyse the intentional acts of consciousness which constitute 'reality'. In passibility, a wholly different kind of reduction is at stake, namely one that is induced by *existential crises*. In the experience of crisis, our 'original belief in the world' or *Urdoxa* is lost.⁴⁴ According to Maldiney, something similar occurs in the *psychotic* experience as it was described by Dasein psychiatrists such as Ludwig Binswanger, Roland Kuhn and Wolfgang Blankenburg in cases of schizophrenia. In both existential and psychotic crisis, the subject suffers from a loss of the confident proximity of things, a loss of what Binswanger called the 'natural self-evidence of being-in-the-world' (*Der Verlust der natürlichen Selbstverständlichkeit*).[45] As such, it is not only the ego of representational consciousness that suffers, but also the selfhood or *Dasein* of existence, which anticipates its life projects by projecting itself in the web of significance, which normally constitutes our being-in-the-world. In both existential and psychotic crises, this ordinary relation to the world is deeply transformed, such that it suspends representational thought and induces existential *disquiet* and *anxiety*.

For Maldiney, in crisis situations our subjective life attains a properly existential dimension because crises throw the subject back upon itself. That is to say, in a crisis the objectifying, imaginary relation of the self to itself encounters its intrinsic limit – a limit that is posed not by the shared symbolic order of normative rules, ideals and laws, but rather by *reality itself*. In a certain sense, existential crises confront the imaginary dimension of the subject to *reality*, in such a way that this confrontation threatens to dissolve the imaginary. Confronted with a crisis, one can sense the *absence* of representations, the *impossibility* of the imaginary subject to keep reality at a distance and freely project itself into it. This is not to say that the subject cannot and will not often *resist* a crisis by turning to imagination. But before reflecting, *reality* drills a short, and often unnoticed, access to the ultimate surprise of *suchness*. As Maldiney writes:

> Pure being in itself, in its brute state, independent of any consideration of its kind or its form, is a monster of astonishment that *deprives us of each relation to the world and whose alterity provokes fear*. Such is the being (including our being itself), which we are thrown into. For however effective it may be in its suchness, it might just as well not have been: nothing would change its opacity. Contingent, gratuitous, it is unjustifiable, 'in excess', outside of meaning.[46]

One is struck then with an astonishment that is closely related to what Heidegger called the first question of metaphysics: *why are there beings at all instead of nothing?*[47] Many may never turn to this question, and yet we are each touched once, Heidegger writes, maybe even now and then, by the concealed power of this question, without properly grasping what is happening to us:

> In great despair, for example, when all weight tends to dwindle away from things and the sense of things grows dark, the question looms. Perhaps it strikes only once, like the muffled tolling of a bell that resounds into Dasein and gradually

fades away. *The question is there in heartfelt joy, for then all things are transformed and surround us as if for the first time, as if it were easier to grasp that they were not, rather than that they are, and are as they are.*[48]

This fundamental amazement faced with a decline of the familiar world and an appearance of the alterity of reality – *when things surround us as if for the first time* – is present not just in crises but also in heartfelt joy (*in einem Jubel des Herzens*). In such moments, it seems easier to understand that things were *not* rather than that they are, and are as they are. For Heidegger and Maldiney, it is the same amazement, which is at work in aesthetic experiences, where it manifests itself in the 'shock' (*Anstoß*) '*that* such work *is* and not rather is not'.[49] Heidegger explains this shock as a 'knocking over' (*umstoßen*) of the familiar face of the world (*das bislang geheuer Scheinende*) and a pushing open of the unfamiliar (*das Ungeheure*), whereby *reality seems to loosen itself from all relations to man*:

> The more solitary a work, set-fast in its *Gestalt*, stands within itself, *the more purely it seems to loosen itself from all relations to man*, and the more easily the shock *that* such work *is*, breaks into the open, and the more essentially the unfamiliar is pushed open, and the until now seemingly ordinary is knocked over.[50]

Heidegger writes that there, where the artist, the process and the circumstances of the production of the work remain unknown, there the shock (*dieser Stoß*), this 'that-it-is' of the work breaks-forth most purely.[51] Like an existential crisis, a work of art thus essentially *knocks over* the familiar, the 'naturally' self-evident (Blankenburg) and opens up the unfamiliar, which is the true face of reality: 'The more essentially this shock comes into the open, the stranger and more solitary the work becomes' (*Je wesentlicher dieser Stoß ins Offene kommt, um so befremdlicher und einsamer wird das Werk*).[52] Did not Deleuze and Guattari envision the same de-subjectifying experience when defining the work of art in terms of '*blocs of sensations*', which *detach* themselves from all relations to the human subject and which present themselves 'in the absence of man'?[53]

For Maldiney, it is this experience of a reality that *loosens itself from all relations to the subject*, which forms the ultimate ground of human existence or *Dasein*. Strictly speaking, however, this ground is an unground or even an abyss, for every question 'why' – such as the question, 'why is there this being at all instead of nothing' – strives to reach such a ground and runs up against an unground or an abyss.[54] The subject did not itself lay the ground of its existence. It did not choose its parents, its body, or the circumstances in which it is thrown. Nonetheless, the individual *becomes the ground of its existence by being receptive* to the event. For Maldiney, this passible receptivity is the deepest inner core driving of a subject's existential (trans-)formation. But how is this possible? What calls the subject to the possible, to transcendence, to existence?

Our passibility to an estranging event makes us receptive to the *indeterminacy of our present in time*. The passible subject discovers the essence of time: the *openness* of the present. When an event appears as entirely groundless, contingent, gratuitous and unjustifiable, reality presents itself as a Nothingness (*le Rien*). For Maldiney, this Nothingness or Emptiness is *the invisible space of the present*. That is to say, in sensing the Nothingness of an event, the subject *senses the openness or the closure of its present*. It is this openness of the present, which Heidegger indicated with the terms *Offenheit, Lichtung, Erschlossenheit* or 'the opening-up of *Dasein* out of its captivation by beings, to the openness of Being' (*die Eröffnung des Daseins aus der Befangenheit im Seienden zur Offenheit des Seins*). When the subject is 'captivated' (*Befangenheit*) by its ontic immersion in the world, the subject is blind to this *openness* of the present. But when it is thrown back upon itself, the subject becomes transparent to its present; the most inner core of its existence then reveals itself as the essence of time: the *openness of the present*.⁵⁵ *To become the ground of its existence, the subject must become one with this openness of its present*. This means that the most inner core of the pathic subject is not simply the existential *being-possible* of *Dasein*, but rather and more profoundly, the *wu wei* of Taoist philosophy. First and foremost, our existence is rooted in the *Nothingness of being*, which is also the *Nothingness of the self*. When the subject is capable of non-action, it reaches this empty core and becomes one with the openness of time.

One understands then why, for Maldiney, 'the real precedes the possible.'⁵⁶ In passibility, our representational relation to the ontic *whatness* of the world and its real or imaginary objects is *reduced* to the pathic *how* of being-with-the-world. This reduction no longer places us in the *seemingly* autonomous element of a pure, self-determining thought (*nous poietikos*), but instead places us in the *real* element of *passivity, indeterminacy* and *openness*.

For Maldiney, this element of passibility concerns by definition formative and transformative experiences: the passible openness to crisis *implies a transformation of the subject*.⁵⁷ The subject who suffers the loss of a loved one takes a pathic attitude to the loss *through* suffering. The subject knows that bearing, enduring and processing this suffering will take time, and will ultimately transform the suffering subject itself. In a similar way, the subject who falls in love with someone surrenders itself with heartfelt joy to the promise of a new life, which will be transformative. For Maldiney, it is this *openness to transformation*, to letting ourselves be transformed by what 'happens' to us, which distinguishes a healthy from a pathological mode of passibility.[58] Crisis arouses the feeling of existing, of feeling challenged and of having to answer to the crisis creatively, with all our resources. While in our daily habitual life, we relate to a familiar and predictable world, crisis transforms us into veritable subjects of a reality that presents itself as an unknown nothingness (*rien, wu*). But this nothingness is not a pure chaos in which the subject is doomed to lose itself. Passibility is open to 'a Nothing (*wu*) which is not the world itself but an event *from which* irradiate all the dimensions, all the rays of the world'.[59] As Johan de Deckere suggested, perhaps one should say, then, with Simone Weil, that the event *fills* an emptiness or a void, which must stand ready and be prepared to *receive* its grace:[60]

> Not to exercise all the power at one's disposal is to endure the void. This is contrary to all the laws of nature. Grace alone can do it. Grace fills empty spaces but it can enter only where there is a void to receive it, and it is grace itself which makes this void.[61]

The *pathos* of individuation

Let us return at this point to the relation between affectivity and psychic individuation. Deleuze's interpretation of the pathic dimension is inconceivable without the Bergsonian idea of a coexistence of many different degrees of duration, which are inferior and superior to that of the human condition.[62] Already in Bergson, this idea led to the affirmation of an *ontological* reality that is inherent to *becoming* (*le devenir*): 'If things are said to endure, it is less in themselves or absolutely than in relation to the Whole of the universe in which they participate insofar as their distinctions are artificial.'[63] For Bergson, the participation in supra- and infra-human temporal structures was possible through the method of intuition. Deleuze fully inscribes himself in this Bergsonian thought when conceiving sensation in terms of a 'zone of indiscernibility' between man and animal.[64] What is at stake here is not a 'sentimental identification' between man and animal, but rather a zone of 'deep identity' between both, and which concerns precisely their participation in the reality of Duration.[65]

For Deleuze, what is at stake in the pathic dimension of sensation is a discovery of the body insofar as it consists of two heterogeneous, opposed regimes: *organization* and *inorganic life*. In a pathic encounter, the body manifests itself as more than an organized system of organs, sensorimotor patterns, instincts, habits, etc. Beneath its organized circuits, the body attests to 'a more profound and almost unlivable Power', which is the power of inorganic life.⁶⁶ As we have seen, this is the vital power of individuation, which creates degrees of energy indetermination in the material world.

The distinction between organization and inorganic life coincides with Deleuze's distinction between our *psychological* duration, which is dominated by organic need, pleasure and utility, and the *ontological* duration, which is the reality of becoming: the reality of Duration itself. In the empirical exercise of sensibility, which characterizes our psychological duration, sensations are related to qualified objects in extensive space and time. Thus, in psychological duration, consciousness rarely coincides with Duration. Our psychological duration is intermingled with spatialized perception, utilitarian behaviour, representational thought, etc. – all of which amount to a closure and dispossession from Duration. But there is one class of experiences, where our spatialized experience of sensations is suspended: when a degree of *energy indetermination* is inscribed into the psychic system, the spatializing mind is momentarily suspended to *an indetermination of time*. Indeed, Deleuze's ontological interpretation of the affective entails an *opening* of our human, psychological consciousness onto the *ontological* reality of Duration. Sensation is not only a power of sensing intensities, but it is also essentially a synthetic power of sensing time itself. But this time, again, is not the temporality of our psychological duration. As the reality of becoming, ontological Duration forms the constitutive *indeterminacy* of the present. As de Deckere puts it:

> Becoming thereby has no 'subject' that would become something else; becoming produces only itself ('its' own differences) and has no fixed stages or poles between which 'something' that remains identical to itself would evolve or transform. It therefore also has no end term or end result (that which 'one' has finally become). The only reality is the identity *of* becoming, which continuously merges into the *panta rei* of another becoming.⁶⁷

This is precisely what it means to say individuation or sensation *endures*: there is an indeterminate mobility of a present that perpetually differs from the past and that produces an open-ended future. For Deleuze, when sensation opens up to this indeterminate becoming of Duration, 'its' psychological duration becomes *unhinged* by irreversible changes and qualitative transformations. For the subject, it is as though its psychological duration is 'thrown out of joint' by a caesura, 'a unique and tremendous event'.⁶⁸ The subject relates to the caesura as to the present of metamorphosis, which takes on an *excessive* presence, exceeding the bounds of the organized circuits of body and mind. As the present of individuation, Duration possesses 'a secret coherence which excludes that of the self' and which turns against the self, 'as though the bearer of the new world were carried away and dispersed by the shock of the multiplicity to which it gives birth: what the self has become equal to is the unequal in itself'.[69]

Subjected to irreversible changes and qualitative transformations, the subject is in a certain sense 'equalized' with the very indeterminacy at the heart of Duration. It is as though the immanent flux of Duration is 'freed' from its falsification in psychological duration, which projects the external form of space over it. In order to experience the intensive reality of individuation properly, it is necessary to feel how Duration *divides itself* and *differentiates itself* according to its own measure. To grasp this unbounded, self-differentiating movement properly, one must come to a pure intuition of its immanent development and its immanent changes.

We can therefore say that pathic sensation, which grasps intensity independently from the extensive form of intuition, which normally organizes it, really grasps the ontological reality of Duration, as the intensive and indeterminate becoming of individuation. The more we penetrate into Duration, the more the substantial fixity of matter seems to *disappear* and the more we grasp there is no real distinction between matter and becoming. Matter *is* intensity, flux, gradients, movements and dynamic tendencies, 'in relation to which forms are contingent or accessory'.[70] Indeed, going beyond psychological duration, sensation extends itself into the pure immanence of *pre-individual* Duration. Sensation grasps this 'obscure' and 'appalling' ground of Nature, 'that ground which has no name' and which Deleuze qualifies as an 'essentially inorganic life', 'the inorganic life of things'.[71]

Volitional intuition

Let us note, finally, that pathic sensation also entails to Deleuze a modification of the *will*, a 'leaping in place of the whole body which exchanges its organic will for a spiritual will'.[72] When human consciousness regains a connection to the enduring mobility of Duration, it creates a *spiritual* kind of will in that it creates an *indetermination* of will. Keeping in mind the essence of inorganic life, namely the production of energy indetermination, the shift from organic to spiritual will consists in the creation of a vital impulse, a vital will towards differentiation and individuation. For Deleuze, this spiritual will is characterized by a Stoic *indifference* to the enterprise of evaluating one's personal interests, motives and desires.[73] But this Stoic will is not a liberation from willing itself, as perhaps Schopenhauer would have had it. Rather, it is a liberation from the organic instinct, which takes hold of the will, and which turns it into a reactive, resentful will. As opposed to the organic will, 'which grasps whatever happens as unjust and unwarranted', spiritual will raises sensibility, as the power of being affected, to its highest level.[74] It changes one's affective *attitude* or *disposition*, such that one *wills* the event. This most elevated level of affectivity, which the spiritual will in us ultimately strives for, is an abysmal *openness* to the event, an *amor fati*.

In its most succinct formulation, Deleuze defines this spiritual will as a 'volitional intuition' in which 'the given' does not *limit* the activity of the will.[75] It is a will 'beyond courage and cowardice', a 'pure grasping of the event' by means of *a will that the event creates in oneself*.[76] This can only be understood in light of what one might call Deleuze's Nietzschean presupposition, namely that human will has a fundamental predisposition towards passivity and ressentiment. Faced with the contingencies of life, the human will always fluctuates between the two extremes of ressentiment, which grasps what happens as unjust and unwarranted, and volitional will, which itself affirms and wills the event. Ressentiment is a reactive, passive state of hostility towards what happens, a 'spirit of revenge' which reduces our power to think and to act, and separates us from what we can do.[77] By contrast, volitional intuition manifests the essence of the will as the 'active' principle that is *open* also to those experiences, such as the experience of suffering (and death), that entail a dimension of *indeterminacy* and *de-subjectivation*. As Deleuze writes:

> Either morality makes no sense at all, or this is what it means and has nothing else to say: not to be unworthy of what happens to us. To grasp whatever happens as unjust and unwarranted (it is always someone else's fault) is, on the contrary, what renders our sores repugnant – veritable *ressentiment*, resentment of the event. (…) Nothing more can be said, and no more has ever been said: to become worthy of what happens to us, and thus to will and release the event, to become the offspring of one's own events, and thereby to be reborn, to have one more birth, and to break with one's carnal birth.[78]

Reactivity and passivity are a perpetual human temptation in that the desire for self-maintenance, stability and order is attached to the bounded organization of the self that one is at any given moment in time. But from this point of view, my life will appear as too weak, too unjustly treated by fate. By contrast, volitional intuition embodies a will to *overcome* the fragility and transience of self in a larger vision, in an expansive sense of self (Nietzsche's *hohe Stimmung*), and in a sublime sense of universal and natural belonging. Volitional intuition expands itself to be included within Nature, and that sublime expansion increases its power, its activity instead of its reactivity. In this case, it is the self that is too weak for life, it is life that is too large for self, scattering its singularities all about, *in no relation to the self at all.*[79] But to attain this sublime level of pure passibility, the agent must let go of each *telos*, each goal of conscious thinking and striving. For this reason, pathic sensations only emerge when they deprive us of our power of saying 'I'. Passibility is not of the punctual order of the I or the self, it cannot be self-present and it is no reflexivity of subjective feeling. We should rather describe a true sublime event in the third person singular: 'it suffers' and 'it wonders' such as 'it rains' or 'one dies'.[80]

7

Erewhon: Infinity and the sublime

For there are two labyrinths of the human mind, one concerning the composition of the continuum, and the other concerning the nature of freedom, and they arise from the same source, infinity.
— Gottfried W. Leibniz[1]

Infinity and the sublime

The human experience of the sublime is strongly connected to the space and time relative to which the human mind must determine itself. The aim of this concluding chapter is to show that both the Kantian and the Deleuzian interpretations of the sublime rely on a particular view of space and time, and on a correlated metaphysical view of its infinity as an actual (Kant) or a virtual (Deleuze) whole. In Kant, we should distinguish the mathematical concept of potential infinity, which is applicable to Newtonian space and time, from a neo-Platonic, metaphysical Idea of actual infinity, which Kant applies to the universe as a self-contained world-whole. Similarly, in Deleuze we find a properly metaphysical concept of infinity, which is rooted in Anaximander's concept of *to apeiron*, and which Deleuze applies to the space and time of thermodynamics as a self-individuating virtual whole. Confronting these differing views of space, time and infinity, this final chapter shows how Kant and Deleuze are led to develop separate, yet interconnected conceptions of the sublime.

In Kant's original view, space and time are pure intuitions, which means that they are constructions of the mind. Contrary to what our natural attitude suggests, the perception of the spatiotemporal, 3D Euclidian structure of the world is not a passive reception of external structures but rather an active construction of the mind. Human experience is a synthetic construction, which results from imposing finite limits or boundaries onto the intuitive continuum: we always only experience local places in global space and local durations in global time, and these are always given as enclosed between finite boundaries. Within this neo-Aristotelian perspective, there is an *ontological primacy* of the continuum over the discrete, which is experienced as a non-compositional, cohesive, primitive and intuitive datum – a continuous whole, without discrete parts.[2] As Kant writes:

> Spatium est quantum, sed non compositum. For space does not arise through the positing of its parts, but the parts are only possible through space; likewise with time. The parts may well be considered *abstrahendo a caeteris*, but cannot be conceived *removendo caetera*.[3]

The function of intuition is essentially to *segment* the spatial and temporal continuum into discontinuous parts, which may be glued or synthesized together. Human consciousness segments the spatial and temporal continuum into an extensive manifold (*Mannigfaltigkeit*) of spatially and temporally determined parts: moments in time and places in space. But these discontinuous parts themselves remain continua. Any present moment in time is merely an imposed boundary between which the temporal continuum takes place. Likewise, the simplest elements of space are merely limits, which we impose upon the spatial continuum.

Within this synthetic perspective, the continuous spatiotemporal flux of human consciousness is a synthetic construction that has an Aristotelian, finitistic status of being a potential infinity. It is constructed by the *finite* unity of self-consciousness (apperception) as the synthetic ordering and unifying principle of the spatiotemporal 3D manifold. The ordered and unified manifold is a potential infinity in the sense that it continuously emerges from a finite act: the finite unity of apperception constitutes the unity and order of the temporal manifold as a potential infinity.

Kant's analysis of the sublime is centred on the idea that it is possible to suspend this synthetic construction of experience when the mind is confronted with vast extensions. In the sublime, imagination is said to institute a momentary regression that suspends both the linear form of time and the extensive form of space that is assumed in the *Critique of Pure Reason*. This regress opens up a new form of intuition, by means of which imagination can instantaneously comprehend an intensive multiplicity (*Vielheit*) as a pre-conceptual unity. Whereas in our normal perception the synthesis of apprehension always intuits a synthetic manifold (*Mannigfaltigkeit*) of temporally determined parts, the sublime regression intuits an intensive multiplicity as an undetermined unity, which is to be conceived as a totality, a whole or a continuum *without* discrete parts. Thus, in the Analytic of the Sublime, Kant opens up the possibility that there are *no explicit boundaries* in intuition. In a sublime experience one intuits, according to Kant, 'a *formless* object' insofar as '*limitlessness* is represented in it, or at its instance, and yet it is also thought as a totality'.[4]

The first aim of this chapter is to show how, for Kant, this sublime intuition of limitlessness brings to mind the neo-Platonic Idea of actual infinity, that is, of a given infinite whole. To this end, I will show how space and time are for Kant infinite in two distinct senses. On the one hand, he often discusses infinity's boundlessly increasing or dynamic, *potential* aspect – for example when speaking of the 'limitlessness in the progression of intuition', the synthetic progressions in experience that can never be completed or the regress of conditions that can never be regarded as absolutely completed.[5] In this same sense, Kant also maintains time is infinite because 'every determinate magnitude of time is possible only through limitations of one single time that underlies it' and time 'must therefore be given as unlimited'.[6] Here, Kant intends Aristotle's conception of potential infinity, which implies that which is such that, given any determinate part of it, there is always more to come. But Kant also discusses space and time in terms of the *all-encompassing* or *static* aspect of actual infinity. He then speaks of space and time as an infinitely complex *whole*, an absolute *totality* or an infinite *given* magnitude. In these occurrences, as I will show, Kant is using a neo-Platonic, metaphysical concept of actual infinity. The properties, which he ascribes to it, are: completeness, wholeness, absoluteness, unconditionality and finally, sublimity. Indeed, Kant's view is not just that 'nature is sublime in those of its appearances the intuition of which brings with them the idea of its infinity', but also that (actual) infinity *is* sublime.[7]

In Deleuze's transcendental empiricism, the central organizing idea is that reality is the continual creation of unpredictable novelty and not the successive realization of pre-existing possibilities. Instead of the Newtonian worldview of a deterministic reality in which all possibilities are pre-existent and time has no creative effect, Deleuze developed the Bergsonian view that reality is fundamentally creative evolution, the continuous creation of new possibilities. To develop this alternative view of an inherently creative reality, Deleuze's metaphysics divides reality into two fundamental planes: one pre-individual plane of Nature and one individual plane of material, living and psychic things. But how might one give a meaning to the concept of a *pre-individual Nature* that is deprived of natural beings? As we have seen, Deleuze's central idea is that insofar as every individual being has a *form* or *structure*, one must conceive of an *a priori* space within which this form individuates itself.[8] In this sense, Euclidian space has traditionally been given an ontological primacy, and many thinkers have conceived it as the body of God. In Newton's metaphysics of space, for example, absolute space or pure extension exists prior to and independently of matter as an affection of God himself, because God is omnipresent or everywhere.[9] The most salient philosophical source of this view was the neo-Platonic tradition, which conceived absolute space as neither a substance nor an accident, but as an emanative effect of God.

But Deleuze's conception of pre-individual Nature stands in stark contrast to the conceptions of space in Newton and Kant. Following a tradition that runs from Leibniz to Maimon, Fichte, Schelling, Hermann Weyl and others, Deleuze defends the view that matter is not a given in pure extension or some passive geometrical or mechanical quantity, but rather it is an active agent that is itself prior to and constitutive of extensive spatiotemporal events.

In this framework, pre-individual space is conceived in terms of Anaximander's indefinite *apeiron*: a primordial extramundane continuum from which 'pure intensity' or 'pure energy' constitutes extended and qualified material, living and psychic things. This leads Deleuze to develop a new Transcendental Aesthetic, distinguishing between an *a priori* intensive space (*spatium*) and time (*duration*), within which processes of individuation unfold, and an *a priori* extensive space, which is related to the phenomenal properties of these dynamics. Accordingly, Deleuze distinguishes between two irreducible ways of apprehending reality: a metaphysical mode, which apprehends Being as a genetic process or creative becoming, and a representational mode, which apprehends qualified things in extension.

What is largely unknown is that Deleuze connected to this Transcendental Aesthetic a new way of conceiving the intuition of the sublime – a topic he repeatedly returned to throughout his work. In accordance with Kant, Deleuze's conception of the sublime is centred on the idea that it is possible to suspend the synthetic construction of representational experience: in a sublime intuition, the content of sense is intuited as an intensive multiplicity of indeterminate parts of a whole. But, as I aim to show, Deleuze does not relate this sublime intuition to the Platonic Idea of an actual infinity, a self-contained infinite Whole. Instead, the sublime is for him an intuitive opening onto the ontological reality that is inherent to the creative becoming of individuation. The feeling of the sublime then becomes an ecstatic intuition of the energetic indetermination driving individuation: an intuition of reality as 'a fundamentally open Whole'.[10]

Actual and potential infinity

Kant's and Deleuze's philosophical approaches to infinity inscribe themselves in a long metaphysical tradition that ranges from Anaximander, Plato and Aristotle up to Descartes, Leibniz and Spinoza. In this opening section, we will compare how the Ancient Greeks conceived of infinity as either an indefinite and unlimited moving element (Anaximander), an actual infinity (Plato) or a potential infinity (Aristotle).

Anaximander's *Apeiron*

In Greek thought, the term for the infinite was *to apeiron*, which literally means 'without limits' ('limit' meaning '*peras*') and hence 'unlimited' or 'unbounded'. Anaximander first introduced the concept into Western philosophy in response to what was at the time (and has remained) a fundamental metaphysical challenge: to identify the primal stuff from which all things are made. According to Anaximander, this primal stuff was *to apeiron*: something neutral, boundless, imperishable, the primal source of all that is. As a sort of indefinite and unbounded moving element, the *apeiron* indicated a primal reality that was unbounded both spatially and temporally and that was all-embracing.[11] One can read the original Greek ἄπειρον as without a limit (ἄ-πειρον) but also as related to πειρα and read it as 'without experience' or 'impassible'. This seems to be Deleuze's reading when he relates the 'unlimited becoming' of the *apeiron* to the 'impassible' incorporeals of the Stoics.[12]

Anaximander conceived *to apeiron* as a divine and metaphysical first principle. Infinity was for him a kind of primal substratum that underlies all the natural processes whereby substances change into one another (and that itself remains changeless). In this context, we should already distinguish two senses of the term 'infinite'. The first is the temporal sense related to the inexhaustible series of cosmic cycles, and the second is that related to the permanence and timelessness of their final substratum.[13] It is in the latter sense that Anaximander uses *to apeiron* as a synonym of the divine and neutral metaphysical principle.

That God is the Indefinite implies that he is not only spatially infinite but also qualitatively indefinite: the divine is without any definable attribute whatsoever. The infinite can in this sense not be exhaustively represented in our thought and remains unknowable.[14] The indeterminate nature of *to apeiron* also implies it is not some sort of physical 'stuff' (atoms, particles, waves, etc.)

from which the world is constituted. Anaximander's doctrine is not a physics but a metaphysics. The infinite is not any sort of matter but rather it is the eternal primordial source of all being, which produces world after world from an inexhaustible fecundity.[15]

But what exactly is Anaximander's Unlimited? Anaximander saw in the multifarious processes around us a fundamental disharmony and imbalance between continuously conflicting 'opposites': hot or cold, dry or wet, light or dark, health or sickness, anger or fear, etc. These 'opposites', then, were for him the primal sources of all continuously changing processes in nature. Anaximander believed that the opposites themselves emerged from and would return to the *apeiron* where they would lose their identity and where all conflict would be overcome.[16] As Sweeney puts it, the *apeiron* was 'a self-animated mass' that produces the opposites but is itself neither hot nor cold, neither dry nor moist.[17] It is simply other than them all because it is their origin. Of the nature of the Indeterminate we can therefore only say: 'it is such as to be that from which the "Opposites" and posterior effects arose, which surrounds the visible universe they constitute, which somehow guides it.'[18]

This characterization leads to an important question: is the Infinite distinct from its products or identical with them? Is Anaximander a dualist or a monist? According to Sweeney, he is monist only insofar as his world has a single originating principle and both it and its principle consist of the same sort of 'stuff' (which, however, is found in the *apeiron* in an indeterminate manner and in things in a determinate manner). But Anaximander is not a monist in the sense that constituted things would be really identical with their primal source. Both levels of reality are intimately related but nonetheless product and cause remain fundamentally different.

In what sense should we say, then, that *to apeiron* is infinite? Most scholars view *to apeiron* as permeating all that exists in the world and yet simultaneously surrounding it also.[19] As the origin of our tremendous and varied universe, it is inexhaustible in resources, as well as itself without origin and end. It is infinite in the sense that it is indeterminate, everlasting, indestructible and without any extrinsic limit.

Note that this concept of *to apeiron* plays a central role in Deleuze's metaphysics. As we have seen, Deleuze makes an ontological distinction between a pre-individual plane of nature (*natura naturans*) and the actual individual beings in nature (*natura naturata*). Simondon called this pre-individual plane simply 'Nature' and inscribed it within the framework of Anaximander:

One could call *nature* this pre-individual reality that the individual carries with it, seeking to recover in the word nature the signification it had for the Presocratics; the Ionian philosophers saw in it the origin of all the species of being, anterior to individuation; nature is the *reality of the possible*, in the form of this *apeiron* from which, according to Anaximander, all individuated form emerges: Nature is not the contrary of man, but the first phase of being, the second being the opposition of the individual and its milieu, which complements that of the individual with respect to the whole.[20]

As we have seen, Deleuze drew several important consequences from this idea of a pre-individual substrate of Nature. Deleuze's *apeiron* is the pre-individual *natura naturans*, which determines the possible ways in which an infinite variety of material, living and psychic forms may become individuated as *natura naturata*.

Pythagoras and Plato: *Peras/Apeiron*

After Anaximander, the Pythagoreans conceived *to apeiron* as something abhorrent: a dark, boundless void beyond the visible heavens. Where Anaximander had understood the Unlimited in terms of perfection and goodness (by taking away conflict and opposition), they saw it as something repellent. Adrian Moore points out they believed this because *to apeiron* had no end in the sense of a limit (*peras*) and it equally had no end in the sense of a purpose or destiny (*telos*).[21] In contrast to the regular cycles of the planets, the recurring patterns in nature and the proportioned structures in the physical world, *to apeiron* appeared to be something senseless, chaotic, indeterminate: a boundlessness without structure, simply waiting to have a limit imposed upon it. The Pythagoreans believed that all that exists in reality was the result of a synthesis between limit and the unlimited void.[22] That is to say, limit is what makes every object exist concretely, by ceaselessly endowing it with its proper form and individuality.[23] What emerged from the imposing of a limit onto the void of the *apeiron* was a beautifully structured, harmonious whole whose parts hung together in unity precisely because of their limitedness and finitude.[24] As such, limit is what determines the logical order of events, by removing them from pure chance or randomness.

Plato's metaphysical approach to the infinite was greatly inspired by the Pythagoreans (in particular by Parmenides). He agreed with the Pythagoreans that Anaximander's *apeiron* was an indeterminate void and all existing things had to acquire determinate limits and structures by the general imposition of a *peras* on *to apeiron*. In this regard, he took a Pythagorean approach to the basic problem of Anaximander: how does reality emerge from *to apeiron*? Plato gives the example of temperature. If my body temperature has a determinate quality, then this is the effect of an imposition of *peras* on *to apeiron*. The optimal healthy state of the human body is expressed in a well-defined proportion that fixes a limit-point at which the body's indefinite capacity to evolve is resolved and beyond which it is senseless and useless to proceed any further.[25] For Plato, the effect of such limiting by *peras* was a world as described by the Pythagoreans: a beautifully ordered whole. But Plato argued that this Pythagorean world was not the real world. It was merely the sensible world of appearances. According to Plato, what actually controlled the synthesis between limit and unlimited, that is, how a *peras* became imposed on *to apeiron*, was a sort of generative cosmic causality, a principle of intelligence or reason, which belonged to the true metaphysical reality (the primal substrate of all things).[26] The latter was the world of Ideas, which were formal archetypes of things in the sensible world, which in turn instantiated them and participated in them in diverse degrees.

On Plato's view, then, this primal world of Ideas had to be metaphysically infinite: it was a timeless eternity. Like Anaximander's *apeiron*, Plato's world of Ideas was eternal in the sense that it could suffer no change, it could suffer neither generation nor decay. Plato also agreed with Anaximander that this infinite realm had to be an indivisible, homogeneous whole. But Plato did not define his account of infinity in terms of the Indefinite or Unlimited. Influenced by the Pythagoreans, Plato viewed the world of Ideas as completely determined and definite by virtue of *peras*. On his view, there could be nothing indeterminate or unlimited about what was real and true and good. Indeed, the fundamental invention of Plato was to say the *infinite can itself have a limit* and in this sense be *actual*. In Plato's original sense, for infinity to be actual means to have a boundary. But this does not imply, for Plato, having a spatio-temporal place. Rather, actual infinity becomes a kind of originary *nowhere*, from which the spatio-temporal now and here *emerges* and which has no corporeal existence, but is purely ideal. This view of actual infinity clearly conflicts with Anaximander's view of the indeterminate nature of infinity: in Anaximander's *apeiron*, things would lose their identity for there are no determinants, no *peras*, and all limits would be overcome.[27] Plato inverts this picture: for him, any legitimate concept of *to apeiron* could only have its home in the bodily world of appearances and not pertain to the world of Ideas.

Now, let us make a second, important observation about Deleuze's reading of these Greek philosophers. When Deleuze calls his philosophy 'a reversal of Platonism' it is precisely this Platonic reinterpretation of Anaximander that is at stake.[28] Reversing Plato means for Deleuze two things. First of all, refuting Plato's dualism, Deleuze advocates a monism in the spirit of Anaximander: the infinite 'One-All' becomes a primal substrate space which is 'unlimited, or at least without precise limits'.[29] It is only *from* this primal Indefinite that material, living and psychic forms (and the dualisms they bring with them) emerge.[30] Secondly, the reversal of Platonism entails a return to Anaximander's conception of *to apeiron* as a primal Becoming: the primal substrate of reality cannot be seen as a timeless eternity. This is a crucial point.

In Plato, the world of Ideas is a timeless, static reality of ideal possibilities determining the various ways in which material things may or may not behave. Deleuze's *apeiron*, by contrast, is essentially *creative* and *becoming*. Deleuze will connect to this a new conception of *peras*.[31] While for Plato *peras* designates pre-existent, ideal structural possibilities that subsist eternally and can be actualized in material reality (thereby determining that reality), for Deleuze *peras* will refer to the power of *singularities* to *create new ideal possibilities*, which in turn individuate *new* realities emerging from the primal Infinite. Unlike Plato's realm of Ideas, for Deleuze, the Infinite will not refer to a static, eternal totality of *pre-given* possibilities – the eternal invariants of all natural forms. Instead, the Infinite will refer to a primal substrate space of creativity, harbouring the open, evolving creation of new possibilities and thus the infinite variability of new natural physical, living and psychic forms. Deleuze's *apeiron* then becomes what he calls with Samuel Butler the '*Erewhon*': an originary 'nowhere' from which emerge *inexhaustibly* ever new, differently distributed 'heres' and 'nows'.[32]

Aristotle's potential infinity

Rejecting the metaphysical appearance/reality distinction found in Anaximander and Plato, Aristotle refuted the idea that actual infinity can exist either physically or as a metaphysical substrate. For him, one can only make sense of the concept of infinity in spatio-temporal terms. And since there is in the natural world of space and time nothing that has no limit or bound, Aristotle rejected the idea that infinity could exist in nature. But Aristotle did acknowledge proofs for the existence of the infinite: time (which seemed to be infinite, both by addition and by division), mathematical numbers and the division of magnitudes. This led him to decisively divorce infinity from physics and engage it exclusively with mathematics: there is no such thing as (actually) infinite physical bodies, but nonetheless mathematicians can engage the *potential* infinity of numbers and magnitudes in their discourse. For example, upon constructing the geometric figure of a straight line, we may extend its segments with no finite limit and divide it into an infinite series of parts.

Aristotle's proposal, then, was to say 'there is no objection to something's being infinite *provided that its infinitude is not there "all at once."*'[33] This means that infinity could only exist *potentially* but not *actually*. As Moore puts it, the potential infinite is that whose infinitude exists, or is given, '*over* time', whereas the actual infinite is that whose infinitude exists, or is given, 'at some point *in* time'.[34] Thus, potential infinity is never wholly present. This conception of potential infinity was an explicit reaction against the Presocratic concept of an infinite All that is linked with actuality. The infinite All of the Presocratics is that which has nothing outside it and thus, is complete and whole precisely because it has no end or limit and, accordingly, encompasses everything. For Aristotle, on the contrary, 'it is not what has nothing outside it that is infinite, but what always has something outside it' (*Physics* 3.6.206b34-207a6). In this sense, infinity exists for him only as a potential: a never-ending process over time, which is *itself finite* at any specific time.

Actual and potential infinity in Kant

The mathematical infinity of space and time

In the Transcendental Aesthetic of the first *Critique*, Kant maintains that space and time are infinite. For example, in a much-debated passage, he writes that 'Space is represented as an infinite *given* magnitude'.[35] At the same time, however, Kant acknowledges that the phenomena we experience in space and time are never infinite.[36] But in what sense can space then be represented as an infinite *given* magnitude? Like Newton, Kant rejects Descartes's identification of matter with extension and defends, accordingly, the concept of absolute (empty) space existing prior to and independently of matter.[37] In Newton, this led to the neo-Platonic idea that absolute space is neither a substance nor an accident, but an emanative effect of God himself, since God is omnipresent or everywhere (and can himself thereby create matter or body as something distinct from pure extension). For Kant, however, space is not the 'sensorium' of God. Although something like Newtonian space remains as the foundation of the sensible world, space is rather the form of *our* sensorium, the form of our pure sensibility.[38]

When Kant writes that space is represented as 'an infinite *given* magnitude', it is our intuitive representation of the *form* of space that is at stake. As he puts it, 'space is merely the form of outer intuition, but not a real object that can be externally intuited, and it is not a correlate of appearances, but rather the form of appearances themselves'.[39] Thus, space taken as an infinite *given* magnitude, concerns the form of space as something infinitely complex, namely as a 'whole' that contains an infinite aggregate of 'parts': 'for all parts of space *in infinitum* exist simultaneously'.[40] But for Kant, this form of space as a complex whole is not an empirical reality. Since the parts of space extend infinitely and can also be divided infinitely, it is impossible to ever attain this whole in empirical intuition.[41] Nothing in our human experience can properly meet the description of such an infinitely complex structure.

We should therefore say that space (as well as time) is for Kant infinite in two distinct senses. On the one hand, he clearly intends infinity's *boundlessly increasing* or *dynamic, potential* aspect. He then speaks of the 'limitlessness in the progression of intuition', the infinite aggregate of parts in experience, the synthetic progressions in experience that can never be completed and of the regress of conditions that can never be regarded as absolutely completed.[42] In a similar sense, he maintains time is infinite because 'every determinate magnitude of time is possible only through limitations of one single time that underlies it' and time 'must therefore be given as unlimited'.[43] Here, the negative properties of mathematical infinity are clearly present: boundlessness, limitlessness, endlessness, potentiality, conditionality, externality. In Aristotelian phrasing, the infinite in this mathematical sense implies that which is such that, given any determinate part of it, there is always more to come.

The actual infinity of the universe as a whole

But Kant also speaks of space and time in terms of an *all-encompassing* or *static* aspect of actual infinity. Kant then speaks of space and time as an infinitely complex *whole*, an absolute *totality* or an infinite *given* magnitude. In these occurrences, he is using a neo-Platonic, metaphysical concept of actual infinity. The positive properties, which he ascribes to it are: completeness, wholeness, absoluteness, unconditionality.

Kant thought that we are metaphysically finite beings in a *metaphysically* infinite universe or world-whole. As such, human beings are part of a universe that forms a self-contained and absolute totality, a complete unified whole. But according to Kant, we could never have any experience or knowledge of this whole. Whatever can be experienced is always finite, partial and *conditioned* (e.g., by particular causes). Our experience of things as conditioned leads to the thought of an infinite series of conditions, each itself conditioned by some further condition. But this infinity is mathematical: it is a potential infinity. The metaphysical infinity of the world as a self-contained and absolute whole, by contrast, posits reality as an *unconditioned* whole.

Infinity and the sublime in Kant

Formlessness, limitlessness and the idea of actual infinity

From its first paragraph onwards, the Analytic of the Sublime (§23) confronts us with a paradoxical idea: while judgments on beauty concern the *form* of the object, 'which consists in limitation' (*Begrenzung*), the sublime by contrast, is to be found in 'a *formless* object' (*einem formlosen Gegenstande*) 'insofar as *limitlessness* [*Unbegrenztheit*] is represented in it, or at its instance, and yet it is also thought as a totality'.[44] What does Kant mean here with a formless object? How can an object be *intuited* as being formless and limitless and yet be *thought* as a totality?

For Kant, what is 'formal in the representation of a thing' concerns 'the agreement of the manifold with a unity'.[45] In the First Critique's Subjective Deduction, Kant described how such a formal unity is produced from an intuitive sensuous manifold through the three synthetic acts of apprehension, reproduction and apperceptive recognition. In the sublime, the formlessness of the object designates the failure of these syntheses to unify the manifold. Strictly speaking, in the sublime, the imagination is confronted not with a 'manifold' but with a 'multiplicity' that 'exceeds' the imagination and that accordingly cannot be unified conceptually. We can already see, therefore, that sublime *limitlessness* or *formlessness* does not designate the mathematical, potential infinity of nature, which can be conceived by our finite understanding. As Kant writes, 'the imagination is adequate for the mathematical estimation of every object (…) because the numerical concepts of the understanding, by means of progression, can make any measure adequate for any given magnitude.'[46] In this process, 'There is no difficulty with apprehension, because it can go on to infinity'.[47] Indeed, 'The imagination, by itself, without anything hindering it, advances to infinity in the composition that is requisite for the representation of magnitude; the understanding, however, guides this by numerical concepts, for which the former must provide the schema.'[48]

However, confronted with objects whose vast magnitude exceeds our imagination, the latter 'sinks back in itself' and brings to mind reason's Idea of an absolute 'whole':[49]

> But now the mind hears in itself the voice of reason, which requires totality for all given magnitudes, (...) hence comprehension in *one* intuition, and it demands a *presentation* for all members of a progressively increasing numerical series, and does not exempt from this requirement even the infinite (space and past time), but rather makes it unavoidable for us to think of it (...) as *given entirely* (in its totality).[50]

In the sublime, it is for Kant thus the neo-Platonic idea of actual infinity that is brought to mind, 'for what is properly sublime cannot be contained in any sensible form, but concerns only ideas of reason'.[51] This becomes all the more clear if we consider Kant's definition of actual infinity as sublime. The sublime is '*absolutely great*' in the sense that it is '*great beyond all comparison*'.[52] As such, Kant distinguishes sublime 'greatness' (*Groß sein; magnitudo*) from mathematical 'magnitude' (*eine Größe sein; quantitas*).[53] It is in these same terms that Kant also defines infinity as an absolute whole:

> The infinite, however, is absolutely (not merely comparatively) great. Compared with this, everything else (of the same kind of magnitude) is small. But what is most important is that even being able to think of it as *a whole* [*ein Ganzes*] indicates a faculty of the mind which surpasses every standard of sense.[54]

Composition and comprehension of spatio-temporal magnitude

To understand why the Idea of actual infinity is brought to mind in the experience of the sublime, we should focus on Kant's statement that the *magnitude* of an object can exceed our imagination. Kant explains the excess of imagination in terms of two processes that are involved in the constitution of the magnitude of spatio-temporal phenomena: 'composition' (*Zusammensetzung*) and 'aesthetic comprehension' (*Zusammenfassung*).

Note, first, that for Kant space and time are continuous magnitudes or what he calls '*quanta continua*' of which we can always only experience 'parts'.[55] We experience always local places in global space and local durations in global time. This is possible only if we impose 'limits' or 'boundaries' onto the continuous magnitudes of space and time.[56] Of course, being continuous magnitudes, space and time do not actually contain any spatial points or temporal instants, but our human intuition forms and imposes those so as to have a finite, limited spatio-temporal experience. We always only experience local parts of space and time, and these are always given as enclosed between boundaries. For Kant, the imagination is the synthetic faculty of human intuition that has this exact function: to impose limits and boundaries on the spatial and temporal continuum.

Now, Kant's distinction between composition and comprehension essentially entails two different ways in which imagination can limit the continuous (intensive and extensive) magnitude of space and time. This is a significant point, because Kant only introduces this distinction in the Analytic of the Sublime. In the first *Critique*, Kant does not yet distinguish between composition and aesthetic comprehension. Let us briefly consider this distinction.

In the first *Critique*, our intuition of the spatio-temporal manifold is produced by what Kant calls 'composition' (*Zusammensetzung*), in which the representation of spatio-temporal parts makes possible the representation of the whole. In this composition, the imagination is always guided by the understanding, which unifies its apprehensions by means of concepts. Accordingly, in the first *Critique*, 'comprehension' of that which is composed always refers to 'logical comprehension' (*comprehensio logica*) in concepts of understanding.[57] As noted, Kant is explicit that imagination's composition and understanding's comprehension are *potentially* infinite processes. By means of numerical concepts, one can easily push the measure of the parts of a manifold up by scale, from a mile to the diameter of the earth, to the distance between observable bodies in the solar system or the Milky Way galaxy, which rotates around the centre of a larger system of such galaxies, and so on *ad infinitum*.[58]

In the Analytic of the Sublime, however, Kant states that the constitution of spatial and temporal magnitudes by imagination not only involves composition but also what he calls 'aesthetic comprehension' (*comprehensio aesthetica*). This is a process whereby imagination *itself* seeks unity and order in that which has been successively apprehended – independently from and prior to the intervention of (numerical, logical) concepts of understanding. In what Kant calls its 'basic measure' (*Grundmaß*), imagination attempts to unify and comprehend (*Zusammenfassung*) the diversity in the spatio-temporal flow of apprehended and reproduced (i.e. composed) parts. But unlike the logical comprehension, which is numerical, this aesthetic comprehension is finite and limited: the vast magnitude of certain phenomena is such that 'comprehension becomes ever more difficult the further apprehension advances, and soon reaches its maximum, namely the aesthetically greatest basic measure for the estimation of magnitude'.[59]

The regression of imagination and the excess of magnitude

According to Kant, when aesthetic comprehension faces its limit, it becomes dissociated from apprehension's synthetic progress *ad infinitum* and instead induces a *non-synthetic regress* that does 'violence' to inner sense and 'suspends' time as the linear, successive form of inner sense. Instead of constituting the magnitude of time as the progressive form of inner sense, the imagination is now said to institute a 'regression' that annihilates this condition of time. As a result, the mind feels itself '*moved*' – a movement, Kant writes, which 'may be compared to a vibration [*Erschütterung*], that is, to a rapidly alternating repulsion from and attraction to one and the same object'.[60] That which it is driven to comprehend appears to be 'excessive' for imagination and it faces 'as it were an abyss, in which it fears to lose itself'.[61] Kant describes this regress in the following passage:

> The measurement of a space (as apprehension) is at the same time the description of it, thus an objective movement in the imagination and a progression; by contrast, the comprehension of multiplicity [*Vielheit*] in the unity not of thought but of intuition, hence the comprehension in one moment [*Augenblick*] of that which is successively apprehended, is a regression, which in turn cancels [*aufhebt*] the time-condition in the progression of the imagination and makes *simultaneity* intuitable. It is thus (since the temporal succession is a condition of inner sense and of an intuition) a subjective movement of the imagination, by which it does violence to the inner sense.[62]

The aesthetic comprehension instantiated by the regression is a comprehension 'in one moment' not of a 'manifold' (*Mannigfaltigkeit*), but of a 'multiplicity' (*Vielheit*). Although Kant does not elaborate on this distinction in the passage on the imaginative regress, it provides an important tool for understanding this specific mode of intuition. As Rudolf Makkreel has shown, the distinction between *Vielheit* and *Mannigfaltigkeit* indicates that 'the plurality-unity relation in aesthetic comprehension differs from that in logical comprehension'.[63] The imaginative regression is dealing with the comprehension of a multiplicity as a unity, *not* with the successive composition of units. Whereas for the logical, cognitive comprehension, the content of sense is regarded as a manifold, that is, a complex of *temporally determined parts*, 'in aesthetic comprehension, by contrast, the content of sense is regarded as a multiplicity of *indeterminate* parts of a whole'.[64] While the unity of the former must be inferred through a concept and involves an objective progress of the imagination, the unity of the latter can be instantaneously comprehended in the subjective regress of the imagination. This why, for Makkreel, the imaginative regress does not annihilate time-consciousness as such, but rather it 'suggests the possibility of negating the mathematical or linear form of time'.[65]

Table 1 Kant's distinction between logical and aesthetic comprehension.

Logical comprehension	Aesthetic comprehension
Manifold	Multiplicity
Temporally determined parts	Temporally indeterminate parts
Conceptual whole	Intuitive whole
Logical ideality	Morphological ideality
Successive synthesis	Non-synthetic regress

Aesthetic comprehension and intensive magnitude

The above-cited passage involves a crucial *Vielheit-Mannigfaltigkeit* distinction, which goes back to the distinction between extensive and intensive magnitudes made in the Anticipations of Perception of the first *Critique*. An extensive magnitude involves a manifold generated by a successive synthesis proceeding from parts to whole. By contrast, Kant states that an intensive magnitude is not apprehended successively, but in an instant. The intensive magnitude, which he calls a degree (*Grad*), represents the multiplicity in the content of sense. It is the '*quantum*' corresponding to 'the matter of sensation' or 'the real of the sensation (...) by which one can *only* be conscious *that* the subject is affected'.[66] Kant writes: 'Now I call that magnitude which can only be apprehended as unity, and in which multiplicity (*Vielheit*) can only be represented through approximation to negation=0, *intensive* magnitude.'[67] Makkreel refers to Paton's interpretation of this obscure passage:

> The multiplicity in an intensive magnitude is not represented by parts outside one another. Instead, 'every degree contains a plurality, because it contains all lesser degrees down to zero'. The multiplicity involved is not of discriminated parts of a manifold, but of degrees of intensity. This multiplicity in unity is given in an instant: yet, apparently, it can be represented *as* a multiplicity only when we imagine a possible diminution of the sensation. Such an imaginative act would require a process in time, and is not easily squared with Kant's assertion that apprehension of intensive magnitude is instantaneous. This difficulty is part of a more general one posed by the Anticipations of Perception. (...) Certainly in the context of the first *Critique,* the idea of an instantaneous *synthesis* through which we intuit multiplicity remains problematic at best.[68]

Table 2 Kant's distinction between logical and aesthetic comprehension in terms of the distinction between extensive and intensive magnitude.

Logical comprehension	Aesthetic comprehension
Extensive manifold	Intensive multiplicity
Temporally determined parts	Temporally indeterminate parts
Successive synthesis	Instantaneous comprehension
Conceptual whole	Qualitative whole
Priority of extensive parts to whole	Priority of intensive whole to parts
Continuous whole with discrete parts	Continuous whole with intensive degrees

From the point of view of the first *Critique* an instant is never sufficient to allow us to apprehend the manifold contained in a given intuition, for it requires temporal discrimination. The manifold contained in an intuition can only be represented by the mind as a manifold if it has the time to do so, that is, if it can distinguish time in the sequence of one impression upon another. Since in the aesthetic comprehension, unlike the logical one, the content of sense is regarded as a multiplicity of *indeterminate* parts of a whole, the unity of the comprehension does not have to be inferred through a concept and does, therefore, not require an objective progress of the imagination. Much rather, from the point of view of the third *Critique*, 'the intuition of multiplicity is more readily conceivable through the idea of an imagination annulling the linear form of time'.[69] 'Thus', Makkreel concludes, in the sublime 'aesthetic comprehension intuits multiplicity as an indeterminate unity, which is to be conceived as a totality or continuum without discrete parts'.[70] It is this sublime intuition of an indeterminate spatio-temporal continuum, which for Kant brings to mind reason's neo-Platonic Idea of a given, truly infinite whole.

Infinity and the sublime in Deleuze

The priority of extension over quality

As a material, bodily figure, the extension of an object is for Kant a primary quality that is filled by sensible secondary qualities (colours, tastes, texture, roughness, etc.), which have an intensive degree or magnitude. Any perceived body is a sensible schema, which is 'filled' with sensible qualities. The relation between spatial extension and qualitative degrees corresponds to that between the successively apprehended parts of an intuited body and the instantaneously sensed multiplicity in intuition. For Kant, extension is thus a universal, *a priori* form for qualities.[71] That is to say, Kant maintains that it is the unity and cohesion of extension (its spatial order, its topology) that confer unity upon qualities. Colour data, for example, are not scattered and without connection. We experience them as belonging to a fixed unity and a fixed form, namely the form of a spatial body. For Kant, there is therefore a primacy of extension with regard to sensed qualities with their intensive degrees: qualities come to fill extension. Our sense of spatial extension, by contrast, does not depend for its cohesive unity and order on the experience of qualities such as tastes or colours.

The priority of intensive space as a whole

In contrast to Kant, Deleuze claims that intensity itself is still prior to both extensity and quality: 'intensity creates the qualities and extensities in which it explicates itself.'[72] Intensity is for Deleuze a dimension of matter that is apart from extension, prior to extension. This means that matter is not merely a passive feature of space-time but it is also an active agent, acting as a metaphysical process or transcendental agent. For Kant, a non-extensive object (or process) cannot be known because this would essentially be a 'non-sensible' object, which is the object of metaphysics.[73] In contrast to this view, Deleuze follows the tradition from Leibniz to Fichte, Schelling, Bergson and others (a tradition that was also extended in Herman Weyl's 'agent theory' of matter), which assumes matter to be non-extensive, and to be a dynamical agent in the sense that it lies behind extensity, that it excites and determines extensity from beyond extensive space and time.[74] Following Kant's transcendental framework, Deleuze calls this extramundane realm of intensive matter a *noumenal* realm of 'pure intensity' or 'pure energy'.[75] But in what sense is intensity not only *transcendent* but also *transcendental*? That is, in what sense is it not only pre-extensive but also a condition of possibility of space and time? How can this extramundane realm of pure intensity constitute the primary and secondary qualities of extended matter, as Deleuze claims?

For Deleuze, as we have seen, the heart of this problem is to understand the principle of the spatial connection between parts in a structural whole (which he called, following Riemann and Bergson, a 'multiplicity'): *how do different spaces become reciprocally related such that they give rise to individuation, organization and the emergence of complex structure?* Deleuze proposed the hypothesis that every extended, qualified phenomenon emerges from an asymmetry (discontinuity) in the continuous substratum space. This asymmetry is induced by a singularity, a critical threshold, in the intensive dynamics between elements in the substratum space. This hypothesis depended therefore greatly on mathematical and physical ideas in thermodynamics and dynamic systems theory, describing bifurcations, singularities, complexification, strange attractors, structural stability, etc. Unlike earlier physical theories, which situate themselves principally in a relatively regular universe (mathematically speaking), these theories focus on the singularities of physical systems rather than their regularities. Morphodynamics in particular studies how complex structure can emerge in natural systems through dramatic changes called bifurcations or catastrophes. Drawing on these ideas, Deleuze argued that singularities and the subsequent individuation of phenomena can only unfold in continuous spaces that are endowed with a certain topological structure and one should therefore conceive a pre-extensive, intensive space as a relational and structural space. His main idea was to conceive this intensive space as a relatively undifferentiated continuum (a space defined by continuous intensive properties) that progressively self-differentiates by undergoing symmetry-breaking, discontinuous transitions (bifurcations). This passage from a relatively undifferentiated to a more differentiated state is the individuating process that gives rise to *extensive, qualified structures* (discontinuous structures with definite metric properties). Thus, in Deleuze's metaphysics, the measurable and divisible metric extensive space we inhabit emerges from an intensive continuum that progressively differentiates itself by undergoing intensive symmetry-breakings.[76] For Deleuze, this self-differentiating movement is a 'sublime principle of difference': a transcendent and transcendental principle of 'pure difference' by which the whole of intensive space differentiates itself into extended, qualified structures.[77]

The intensive continuum as an *Apeiron*

Being pre-extensive, the intensive continuum is for Deleuze essentially like Anaximander's *apeiron*: for the elements that it consists of, the pure intensive differences are not external relations between pre-existing identities, but generative, individuating relations. Like the *apeiron*, intensive space is 'a world *without identity*, without resemblance or equality'.[78] On this primal level of reality, matter exists only as an intensive differential flux rather than a thing.

Deleuze tells us that this original intensive space is what Plato already discerned in Anaximander's *apeiron* when he excluded it from the world of Ideas and attributed it to the illusory world of sensibility: 'an unlimited becoming without measure, a veritable becoming-mad which never rests'.[79] What is decisive in this conception of intensive space as *apeiron* is Deleuze's view that it is the metaphysical substrate from which emerges not only spatio-temporally extended matter, but also living and psychic systems. As we have seen, even *Ideas* emerge from the *apeiron*.

The self-individuating continuum

Deleuze's disagreement with Kant essentially concerns the latter's conception of the world of spatiotemporal appearances as a causally closed, deterministic world that harbours no creativity, autonomy, teleology or subjectivity. The Kantian world of appearances is causally closed in the sense that every event, every change or every phenomenon occurs in a conditioned series closed under universal physico-mathematical laws. It follows that nothing occurring in nature could have been otherwise and be contingent in the sense of being unconditioned by a law of nature. Contingency means for Kant phenomena that really, empirically, naturally, might have been otherwise. Real contingency means the real, physical possibility of a thing that is unconditioned by natural law. For Kant, physical nature is *never* contingent in this sense. As a result, the causal closure of the natural world separates it from the realm of autonomy and freedom, that is, from subjectivity, self-organization, creativity and spontaneity. But such a separation, Deleuze claims, is experientially and phenomenologically false. Living and psychic systems testify to continuous processes of contingent and creative evolution, change, or to use Deleuze's terms: *differentiation* as a *creative becoming*.

In living and psychic systems, differentiation is a contingent process of individuation: a process that creates new realities that did not subsist beforehand even virtually, logically, or abstractly. Indeed, differentiation is the *creation of new possibilities* ('virtualities'), which subsequently become actualized by individuation.[80] Deleuze thus denies the possibility of predicting *a priori* the evolutionary dynamics of processes of living and psychic individuation in the Kantian sense of the determination of their *a priori* space and time.[81] Deleuze maintains that all processes of individuation in nature occur from within the primal space of pure intensity. The space of pure intensity provides an energetic source of activity by which living and psychic systems can create and actualize new virtual possibilities. But this does not mean that intensive space is a totality of all possibilities that is fixed once and for all, a Platonic actual infinity. This would be precisely not what Deleuze has in mind. In the *apeiron*, new possibilities are *created*: it evolves contingently over time. The *apeiron* or *Erewhon* is itself the indeterminate, intensive Whole and within it new possibilities are created by differentiation.[82] In fact, Deleuze does sometimes compare the primal, intensive substrate from which material, living and psychic systems emerge to the One-Whole of the Platonists.[83] But unlike the latter, this Whole is 'a single Time' that forms a totality: a Bergsonian 'Duration' or 'virtual becoming' consisting of 'different intensities or degrees in virtual coexistence, in a single Time, in a simple Totality'.[84]

Pure intuition and the concept of the sublime

For Kant, the appearance of matter is possible only as representation. For Deleuze, by contrast, there is a kind of appearance of matter that does not arise in representation. As we have seen, matter is for Deleuze not simply a passive given in extension but an active energetic process prior to spatiotemporal extension. This claim leads Deleuze to distinguish between an *a priori* of intensive spatiality, within which generative processes of individuation unfold, and an *a priori* of extensive space, which is related to the empirical properties of these individuating dynamics. Accordingly, Deleuze's Transcendental Aesthetic distinguishes between two irreducible modes of apprehending reality: a metaphysical, properly transcending and sublime mode, which apprehends Being as a genetic process or creative becoming, and a representational, empirical mode, which apprehends qualified objects in extension.

For Deleuze, the perceptual, volitional and thinking reality of consciousness rarely participates in the intensive substrate space of individuation: 'it is by no means certain that either the I or the Self falls within the domain of individuation.'[85] One should rather say that individuation is a primary, energetic condition of consciousness, its creative essence and potentiality, but not its usual character. Instead, the reality of consciousness 'closes itself off' from the creative, self-differentiating becoming of individuation: it 'alienates itself' in the actual psychic structures and forms that individuation creates.[86] The source of this alienation is the habits formed in psychic life, but as we have seen, it is more fundamentally the mind's representational logic of recognition, which submits psychic life to an imaginary identity principle.

In representational intuition, the intensive reality of matter is always sensed such that it appears *relative* to the pragmatic or cognitive interests of the subject. The empirical exercise of sensibility does open onto the intensive reality of matter, but in order that it may appear in representational consciousness, it must be integrated into its specific representational forms and structures: habits, memories, desires, concepts, etc. This process of integration consists in contracting the intensive vibrations of matter into homogenous qualities, which become subordinated to the extensive form (schema) of spatiotemporal objects. Intensive matter is thereby formed as an extensive qualified body that is prepared for conceptual recognition.

But according to Deleuze, the contractions of intensive quantities of matter can also exceed this empirical exercise of sensibility and lead to a transcending and transcendental exercise whereby intensity induces a process of psychic individuation. By virtue of its fundamentally energetic and temporal nature, consciousness retains a possible connection to the self-differentiating movement of individuation. In order for consciousness to actualize its conative capacity for individuation, psychic energy must *detach* itself from its actual attachments to objects and to the narcissistic self, and become a 'neutral and displaceable energy'.[87] Deleuze calls this the creation, in living or psychic systems, of a certain degree of energetic 'indetermination', which obstructs a sensation of intensity from being prolonged into a determined cognitive, volitional or behavioural act and instead inscribes an excess of potential energy in the psychic organization.[88] Intuitively, intensive energy is then sensed as a differentiable 'multiplicity' endowed with critical thresholds or singular points that make a sensation become *salient* as an affective experience that cannot be anticipated or recognized in representation. One senses, then, intensive singularities or limit values that belong to the structural order of pre-phenomenal space (*apeiron*) itself – limits that are not derivative of the subjective mind but rather belong to the intensive continuum of individuation.[89] As Gilbert Simondon writes in a passage that is worth citing here in full:

> Spirituality would have no signification if there were not this luminous adherence to the present, this manifestation that gives an absolute value to the instant and consummates within itself sensation, perception and action. Spirituality is not another life, nor is it the same life; it is other and same, it is the signification of the coherence of the other and the same in a superior

life. (…) Spirituality (…) is the fact that the individuated being is not entirely individuated but still contains a certain charge of non-individuated, pre-individual reality that it preserves and respects, living with the awareness of its existence instead of retreating into a substantial individuality. Spirituality is the respect of this relation of the individuated and the pre-individual. It is essentially affectivity and emotivity. Pleasure and pain, sadness and joy are the extreme differentials that arise from this relation within the subject between the individual and the preindividual; one shouldn't speak merely of affective states, but rather of affective exchanges – exchanges between the pre-individual and the individuated in the subjective being. Affectivity and emotion are movements between the natural indetermined and the *here-and- now* of actual existence; it is through affectivity that this rising of the indetermined emerges towards the present.[90]

In an unmistakable reference to the comprehension of formlessness in the Kantian sublime, Deleuze writes this relation to the energetic source of individuation excites within the subject both terror and attraction:

It [individuation] involves fields of fluid intensive factors, which no more take the form of an I than of a Self. Individuation as such, as it operates beneath all forms, is inseparable from a pure ground that it brings to the surface and trails with it. It is difficult to describe this ground, or the terror and attraction it excites. (…) For this ground, along with the individual, rises to the surface yet assumes neither form nor figure. It is there, staring at us, but without eyes. (…) It is the indeterminate [*apeiron*], but indeterminate in so far as it continues to embrace determination.[91]

But this outside is also (…) the true interiority of time, that is the whole which changes, and which by changing perspective, constantly gives real beings that infinite space which enables them to touch the most distant past and the depths of the future simultaneously, and to participate in the movement of its own 'revolution'.[92]

In psychic life, the singularities triggering psychic individuation are critical thresholds that form 'sensitive points': points of tears and joy, of sickness and health, of hope and anxiety.[93] These critical thresholds present themselves affectively as an excess of potential energy that obstructs the representational determination of sensation and 'forces' differentiation to occur in the psychic organization.[94] Deleuze describes this experience of intensity as a sublime encounter that 'carries each faculty to its own limit' and induces a transcending and transcendental exercise of the mental faculties.[95] In this encounter, psychic energy induces 'a compulsion to think which passes through all sorts of bifurcations, spreading from the nerves and being communicated to the soul in order to arrive at thought'.[96] Sensibility first transmits its constraint to the imagination, which in turn is forced to confront its own limit, 'its *phantasteon*, its maximum which is equally the unimaginable, the unformed or the deformed in nature'.[97] Finally, when human thought confronts intensity as a differentiable multiplicity, the mind is put in a state of 'perplication', which moves and 'perplexes' thought – not because of any doubt, astonishment or hesitation, but because of the confrontation with the peculiar neutrality and impersonality of individuation itself.[98] Perplexed and faced with the limits of representation, human thought is finally forced to pose a problem as the object of an Idea. For example: my wound existed before me, how will I embody it?

Deleuze writes that Kant himself 'had the liveliest presentiment of such [intensive] notions participating in a phantasmagoria of the imagination, irreducible both to the universality of the concept and to the particularity of the now here [: the diversity to which categories apply in representation]'.[99] While imagination's synthesis is excised upon the diverse here and now, and the synthetic units or categories are continuous universals, which condition all possible experience, in the sublime 'the Kantian schemata would take flight and point beyond themselves in the direction of a conception of differential Ideas':[100]

> For where do Ideas come from, with their variations of relations and their distributions of singularities? Here, too, we follow the path to the bend at which 'reason' plunges into the beyond.[101]

The sublime transcendence of the Idea

But in what sense, then, is the emergence of the Idea for Deleuze *transcendent* to human consciousness? It is so, in the sense that we dwell in the creative element of thought *without being able to convert its intuition into a knowledge and without being able to appropriate its dynamics in a self-initiated cognitive or volitional act*. Only 'intuition' and 'sensation' allow one to grasp this creative movement and its driving *conatus* from within.

The Idea is defined as a creative and differentiating structure that organizes a certain degree of energetic 'indetermination' in the mind.[102] In the human mind, an Idea emerges when a sensation is not prolonged into a determined cognitive, volitional or behavioural act, but when instead an energetic indetermination is induced into the psychic organization (the 'self') as an excess of potential energy. On the basis of this energetic indetermination, then, individuation can introduce differentiation and creativity into psychic life. Like an evolutionary structure of life that becomes differentiated over time, or an undifferentiated embryo that is differentiated in embryogenesis, psychic individuation introduces a creative differentiation in the mnemonic, imaginary or conceptual contents of the mind. But this creative and differentiating process is not the action of a subjective faculty, such as human reason. In Deleuze's philosophy, the Idea is grounded in an extra-subjective element that does not belong to the register of consciousness – at most a very rudimentary, morphodynamic form of consciousness, as he puts it on some occasions.[103] This means that psychic creativity and differentiation are never a self-initiated, voluntary cognitive process. Rather, it is necessary to 'force' the differentiation of thought from bodily dynamical processes, which create a kind of involuntary tension between thought and its embodied, energetic support.[104]

A central attribute of this tension between thought and its energetic support is that it *de-subjectivizes* thought by detaching mental energy from its libidinal, objectal investments. Deleuze often speaks of 'dissolving' the psychic organization (the self) and invites us to conceive of this process in terms of the Nietzschean will to power, which is essentially distinct from an individual, subjective will.[105] Psychic individuation is enacted by a will that acts in the energetic, morphodynamic depths of the body, 'enveloping' intensive differences without yet having any memories, imaginations, representations or even the slightest aspiration of a goal, such as pleasure. Instead, the will at work in individuation coincides with the pre-individual circulation of intensive energy and acts in it as an immemorial, morphogenetic condition of psychic life.

For Deleuze, the sublime emergence of an Idea thus presupposes that psychic life can *detach* itself from its organized, differentiated structures – the imaginary self and its objectal investments – and *attach* itself once again to the creative, differentiating movement of individuation. In detaching itself from the self and its objectal attachments, psychic life goes beyond the constraints of its 'pleasure principle' and regains an impersonal, bodily will to power that strives for differentiation. In the Deleuzian sublime, we can therefore speak of an individuation *without* a subject: an individuation in which the subject itself *disappears*.

Conclusion

In this book, I have sought to show that Deleuze's metaphysics opens up a novel approach to the sublime, which just as Kant's should be understood in relation to his conception of infinity and his transcendental theory of Ideas.

Kant's conception of the sublime takes its point of departure in the idea that space and time are continuous magnitudes (*quanta continua*) of which the human mind can always only experience limited parts. This is possible only if the mind imposes limits or boundaries onto the intuitive continuum. In normal, representational experience, this limiting is achieved by a synthetic, apprehensive act of composing different successive extensive parts, which are filled by sensible qualities with an intensive degree. Any perceived body is a sensible schema, whose synthesized parts precede and make possible the perceived, qualified whole. Thus, any perceived bodily whole is a synthetic *construct* of integrated parts. By virtue of mathematical concepts, the measurable scale or degree of this synthetic magnitude is for Kant potentially infinite: by virtue of mathematical concepts, one can intuitively measure, compare and represent to oneself the magnitude of a mountain, a planet, a solar system or even the Milky Way galaxy, which rotates around the centre of a larger system of such galaxies, and so on *ad infinitum.*

Although all sensible objects are magnitudes the extent of which we can principally estimate and measure, our intuitive acts of synthesis can be disturbed and exceeded when faced with *vast* extensions. Confronted with vast magnitudes, our intuitive syntheses may fail to unify the limits and boundaries that we require to integrate the extensive parts of a manifold into a unified whole. Instead, human intuition seems then to be confronted with a *formless* magnitude: a synthetic manifold whose magnitude lacks conceptual order and unity, and thus appears to be differential and indeterminate. As a result of this intuition of an excessive magnitude, limitlessness and formlessness are represented in the object.

According to Kant, such a sublime intuition involves two remarkable modifications of our intuition of space and time. On the level of time, intuition does violence to our inner sense because it suspends the synthetic construction of phenomenal time as the linear, successive form of inner sense. On the level of space, intuition does not sense the spatial object as an extensive manifold of discrete, limited parts, but rather it senses an intensive multiplicity as a whole consisting of continuous, indeterminate parts or degrees. Given the modification of time-consciousness, this intuition moreover senses the spatial multiplicity as an instantaneous whole, whose unity need not be inferred through concept formation but can instead be instantaneously sensed. Thus, in the Kantian sublime, intuition senses multiplicity as indeterminate unity, which is to be conceived as an intuitive continuum or totality without discrete parts. It is this sublime intuition, which for Kant brings to mind reason's neo-Platonic Idea of a *given truly infinite whole*.

In Deleuze's metaphysics, a sublime intuition enables us to sense that intensive individuation is *reality itself* and that any extensive and qualified material thing or biopsychic structure is but a finite *result* of a process of individuation. Such a sublime intuition suspends representational thought, which has the tendency to see reality in terms of static substances with fixed identities, resemblances and generalities. For Deleuze, however, individuation as a generative process *alienates itself* in the material *forms* that it creates: by actualizing and differentiating itself, the actual individual loses contact with individuation. Whether it is a physiological function or a psychic habit, every actualized form is an arrest of individuation, and it could be said that actual form turns on itself and closes itself. By virtue of its energetic and temporal nature, however, psychic life can be forced to open itself beyond its closure and re-attach itself to the creative dynamics of individuation. When a degree of energy indetermination is forced upon the psychic organization, the individual is surrendered to the formless multiplicity from which ideal structures emerge. This formless depth or indeterminate *apeiron* makes its appearance only when an excessive energetic indetermination is forced upon the subject's will, producing what amounts to a kind of undifferentiated embryo of thought.[106]

For Deleuze, this energetic condition of psychic individuation is sublime, not merely because it lacks any substantiality, sensible form, assignable function or conceptual signification, but also because it lacks any subjective intentionality whatsoever. In the individual mind, this sublime energetic *locus* 'forms' a kind of immemorial and phantasmagoric no man's land: an *Erewhon*, from which emerge inexhaustibly ever new psychic structures, expressing the infinite potentials of psychic life. This is how the immanent sublime affirms the *apeiron* and sustains a spiritualism of depth: it makes the mind live in the intensive element of individuation, constituting a reason that 'rumbles in its crater'.[107] This is what remains, in Deleuze's transcendental philosophy, of reason's transcendence within the constellation of the sublime or of the *Erewhon*.

Notes

Introduction

1. This idea underlies Robert Doran's thorough study on the sublime in Longinus, Burke and Kant. See Robert Doran, *The Theory of the Sublime from Longinus to Kant* (Cambridge: Cambridge University Press, 2015).
2. Immanuel Kant, *Critique of the Power of Judgment*, trans. Paul Guyer and Eric Matthews (Cambridge: Cambridge University Press, 2000), 5:192; 5:255; 5:265.
3. Immanuel Kant, *Critique of Practical Reason*, trans. Mary J. Gregor (Cambridge: Cambridge University Press, 1996), 5:73.
4. Jocelyn Benoist points out that the roots of this idea lay in the second chapter of the Analytic of Practical Reason, 'On the concept of an object of pure practical reason,' which considers the *feeling* of pleasure or displeasure as a receptivity belonging to inner sense. Cf. Jocelyn Benoist, *Kant et les limites des la synthèse. Le sujet sensible* (Paris: P.U.F., 1996), 290–1.
5. Kant holds that 'the moral law unavoidably humiliates every human being when he compares with it the sensible propensity of his nature' but it also 'awakens *respect*' and 'one can in turn never get enough of contemplating the majesty of this law, and the soul believes itself elevated in proportion as it sees the holy elevated above itself and its frail nature.' See Kant, *Critique of Practical Reason*, 5:74; 5:77.
6. Gilles Deleuze, *Difference and Repetition*, trans. Paul Patton (New York/London: Continuum, 1994), 147.
7. I am paraphrasing here Daniel Andler, whose work on rationality and context has done a great deal in framing my thinking in this book, especially in Chapter 5. See Daniel Andler, The Normativity of Context, *Philosophical Studies* 100: 299 (2000).
8. For this duality, see Tano Posteraro, Assemblage Theory and the Two Poles of Organic Life, *Deleuze & Guattari Studies* 14 (3): 402–32 (2020).
9. Michael Friedman, Newton and Kant on Absolute Space: From Theology to Transcendental Philosophy, in *Constituting Objectivity. Transcendental Perspectives on Modern Physics*, ed. Michel Bitbol, Pierre Kerszberg and Jean Petitot (Dordrecht: Springer, 2009), 36.
10. As René Thom notes, it is likely that the term 'nature' derives from the Latin '*natus*', or 'born'. Nature would then originally mean the universal structural form of all birth, the universal creative form of all living or quasi-living beings. See René Thom, Sur la notion de Nature: la Nature et les êtres, in *Science et philosophie de la*

Nature. Un nouveau dialogue, ed. Luciano Boi (Bern/Berlin/Bruxelles/Frankfurt am Main/New York/Oxford/Wien: Peter Lang, 2000), 174.

11 Gilles Deleuze, *Expressionism in Philosophy: Spinoza*, trans. Martin Joughin (New York: Zone Books, 2005), 169–86.
12 Cf. Henri Atlan, Internal Purposes, Vitalism, and Complex Systems, in *Selected Writings on Self – Organization, Philosophy, Bioethics, and Judaism*, ed. Stefanos Geroulanos and Todd Meyers (New York: Fordham University Press, 2011), 179. As Atlan emphasizes, the *conatus* may not be confused with a mere principle of static homeostasis.
13 Deleuze, *Expressionism in Philosophy*, 87.
14 Cf. Stefanos Geroulanos and Todd Meyers, Introduction, in *Selected Writings on Self-Organization, Philosophy, Bioethics, and Judaism*, ed. Stefanos Geroulanos and Todd Meyers (New York: Fordham University Press, 2011), 18.
15 Deleuze's life-long engagement with the sublime can be periodized as follows. First, from the 1963 Kant book up to 1968 with *Difference & Repetition*, we find an engagement with the sublime in the context of Kant's faculty doctrine and Deleuze's own genetic faculty doctrine; secondly, in 1978 we find an engagement with the sublime in Deleuze's Kant lectures; thirdly, from 1981 until 1983, Deleuze extensively deals with the sublime in his lectures on painting and cinema; subsequently, the two volumes on cinema, *The Movement-Image* and *The Time-Image*, develop a Bergsonian interpretation of the sublime in terms of the intuition of duration. Finally, in 1986, Deleuze writes an essay 'On four poetic formulas which might summarize the Kantian philosophy', in which the sublime is characterized as 'an unregulated exercise of all the faculties, which was to define future philosophy'.
16 Gilles Deleuze, *Cinema 1. The Movement-Image*, trans. H. Tomlinson and B. Habberjam (Minneapolis: University of Minnesota Press, 1997), 9, 23, 38–9.
17 Gilles Deleuze, *Spinoza, Practical Philosophy*, trans. Robert Hurley (San Francisco: City Lights Books, 1988), 18–19.
18 Cf. Deleuze, *Difference and Repetition*, 255–6.
19 Gilles Deleuze, *Bergsonism*, trans. Hugh Tomlinson and Barbara Habberjam (New York: Zone Books, 1991), 104.

Chapter 1

1 Quote from Gilles Deleuze and Félix Guattari, *What Is Philosophy?*, trans. H. Tomlinson and L. Burchill (London/New York: Verso, 1994), 11, translation modified.
2 Psychologism refers to the fallacy of trying to base normative principles on factual premises. In logic and mathematics, psychologism entails trying to establish

the validity of logical and mathematical principles by appealing to empirical facts of human psychology. At the end of the nineteenth century, Frege and Husserl vigorously attacked this psychologism in the philosophy of mathematics and logic, arguing that it confuses the normative with the empirical and makes the laws of logic merely probable and contingent rather than necessary. Kant himself made several remarks that anticipate this criticism of psychologism. For example, in the first *Critique*, he writes that 'pure logic (…) has no empirical principles, thus it draws nothing from psychology (as one has occasionally been persuaded), which therefore has no influence at all on the canon of the understanding. It is a proven doctrine, and everything in it must be completely *a priori*'. See Kant, *Critique of Pure Reason*, trans. Paul Guyer and Allen W. Wood (Cambridge: Cambridge University Press, 1998), A54/B78. For a nuanced and insightful discussion of a remaining 'weak' psychologism in Kant's transcendental philosophy, see Patricia Kitcher, *Kant's Transcendental Psychology* (New York/Oxford: Oxford University Press, 1993).
3. Peter Strawson, *The Bounds of Sense. An Essay on Kant's Critique of Pure Reason* (London: Methuen, 1966), 16, 19, 32.
4. Deleuze, *Difference and Repetition*, 143.
5. Gilles Deleuze, *Kant's Critical Philosophy. The Doctrine of the Faculties*, trans. Hugh Tomlinson and Barbara Habberjam (London: The Athlone Press, 1984), 13.
6. For the problem of transcendental genesis in Derrida's reading of Husserl, see Paola Marrati, *Genesis and Trace. Derrida Reading Husserl and Heidegger* (Stanford: Stanford University Press, 2005). It should be noted that despite his quoted distinction between Kant's concept of transcendental subjectivity and an empirical or psychological subjectivity, Deleuze at times does criticize Kant's first *Critique* for tracing the transcendental structures from the empirical acts of a psychological consciousness and for thereby committing, at least partially, the fallacy of psychologism. In Deleuze's view, the task of a genetic faculty doctrine is precisely to avoid the dangers of psychologism. Cf. Deleuze, *Difference and Repetition*, 135.
7. See Noam Chomsky, *Aspects of the Theory of Syntax* (Cambridge, MA: The MIT Press, 1964).
8. Cf. ibid., 6. Put very simply, a universal grammar is for Chomsky a system of cognitive principles, conditions, rules that are elements of all particular human languages and make our learning and competence of them possible.
9. Noam Chomsky, *Reflections on Language* (New York: Pantheon, 1975), 43.
10. In neuroscience, the Kantian approach to spatial cognition was inaugurated by John O'Keefe and Lynn Nadel in their 1978 *The Hippocampus as a Cognitive Map*, which argued the hippocampus provides organisms with an *a priori* Euclidean framework. See John O'Keefe and Lynn Nadel, *The Hippocampus as a Cognitive Map* (Oxford: Oxford University Press, 1978). See also John O'Keefe, Kant and the

Sea-Horse: An Essay in the Neurophilosophy of Space, in *Spatial Representation: Problems in Philosophy and Psychology*, ed. N. Eilan, R. McCarthy and B. Brewer (Oxford: Oxford University Press, 1999), 43–64. More recently, Stanislas Dehaene and Elizabeth Brannon argued for a 'Kantian research program' in cognitive neuroscience as part of the *Human Brain Project*, investigating the 'neural mechanisms by which Kantian intuitions [of space, time and number] might universally arise'. For Dehaene and Brannon, 'If Immanuel Kant or Blaise Pascal were born today, they would probably be a cognitive neuroscientist!' See Stanislas Dehaene and Elizabeth M. Brannon, Space, Time, and Number: A Kantian Research Program, *Trends in Cognitive Science, Special Issue* 14 (12): 517–19 (2010).

11 Cf. Lorne Falkentsein, *Kant's Intuitionism. A Commentary on the Transcendental Aesthetic* (Toronto, Buffalo, London: University of Toronto Press, 1995), 12.

12 Cf. Jean Petitot, *Neurogéométrie de la vision. Modèles mathématiques et physiques des architectures fonctionnelles* (Paris: Les Éditions de l'École Polytechnique, 2008), 396–7.

13 Cf. Chomsky, *Reflections on Language*, 9–10.

14 Cf. ibid., 133: 'Creativity is predicated on a system of rules and forms, in part determined by intrinsic human capacities. Without such constraints, we have arbitrary and random behaviour, not creative acts.'

15 Chomsky, *Aspects of the Theory of Syntax*, 9. This creative property of syntax is what classical computationalists such as Jerry Fodor and Zenon Pylyshyn call the 'productivity' or 'generativity' of the 'language' of thought, which entails it can generate an indefinite number of expressions from finite means. See Chapter 4 for a brief discussion.

16 Cf. Jean Petitot, *Morphogenesis of Meaning*, trans. Franson Manjali (Bern, Berlin, Bruxelles, Frankfurt a.M., New York, Wien: Peter Lang, 2004), 121–2: 'In fact, natural syntax is not at all recursive in the technical sense of the term. (…) Instead of starting from the primitive concept of a derivation rule, a "good" syntactic theory must explain the dramatically limited range of iterations in natural language.'

17 Cf. Massimo Piattelli-Palmarini, Evolution, selection and cognition: From 'learning' to parameter setting in biology and in the study of language, *Cognition* 31: 4 (1989).

18 Jerry Fodor, *The Modularity of Mind* (Cambridge: The MIT Press, 1983), 10–12, 22. For Fodor, there is both a vertical and a horizontal order among the cognitive faculties.

19 Kant, *Critique of Pure Reason*, B129–30.

20 Ibid., A77–8/B102–3.

21 Ibid.

22 Cf. ibid., B139–40.

23 Deleuze, *Kant's Critical Philosophy*, 49–50, translation mine.

24 Ibid., 60–1, emphasis mine.

25 Gilles Deleuze, The Idea of Genesis in Kant's Aesthetics, in *Desert Islands and Other Texts 1953–1974*, ed. David Lapoujade, trans. Michael Taormina (New York: Semiotext(e), 2004), 61.
26 Ibid.
27 Kant, *Critique of the Power of Judgment*, 20:222.
28 Ibid., 5:189.
29 Ibid., 20:222. In the first *Critique*, the Transcendental Aesthetic was an Aesthetic of cognition, that is of 'the relation of the representation to an object, as an appearance, *for the cognition of that object*' (ibid., 20:221, emphasis mine). For this important distinction between sensation and feeling, see Benoist, *Kant et les limites de la synthèse*, 287–98.
30 Deleuze, *Kant's Critical Philosophy*, 3–4, cf. Kant, *Critique of the Power of Judgment*, 5:204.
31 Kant, *Critique of the Power of Judgment*, 20:224.
32 Ibid., 20:231. Cf. Gérard Lebrun, *Kant et la fin de la métaphysique. Essai sur la 'Critique de la faculté de juger'* (Paris: Collin, 1970), 353–4.
33 Kant, *Critique of the Power of Judgment*, 20:224; 5:226.
34 Deleuze, The Idea of Genesis in Kant's Aesthetics, 69.
35 Ibid., 61.
36 Cf. Kant, *Critique of the Power of Judgment*, 5:373.
37 Ibid., 5:373.
38 See Rachel Zuckert, *Kant on Beauty and Biology. An Interpretation of the Critique of Judgment* (Cambridge: Cambridge University Press, 2007), 5, 14, 193; Jennifer Mensch, *Kant's Organicism. Epigenesis and the Development of Critical Philosophy* (Chicago/London: The University of Chicago Press, 2013), 9.
39 Boris Demarest, System and Organism: In Defence of an Analogy, in *Objectivity after Kant: Its Meaning, Its Limitations, Its Fateful Omissions*, ed. Gertrudis Van de Vijver and Boris Demarest (Hildesheim: Georg Olms Verlag, 2013), 110–11.
40 Kant, *Critique of the Power of Judgment*, 5:374.
41 Ibid., 5:374.
42 Ibid., 5:369.
43 Ibid., 5:378, emphasis mine.
44 Ibid., 5:375, note.
45 Ibid., 5:373.
46 Ibid.
47 As we will see in Chapter 4, Deleuze defines structuralism in terms of a similar 'structural space' that is divided into regions with positional values. In structures, symbolic elements engage in constitutive, generative relations of 'reciprocal determination'. Genetically, they are constructed from the unfolding of singularities, which differentiate and organize a space into a structural space.
48 Cf. Kant, *Critique of the Power of Judgment*, 5:360.

49 Cf. ibid., 5:424.
50 Francisco J. Varela, *Principles of Biological Autonomy* (New York/Oxford: Elsevier North Holland, 1979), 13.
51 For a more detailed development of this suggestion applied to Kant's faculty doctrine, see Louis Schreel, Conatus and Feeling of Life: A Genetic Shift in Kant's Faculty Doctrine?, *Deleuze and Guattari Studies* 16 (3): 402–27 (2022).
52 Cf. Ernst Cassirer, Structuralism in Modern Linguistics, Word, Volume 1, Issue 2, 1945, 110: 'To put it shortly, we may say that language is "organic," but not that it is an organism. It is organic in the sense that it does not consist of detached, isolated, segregated facts. It forms a coherent whole in which all parts are interdependent upon each other.'
53 Gilles Deleuze, How Do We Recognize Structuralism?, in *Desert Islands and Other Texts 1953–1974*, ed. David Lapoujade, trans. Michael Taormina (New York: Semiotext(e), 2004), 179.
54 Jean Petitot, *Morphogenesis of Meaning*, 23.
55 Cf. Jean Petitot, *Les catastrophes de la parole. De Roman Jakobson à René Thom* (Paris: Maloine, 1985), 28.
56 For a comprehensive discussion which leaves the question open, see Alicia Juarrero Roqué, Self-Organization: Kant's Concept of Teleology and Modern Chemistry, *Review of Metaphysics* 39 (1): 107–35 (September 1985).
57 Cf. Gerry Webster and Brian Goodwin, History and Structure in Biology, *Perspectives in Biology and Medicine* 25 (1): 48, 51 (1981); Brian Goodwin, Structuralism in Biology, *Science Progress* 74 (2) (294): 227–43 (1990).
58 In recent years, this neo-Aristotelian approach to Kant's legacy has been taken by Denis Walsh, *Organisms, Agency, and Evolution* (Cambridge: Cambridge University Press, 2015) and Alvaro Moreno and Matteo Mossio, *Biological Autonomy. A Philosophical and Theoretical Inquiry* (Dordrecht, Heidelberg, New York, London: Springer, 2015).

Chapter 2

1 Quote from Gottfried Wilhelm Leibniz, *New Essays on Human Understanding*, trans. Alfred Gideon Langley (Chicago/London: The Open Court Publishing Company, 1916), 112.
2 Julia Jorati, Leibniz's Ontology of Force, in *Oxford Studies in Early Modern Philosophy. Volume VIII*, ed. Daniel Garber and Donald Rutherford (Oxford: Clarendon Press, 2018), 189–224. I rely in my introductory, terminological clarifications on Jorati's insightful exposition of Leibniz's typology of forces.
3 Leibniz, *New Essays on Human Understanding*, 169.

4 Ibid., 169–70.
5 Ibid., 112.
6 Deleuze, *Spinoza, Practical Philosophy*, 18–19.
7 Marcus Willaschek, Jürgen Stolzenberg, Georg Mohr and Stefano Bacin (ed), *Kant-Lexikon. Band 1* (Berlin/Boston: de Gruyter, 2015), 1290, my translation.
8 Cf. Stefan Heßbrüggen-Walter, *Die Seele und ihre Vermögen. Kants Metaphysik des Mentalen in der Kritik der Reinen Vernunft* (Paderborn: Mentis, 2004), 58, 72, 76–7.
9 Cf. ibid., 135.
10 Kant, *Critique of Pure Reason*, B676.
11 Immanuel Kant, *Kant's Gesammelte Schriften*, Hrsg. V. d. Deutschen Akademie der Wissenschaften zu Berlin. Band XXVIII (Berlin: de Gruyter, 1968), 27.
12 Ibid., 434, my translation.
13 Heßbrüggen-Walter, *Die Seele und ihre Vermögen*, 138, note 396.
14 Lerry Loemker, *Gottfried Wilhelm Leibniz: Philosophical Papers and Letters*, 2nd edition (Boston: D. Reidel Publishing Co., 1969), 433.
15 Ibid.
16 Gottfried Wilhelm Leibniz, *Leibniz's 'New System' and Associated Texts*, trans. and ed. Roger Woolhouse and Richard Francks (New York: Oxford University Press, 1997), 21, emphasis mine.
17 In *The Metaphysical Foundations of Logic*, Heidegger stresses this distinction between a mere potentiality and Leibniz's conception of the conatus or '*vis activa*'. See Martin Heidegger, *The Metaphysical Foundations of Logic*, trans. Michael Heim (Bloomington: Indiana University Press, 1992), 82. For a detailed, enlightening analysis of this distinction, which has continuously guided my thinking in this chapter, see also Rudolf Bernet, *Force, Drive, Desire. A Philosophy of Psychoanalysis*, trans. Sarah Allen (Evanston: Northwestern University Press, 2020), 47–86. Already in the early *Thoughts on the True Estimation of Living Forces* Kant praised Leibniz's idea of an internal, active force (*vis activa*) that inheres in every body and that is so fundamental that it belongs to a body prior to its extension. Leibniz's claim was that active force is more fundamental in nature than extension. Since force is prior to extension, matter and space (which are extensive) cannot be primitives: before they emerged nature began with force. Kant here defended what he took to be the essentially metaphysical (Aristotelian) import of the concept of the active force against the reductivism he saw at work in Wolff's identification of active force with the mechanical force of bodies.
18 Heidegger, *The Metaphysical Foundations of Logic*, 82.
19 Ibid., 85.
20 Ibid., 99.
21 Ibid., 90.
22 Ibid., 91.
23 Cf. ibid., 72–3, 89–91, 96.

24 Ibid., 97.
25 Ibid., 91.
26 Leibniz, *New Essays on Human Understanding*, 166.
27 Ibid., 167.
28 Ibid., 192.
29 Ibid., 163.
30 For a detailed analysis of the way Leibniz's concept of the *vis activa* influenced Kant's faculty doctrine, see Heßbrüggen-Walter's intricate exegesis in *Die Seele und ihre Vermögen*. Note that Kant did not think that all the different faculties can be reduced to one single substantial power of cognition, as in Leibnizian or Wolffian metaphysics, which considered all faculties of the mind to be different manifestations of a single 'fundamental power' of representation (the *vis repraesentativa* as the basic power of the soul) (cf. Kant, *Critique of Pure Reason*, A648/B676–7 & Kant, *Critique of the Power of Judgment*, 20:206). Instead, he followed Crusius' view that the diversity of our mental capacities is so fundamental that they could not be conceived as the effect of one single causal substance. To account for the unification of the soul, Crusius pointed to the *cohesion* between the fundamental mental powers: they had to relate to each other in a specifically cohesive way, such that together they could form a unified being. For Crusius, this kind of cohesive connection already entailed that the act of one power had to always be a conditioning *correlate* of the act of another power (cf. Heßbrüggen-Walter, *Die Seele und ihre Vermögen*, 105–6). The mental powers could interact and their *cohesive* interaction could generate effects, which a power taken in isolation would not be capable of.
31 Béatrice Longuenesse, *Kant and the Capacity to Judge. Sensibility and Discursivity in the Transcendental Analytic of the* Critique of Pure Reason, trans. Charles T. Wolfe (Princeton: Princeton University Press, 1998), 7, 163–6, 396.
32 Gilles Deleuze, *Expressionism in Philosophy*, 227–8.
33 Cf. Henri Atlan, *The Sparks of Randomness, Vol. 1. Spermatic Knowledge*, trans. Lenn J. Schramm (Stanford, CA: Stanford University Press, 2010), 259.
34 Deleuze, *Expressionism in Philosophy*, 233.
35 Benedict Spinoza, *Ethics*, trans. Edwin Curley, in *A Spinoza Reader* (New Jersey: Princeton University Press, 1994), 155–6.
36 Deleuze, *Expressionism in Philosophy*, 255.
37 Gilles Deleuze, *Nietzsche and Philosophy*, trans. Hugh Tomlinson (London/New York: Continuum, 2002), 39.
38 Deleuze, *Expressionism in Philosophy*, 257, translation altered.
39 Ibid., 220–1.
40 Deleuze, *Spinoza, Practical Philosophy*, 104.
41 Deleuze, *Expressionism in Philosophy*, 261; Deleuze, *Spinoza, Practical Philosophy*, 102–3.

42 Deleuze, *Spinoza, Practical Philosophy*, 23.
43 Ibid.
44 Ibid., 26.
45 Ibid., 23.
46 For an in-depth study of these connections, see Günter Abel, *Nietzsche: Die Dynamik der Willen zur Macht und die ewige Wiederkehr* (Berlin/New York: de Gruyter, 1984).
47 For the priority of creation and growth over conservation and self-preservation in Nietzsche, see Didier Franck, *Nietzsche et l'ombre de Dieu* (Paris: P.U.F., 2014), 299–301, and for a comparative study of this priority in both Nietzsche, Schopenhauer and Bergson, see Arnaud François, *Bergson, Schopenhauer, Nietzsche. Volonté et réalité* (Paris: P.U.F., 2008).
48 Friedrich Nietzsche, *Beyond Good and Evil*, ed. Rolf-Peter Horstmann and Judith Norman (Cambridge/New York/Melbourne/Madrid/Cape Town/Singapore/São Paulo: Cambridge University Press, 2002), §13.
49 Friedrich Nietzsche, *The Will to Power*, ed. Walter Kaufmann, trans. Walter Kaufmann and R. J. Hollingdale (New York: Vintage Books, 1968), 367.
50 Deleuze, *Nietzsche and Philosophy*, 57, 64.
51 Ibid., 34.
52 Ibid., 64.
53 Nietzsche, *The Will to Power*, 401, translation altered.
54 Deleuze, *Nietzsche and Philosophy*, 35.
55 Nietzsche, *The Will to Power*, 366.

Chapter 3

1 Quote from Henri Bergson, *Creative Evolution*, trans. Arthur Mitchell (New York: Random House, 1944), 14.
2 For the relation between Bergson's process metaphysics and the block universe framework, see Doug McLellan, Bergson's Paradox and Cantor's, self-published at http://bergsonian.org/wp-content/uploads/2020/01/bergsons_paradox.pdf, 2019.
3 Henri Bergson, The Possible and the Real, in *The Creative Mind*, trans. Mabelle L. Andison (New York: Philosophical Library New York, 1946), 108.
4 Gilbert Simondon, *Individuation in Light of Notions of Form and Information*, trans. Taylor Adkinds (Minneapolis/London: University of Minnesota Press, 2020), 13, 68–9.
5 Ibid., 37.
6 Cf. John Collier, Self-Organization, Individuation and Identity, *Revue international de philosophie* 228 (2): 151–172 (2004).

7 Simondon, *Individuation in Light of Notions of Form and Information*, 35. Cf. James DiFrisco, Hylomorphism and the Metabolic Closure Conception of Life, *Acta Biotheoretica* 62 (4): 499–525 (2014).

8 See Nick Lane, *Transformer: The Deep Chemistry of Life and Death* (London: Profile Books, 2022).

9 See, for example, Zenon Pylyshyn, *Computation and Cognition. Toward a Foundation for Cognitive Science* (Cambridge/London: The MIT Press, 1986), 161–8.

10 For a timely process metaphysical critique of this assumption, see Mark Bickhard, Process and Emergence: Normative Function and Representation, in *Process Theories. Crossdisciplinary Studies in Dynamic Categories*, ed. Johanna Seibt (Dordrecht: Springer, 2003), 121–55.

11 Simondon, *Individuation in Light of Notions of Form and Information*, 138, 151–2.

12 Ibid., 160.

13 See Alessandro Sarti and David Piotrowski, Individuation and Semiogenesis: An Interplay Between Geometric Harmonics and Structural Morphodynamics, in *Morphogenesis and Individuation*, ed. Alessandro Sarti, Federico Montanari and Francesco Galofaro (Cham/Heidelberg/New York/Dordrecht/London: Springer, 2015), 50.

14 Bickhard, Process and Emergence, 123.

15 Simondon, *Individuation in Light of Notions of Form and Information*, 29.

16 Ibid., 51.

17 Ibid., 47.

18 Ibid., 50, 158.

19 Ibid., 225.

20 Ibid., 223.

21 Ibid., 5.

22 Ibid.

23 Ibid.

24 In physics, 'free energy' refers to the energy available to power work, rather than being dissipated as heat.

25 Ilya Prigogine and Isabelle Stengers, *La nouvelle alliance. Métamorphose de la science* (Paris: Éditions Gallimard, 1986), 189.

26 Simondon, *Individuation in Light of Notions of Form and Information*, 269.

27 Ibid., 245, 383, note 4.

28 Ibid., 352.

29 Simondon, *Individuation in Light of Notions of Form and Information*, 343.

30 Deleuze, *Bergsonism*, 48–9.

31 Cf. Henri Bergson, *Matter and Memory*, trans. Nancy M. Paul and W. Scott Palmer (New York: Zone Books, 1991), 207.

32 Ibid.
33 Bergson, *Time and Free Will*, 99.
34 Henri Bergson, *Creative Evolution*, trans. Arthur Mitchell (New York: Random House, 1944), 266–7; cf. James DiFrisco, *Élan Vital* Revisited: Bergson and the Thermodynamic Paradigm, *The Southern Journal of Philosophy* 53 (1): 54–73 (2015).
35 Bergson, *Creative Evolution*, 268.
36 Deleuze, *Bergsonism*, 51.
37 I owe this reading of Bergson's notions of memory and metabolism to the brilliant work of James DiFrisco, who has extended these ideas to contemporary discussions in philosophy of science on levels of organization. See James DiFrisco, Organization and Inorganic Life in Bergson, M.Phil diss., Institute of Philosophy, KU Leuven, Leuven (2011); DiFrisco, *Élan Vital* Revisited; James Difrisco, Time Scales and Levels of Organization, *Erkenntnis* 82 (4): 795–818 (2017). One can find a similar Bergsonian inspiration applied in Giuseppe Longo and Maël Montévil's work on biological time and biological rhythm. See Giuseppe Longo and Maël Montévil, *Perspectives on Organisms. Biological Time, Symmetries and Singularities* (Berlin/Heidelberg: Springer, 2014).
38 Cf. Deleuze, *Bergsonism*, 86–7.
39 For this intricate relation between metabolism and duration, see Difrisco, Organization and Inorganic Life in Bergson and DiFrisco, *Élan Vital* Revisited: Bergson and the Thermodynamic Paradigm.
40 Cf. Bergson, *Matter and Memory*, 56–7; Deleuze, *Difference & Repetition*, 258.
41 Bergson, *Matter and Memory*, 210.
42 Ibid., emphasis mine.
43 Cf. Bergson, *Creative Evolution*, 14.
44 Ibid.
45 Ibid., 265.
46 Peter A. Corning and Stephen Jay Kline, Thermodynamics, Information and Life Revisited, Part I: 'To Be or to Entropy', *Systems Research and Behavioral Science*, 15, 1998, 276.
47 Bergson, *Creative Evolution*, 266–7.
48 Ibid., 268.
49 Corning and Kline, Thermodynamics, Information and Life Revisited, Part I, 277.
50 Bergson, *Creative Evolution*, 268.
51 Ibid., 274, 278.
52 Ibid., 270.
53 Ibid., 282.
54 Ibid., 274.
55 Cf. Klaus Mainzer, *Thinking in Complexity. The Computational Dynamics of Matter, Mind, and Mankind. Fifth Edition* (Berlin/Heidelberg/New York: Springer, 2007), 62.

56 See Noah Moss Brender's brilliant account in Noah Moss Brender, Sense-Making and Symmetry – Breaking: Merleau-Ponty, Cognitive Science, and Dynamic Systems Theory, *Symposium* 17 (2): 267 (Fall/Autumn 2013).
57 Deleuze, *Difference and Repetition*, 251.
58 Gabor Forgacs and Stuart A. Newman, *Biological Physics of the Developing Embryo* (Cambridge: Cambridge University Press, 2005), 180. See also Noah Moss Brender, Symmetry-Breaking Dynamics in Development, *Phenomenology and the Cognitive Sciences* 16: 585–96 (2017).
59 Cf. Moss Brender, Symmetry-Breaking Dynamics in Development, 589–90.
60 Forgacs and Newman, *Biological Physics of the Developing Embryo*, 51.
61 Ibid., 52.
62 J. B. Gurdon and P.-Y. Bourillot, Morphogen Gradient Interpretation, *Nature* 413: 797–803 (2001).
63 Cf. Petitot, *Morphogenesis of Meaning*, 32.
64 Deleuze, *Difference and Repetition*, 251.
65 Ibid.
66 Ibid., 251–2. Cf. Forgacs and Newman, *Biological Physics of the Developing Embryo*, 54.
67 As is well known, the concept of ontological difference was first introduced by Martin Heidegger, who used it to indicate the difference between Being and beings. For Heidegger, this difference entailed that Being itself cannot be represented as a thing or an entity (a being) but rather entails an event, a process.
68 Deleuze, *Bergsonism*, 104.
69 Ibid.
70 Cf. ibid., 93.
71 Bergson, *Creative Evolution*, 142.
72 Deleuze and Guattari, *Capitalism and Schizophrenia II: A Thousand Plateaus,* 499.

Chapter 4

1 Quote from Gilles Deleuze, How Do We Recognise Structuralism? In *Desert Islands and Other Texts 1953–1974*, ed. David Lapoujade, trans. Michael Taormina (New York: Semiotext(e), 2004).
2 When discussing the mathematical origins of structuralism, Deleuze also points to the domain of differential calculus, 'specifically in the interpretation which Weierstrass and Russell gave to it, a *static and ordinal* interpretation, which definitively liberates calculus from all reference to the infinitely small, and integrates it into a pure logic of relations'. See Deleuze, How Do We Recognize Structuralism?, 176.
3 Deleuze, How Do We Recognize Structuralism?, 174.

4　Computational functionalism rests on the claim that high-level cognition requires a highly specific cognitive architecture, namely one that gives cognitive states a combinatorial syntactic and semantic structure (which forms a 'language of thought'). There are several good arguments for this claim, which rest primarily on four closely related properties of cognition: the *systematicity*, *compositionality* and *productivity* of cognition, as well as its *inferential coherence*. For a detailed discussion, see Jerry A. Fodor and Zenon W. Pylyshyn, Connectionism and Cognitive Architecture: A Critical Analysis, *Cognition* 28: 3–71 (March 1988).

5　Cf. Dario Compagno's instructive introduction on the relations between transcendental philosophy and semiolinguistics in *Quantitative Semiotic Analysis*, ed. Dario Compagno (Cham: Springer, 2018), 1–29.

6　Cf. Fodor and Pylyshyn, Connectionism and Cognitive Architecture.

7　Deleuze, How Do We Recognize Structuralism?, 179.

8　Cf. Petitot, *Les catastrophes de la parole*, 20; Petitot, *Morphogenesis of Meaning*, 93.

9　Jean Petitot, Morphodynamics and the Categorical Perception of Phonological Units, *Theoretical Linguistics* 15 (1–2): 36 (1988).

10　Deleuze, How Do We Recognize Structuralism?, 174.

11　In his *Prolegomena to a Theory of Language,* the Danish structuralist linguist Louis Hjelmslev equally emphasizes the essential methodological importance of this category of reciprocal dependence relations: 'It soon becomes apparent that the important thing is not the division an object into parts, but to adapt the analysis in such a way that it conforms to reciprocal dependencies that exist between these parts and that allows us to give an adequate account for these dependencies.' See Louis Hjelmslev, *Prolegomena to a Theory of Language*, trans. Francis J. Whitfield (Madison: The University of Wisconsin Press, 1963), 22, translation altered.

12　Cf. Edmund Husserl, *Logical Investigations, Volume 2*, trans. J. N. Findlay, ed. Dermot Moran (London/New York: Routledge, 2001), 7–8.

13　Ibid., 12.

14　Cf. Husserl's analysis of the expressive sign in the first *Logical Investigation*.

15　Edmund Husserl, The Origin of Geometry, in Jacques Derrida, *Edmund Husserl's Origin of Geometry: An Introduction*, trans. John P. Leavey (Stony Brook, NY: Nicolas Hays, 1978), 160.

16　Ibid.

17　Ibid., 161.

18　Émile Benveniste, *Problèmes de linguistique générale 1* (Paris: Éditions Gallimard, 1966), 259, my translation.

19　Paul Ricoeur, *The Conflict of Interpretations*, trans. and ed. Don Ihde (London: The Athlone Press, 2000), 52, 53.

20　Ibid., 33.

21　Ibid.

22 Deleuze, How Do We Recognize Structuralism?, 177.
23 Cf. Petitot, *Morphogenesis of Meaning*, 11.
24 Jean Petitot, Morphodynamics and Attractor Syntax: Constituency in Visual Perception and Cognitive Grammar, in *Mind as Motion: Explorations in the Dynamics of Cognition*, ed. R. F. Port and T. van Gelder (Cambridge: The MIT Press, 1995), 231.
25 It is interesting to note that René Thom's 1970 paper 'Topologie et linguistique' published in *Essays on Topology and Related Topics*, made a similar claim to Deleuze's, proposing basic topological schemata of sentences.
26 Petitot, *Morphogenesis of Meaning*, 69.
27 Ibid., 11.
28 Cf. Deleuze, *Difference and Repetition*, 251.
29 Deleuze, How Do We Recognize Structuralism?, 174.
30 Jean Petitot, Identité et Catastrophes (Topologie de la différence), in *L'identité*, ed. Claude Lévi-Straus (Paris: Quadrige/P.U.F. 1977), 115.
31 Deleuze, *Difference and Repetition*, 183.
32 Ibid., 193, 203–6.
33 See Jean Petitot, *Cognitive Morphodynamics. Dynamical Morphological Models of Constituency in Perception and Syntax*, in collaboration with René Doursat (Bern/Berlin/Bruxelles/Frankfurt am Main/New York/Wien: Peter Lang, 2011), 19.
34 Ibid., 22.
35 Ibid., 19–20.
36 B. Ishkhanyan, M. H. Christiansen, A. Højen, K. Tylén, D. Bleses, R. Fusaroli, … C. Dideriksen (2021, December 22). Cross-linguistic Differences in Categorical Perception: Comparison of Danish and Norwegian. Retrieved from osf.io/qcjgt.
37 Petitot, *Morphogenesis of Meaning*, 83. Contrary to what was initially assumed, we now know that categorical perception is not specifically phonetic, that is, linguistic, but also exists in the perception of musical timbres, musical intervals, colours, etc.
38 See Eric R. Kandel, James H. Schwartz and Thomas M. Jessell et al., *Principles of Neural Science, Fifth Edition* (New York: McGraw-Hill Companies, 2000), Chapter 60: Language.
39 Petitot, *Morphogenesis of Meaning*, 76, 94.
40 Ibid., 11.
41 Ibid., 100, 102–3.
42 Jean Petitot, Le Physique, le Morphologique et le Symbolique. Remarques sur la Vision, *Revue de synthèse* 111: 139–83 (1990), 145, my translation.
43 Ibid.
44 Ibid., 146.
45 Cf. Karl Friston, The Fantastic Organ, *Brain* 136: 1328–32 (2013).

46 Alain Berthoz, *The Brain's Sense of Movement*, trans. G. Weiss, (Cambridge/London: Harvard University Press, 2000), 22, 165–7.
47 Cf. Eric Kandel, *Reductionism in Art and Brain Science. Bridging the Two Cultures* (New York: Columbia University Press, 2016), 22.
48 The reason why significant factors of a physical environment cannot be considered to be purely physical is that nothing physical is significant in and of itself, but only *for* a certain system. For this reason, classical computationalists such as Pylyshyn argue for a divide between the physical and the symbolical: what is informationally meaningful for a cognitive system cannot be analysed purely physically.
49 Petitot considers Marr's 2 1/2D sketch to correspond quite neatly to Husserl's analysis of 'adumbrative' perception in *Thing and Space* and *Ideas I*. Like Marr, Husserl investigates how objects immersed in an external objective 3D space can be constituted from 2D 'adumbrations' (*Abschattungen*). See Petitot, *Cognitive Morphodynamics*, 114.
50 Cf. Petitot, *Cognitive Morphodynamics*, 113.
51 David Marr, *Vision* (Cambridge/London: The MIT Press, 2010), 67. Cited in: Petitot, Le Physique, le Morphologique et le Symbolique, 157.
52 Petitot, Le Physique, le Morphologique et le Symbolique, 157.
53 Marr, *Vision*, 71.

Chapter 5

1 Deleuze follows here not only Bergson but also Freud. In his metapsychology, Freud distinguished two major mental systems, namely that ego (corresponding to our externally oriented consciousness) and the id (corresponding to the internal body). Freud conceived the bodily origins of the ego in terms of a 'surface entity' or 'a projection of a surface', by which he meant that the ego is ultimately derived from bodily sensations, chiefly from those springing from the surface of the body. The ego may thus be regarded as a mental projection of the surface of the body, besides representing the superfices of the mental apparatus. See Sigmund Freud, *The Ego and the Id. Standard Edition* (London: Hogarth Press, 1923).
2 Jean Petitot, Les Deux Indicibles ou la Sémiotique Face à l'Imaginaire Comme Chair, in *Exigences et Perspectives de la Sémiotique: Receuil d'Hommages Pour Algirdas Julien Greimas/Aims and Prospects of Semiotics. Essays in Honor of Algirdas Julien Greimas*, ed. Herman Parret and Hans-George Ruprecht (Amsterdam: John Benjamins Publishing Company, 1985), 284.
3 Cf. Petitot, *Morphogenesis of Meaning*, 37.
4 Cf. Jerry Fodor, *The Language of Thought* (New York: Thomas Y. Crowell Company, 1975), 77; Jerry Fodor, *The Mind Doesn't Work That Way* (Cambridge: The MIT Press, 2001), 14–19.

5   Jerry Fodor, Propositional Attitudes, *The Monist* 61 (4): 519 (1978).
6   Cf. Hubert Dreyfus, Introduction, in *Husserl, Intentionality and Cognitive Science*, ed. Hubert L. Dreyfus and Harrison Hall (Cambridge/London: The MIT Press, 1984), 7–8. I am not concerned here with the inadequacies of Deleuze's Fregean interpretation of Husserl's noema. I am also not concerned here with what are, I believe, important differences between Husserl and Fodor concerning intentionality and propositional attitudes (i.e. why Husserl is not, on my view, a computationalist). For the sake of argument, in the context here discussed (namely propositional predication), and at the superficial level of detail here adopted, I believe the comparison between Husserl, Frege and Fodor largely holds. For said inadequacies, see Nicolas de Warren, Anarchy of Sense: Husserl in Deleuze, Deleuze in Husserl, *Paradigmi. Rivista di critica filosofica*, n. 2, 2014. For the idea that Husserl may have held what Fodor calls the computational theory of mind, see Jesse Daniel Lopes, How Do Mental Processes Preserve Truth? Husserl's Discovery of the Computational Theory of Mind, *Husserl Studies* 36 (1): 25–45 (2020).
7   Cf. Matteo Bianchin, Husserl on Meaning, Grammar, and the Structure of Content, *Husserl Studies* 34 (2): 101–21 (2018).
8   Edmund Husserl, *Cartesian Meditations. An Introduction to Phenomenology*, trans. Dorion Cairns (The Hague/Boston/London: Martinus Nijhoff Publishers, 1977), 53–4, cited in Dreyfus, *Husserl, Intentionality and Cognitive Science*, 18.
9   See Dreyfus, *Husserl, Intentionality and Cognitive Science*, 19.
10 Ibid.
11 Deleuze, *Difference and Repetition*, 131.
12 See Fodor, *The Language of Thought*.
13 Cf. Daniel Dennett, A Cure for the Common Code, in *Brainstorms: Philosophical Essays on Mind and Psychology* (Cambridge, MA: The MIT Press, 1981) & Lopes, How Do Mental Processes Preserve Truth?.
14 Cf. Fodor and Pylyshyn, Connectionism and Cognitive Architecture, 31; Fodor, *The Mind Doesn't Work That Way*, 15.
15 Deleuze, *Difference and Repetition*, 138.
16 Cf. Theodor W. Adorno, *Negative Dialectics*, trans. E. B. Ashton (London/New York: Routledge, 2004), 157.
17 Hilary Putnam, *Reason, Truth and History* (Cambridge: Cambridge University Press, 1981), 49.
18 Theodor W. Adorno, *Negative Dialectics*, 182.
19 Ibid., 181.
20 Cf. Nick Lane, *Power, Sex, Suicide. Mitochondria and the Meaning of Life* (Oxford: Oxford University Press, 2005), 25.
21 I follow here the remarkable work of Allesandro Sarti, Giovanna Citti and David Piotrowski in Allesandro Sarti, Giovanna Citti and David Piotrowski, *Differential Heterogenesis: Mutant Forms, Sensitive Bodies* (Cham: Springer, 2022).

22 See Fodor, *The Mind Doesn't Work That Way*, chapter 2: Syntax and Its Discontents.
23 My approach to the singularity of context has benefitted immensely from the work on situated cognition of Daniel Andler, which builds on Jon Barwise and John Perry's work on situated inference. See Daniel Andler, *Intelligence artificielle, intelligence humaine: la double énigme* (Paris: Gallimard, 2023); Daniel Andler, *La silhouette de l'humain. Quelle place pour le naturalisme dans le monde d'aujourd'hui?* (Paris: Gallimard, 2016); Daniel Andler, Context: the case for a principled epistemic particularism, *Journal of Pragmatics* 35: 349–71 (2003); Andler, The Normativity of Context, 273–303; Jon Barwise and John Perry, *Situations and Attitudes* (Cambridge/London: The MIT Press, 1983).
24 Deleuze, *Difference and Repetition*, 68.
25 For a philosophical introduction to the predictive processing approach, see Andy Clark, *Surfing Uncertainty. Prediction, Action and the Embodied Mind* (Oxford: Oxford University Press, 2016).
26 Deleuze, *Difference and Repetition*, 135.
27 Cf. Deleuze, *Bergsonism*, 21.
28 Cf. Deleuze, *Nietzsche and Philosophy*, 94: 'The point of critique is not justification but a different way of feeling: a different sensibility.'
29 Cf. Theodor W. Adorno, *Negative Dialectics*, 182.
30 Cf. Adorno's characterization of negative dialectics: 'Objectively, dialectics means to break the compulsion to achieve identity, and to break it by means of the energy stored up in that compulsion and congealed in its objectifications.' Theodor W. Adorno, *Negative Dialectics*, trans. E. B. Ashton (London/New York: Routledge, 2004), 157.
31 Cf. Deleuze, *Difference and Repetition*, 165.
32 Ibid., 140.
33 I owe this example to Daniel Andler, The Normativity of Context, 298.
34 One is reminded here of Einstein's famous thought experiments, such as imagining freely falling elevators in space at different velocities. In these eidetic phantasies, Einstein came to his famous equivalence principle, concerning the equivalence of gravitational and inertial mass.
35 Deleuze, *Difference and Repetition*, 23.
36 Ibid., 192.
37 Ibid., 180.
38 For a deeper discussion of the singularity of context, see Daniel Andler's approach to situational intelligence in Daniel Andler, *Intelligence artificielle, intelligence humaine: la double énigme*.
39 Deleuze, *Difference and Repetition*, 26.
40 Ibid., 139.

Chapter 6

1. Simone Weil, *Gravity and Grace*, trans. Emma Crawford and Mario von der Ruhr (London/New York: Routledge Classics, 2003), 10.
2. Deleuze, *Difference and Repetition*, 230.
3. Ibid., 236: 'the paradoxical existence of a "something" which simultaneously cannot be sensed (from the point of view of the empirical exercise) and can only be sensed (from the point of view of the transcendent exercise).'
4. Gilles Deleuze, *Francis Bacon: The Logic of Sensation*, trans. Daniel W. Smith (London/New York: Continuum, 2003), 178, note 1. Three years later, Deleuze uses the exact same terms in his preface to the English translation of his book on Kant's faculty doctrine to point out the novelty of the third *Critique*: 'It is no longer the aesthetic of the *Critique of Pure Reason*, which considered the sensible as a quality, which could be related to an object in space and time; it is not a logic of the sensible, nor even a new *logos* which would be time. It is an aesthetic of the Beautiful and the Sublime, in which the sensible is valid in itself [*où le sensible vaut pour lui-même*] and unfolds in a *pathos* beyond all logic, which will grasp time in its surging forth, in the very origin of its thread and its giddiness.' Deleuze, On Four Poetic Formulas That Might Summarize the Kantian Philosophy, 34.
5. Henri Maldiney, *Regard Parole Espace* (Paris: Les Éditions du CERF, 2012), 189.
6. Ibid., 189. For a detailed discussion of Straus and Maldiney's conception of the pathic, see Louis Schreel, Passibility: The Pathic Dimension of Subjectivity, in *Phenomenology, Neuroscience and Clinical Practice. Transdisciplinary Experiences*, ed. Francesca Brencio (Berlin: Springer, 2024).
7. Maldiney, *Regard Parole Espace*, 45, note 2.
8. Ibid., 189; cf. Henri Maldiney, *Art et Existence* (Paris: Klincksieck, 2003), 27.
9. Edmund Husserl, *Ideas Pertaining to a Pure Phenomenology and to a Phenomenological Philosophy. First Book*, trans. F. Kersten (The Hague/Boston/Lancaster: Martinus Nijhoff Publishers, 1983), 203; cited in Maldiney, *Art et Existence*, 239, note 101.
10. Ibid.
11. Maldiney, *Art et existence*, 239, note 101.
12. Erwin Straus, Die Formen des Räumlichen. Ihre Bedeutung für die Motorik und die Wahrnehmung, in *Psychologie der Menschlichen Welt. Gesammelte Schriften von Erwin Straus* (Berlin/Heidelberg: Springer Verlag, 1960), 151.
13. Maldiney, *Regard Parole Espace*, 189.
14. Ibid., 187.
15. Ibid., 111.
16. Ibid.

17 Straus, Die Formen des Räumlichen, 168; Erwin Straus, *Du sens des sens. Contribution à l'étude des fondements de la psychologie*, trans. Georges Thinès and Jean-Pierre Legrand (Grenoble: Éditions Jérôme Millon, 2000), 284, 294.
18 Straus, Die Formen des Räumlichen, 168; Straus, *Du sens des sens*, 276.
19 Cf. Alain Berthoz and Jean-Luc Petit, *Phénoménologie et physiologie de l'action*, (Paris: Odile Jacob, 2006), 279–81.
20 Straus, Die Formen des Räumlichen, 167.
21 Henri Maldiney, *Penser l'homme et la folie* (Grenoble: Éditions Jérôme Million, 2007), 120, 281.
22 Maldiney, *Penser l'homme et la folie*, 265, my translation.
23 Ibid., 268–73.
24 Ibid., 270.
25 Cf. ibid., 271: 'The originality of Heidegger is to have conceived the opening up of the living being to its *Umwelt* in terms of drive and to have understood its behavior as a process of disinhibition', my translation.
26 Matthieu Guillot, Entretien avec H. Maldiney, *L'Ouvert*, n° 5, Lyon, 2012, 80.
27 Maldiney, *Penser l'homme et la folie*, 278.
28 Cf. Michel Bitbol, Neurophenomenology of Surprise, in *Surprise at the Intersection of Phenomenology and Linguistics*, ed. Nathalie Depraz and Agnès Celle (Amsterdam/Philadelphia: John Benjamins Publishing Company, 2019), 11.
29 David J. Velleman, The Way of the Wanton, in *The Possibility of Practical Reason, 2nd Edition* (MI: Michigan Publishing, University of Michigan Library, 2014).
30 Cf. Henri Maldiney, *L'art, l'éclair de l'être* (Paris: Les Éditions du CERF, 2012), 14–19.
31 Ibid., 19.
32 Maldiney, *Art et existence*, 116, 119.
33 Today, the concept of *wu wei* is often related to the psychological concept of 'flow' as developed by Mihaly Csikszentmihalyi. Actors in flow present the same paradoxical idea of an action without agency, in the sense that actors in flow have dispensed with self-regulation. Their actions are characterized by a mindless indifference to the enterprise of evaluating one's own desires and motives. See Velleman, The Way of the Wanton; Brian Bruya, Action without Agency and Natural Human Action: Resolving a Double Paradox, in *The Philosophical Challenge from China*, ed. Brian Bruya (Cambridge: The MIT Press, 2015).
34 Cf. Martin Heidegger, Der Ursprung des Kunstwerkes, in *Holzwege* (Frankfurt am Main: Vittorio Klostermann, 2003), 59: '*All art*, as letting-happen the advent of the truth of beings as such, is *in its essence Dichtung*. The essence of art, in which the artwork and the artist at once rest, is the setting-itself-to-work of truth.'
35 Ibid., 71.
36 Ibid., 70.
37 Ibid., 55.
38 Henri Maldiney, *Ouvrir le rien. L'art nu* (Paris: Éditions Les Belles Lettres, 2010), 55.

39 Ibid.
40 Ibid., 62–3, 99.
41 Maldiney, *L'art, l'éclair de l'être,* 14.
42 Maldiney, *Ouvrir le rien. L'art nu,* 84.
43 Heidegger, *Der Ursprung des Kunstwerkes,* 55. Estrangement should be understood here not in the Hegelian-Marxist sense of being dispossessed of oneself. In Maldiney and Heidegger's philosophy, estrangement is closer to what Nietzsche called *nihilism*: being enclosed within a self that is no longer *affected* or moved by anything.
44 Henri Maldiney, Existence: crise et création, in *Maldiney. Une singulière présence,* ed. Renaud Barbaras et al. (Paris: Éditions Les Belles Lettres, 2014), 220.
45 Wolfgang Blankenburg, *Der Verlust der natürlichen Selbstverständlichkeit. Ein Beitrag zur Psychopathologie symptomarmer Schizophrenien* (Stuttgart: Ferdinand Enke Verlag, 1971).
46 Maldiney, *Ouvrir le rien. L'art nu,* 37, translation and emphasis mine.
47 Martin Heidegger, *Introduction to Metaphysics,* trans. G. Fried and R. Polt (New Haven/London: Yale University Press, 2000), 1.
48 Ibid., 1–2, emphasis mine.
49 Heidegger, Der Ursprung des Kunstwerkes, 53, translation mine.
50 Ibid., 54, translation and emphasis mine.
51 Ibid., 53.
52 Ibid.
53 Gilles Deleuze and Félix Guattari, *What Is Philosophy?,* trans. H. Tomlinson and L. Burchill (London/New York: Verso, 1994), 164.
54 Cf. Heidegger, *Introduction to Metaphysics,* 3.
55 Cf. Gerard Visser, *Niets cadeau. Een filosofisch essay over de ziel* (Amsterdam: Valkhof pers, 2010), 121–2.
56 Maldiney, *Penser l'homme et la folie,* 291, 302.
57 Ibid., 291, 304.
58 Cf. Maldiney, Existence: crise et création, 221: 'The mark of the pathological is not the crisis but, on the contrary, its impossibility. (…) It is not the crisis but the foreclosure of each critical state which constitutes the pathological', my translation. For Maldiney, psychotic delusions can be seen as a protective shield that protects the subject against the advent of any new, unexpected events. In pathology, no new events are received but rather one and the same event is time and again relived, functioning as a kind of black hole around which the subject circles. Cf. Maldiney, *Penser l'homme et la folie,* 233.
59 Maldiney, *Penser l'homme et la folie,* 233.
60 Johan de Deckere, Onvoorstelbaar lijden: over picturale aanwezigheid, in: *Onheil, pijn, bloed. Voorstellingen van lijden,* ed. Marc Verminck (Ghent: A&S Books/deBuren, 2009), 175, my translation.

61 Simone Weil, *Gravity and Grace*, trans. Emma Crawford and Mario von der Ruhr (London/New York: Routledge Classics, 2003), 10.
62 Ibid., 181.
63 Deleuze, *Bergsonism*, 77.
64 Deleuze, *Francis Bacon*, 21–3.
65 Ibid., 25, 37, 42, 44–6.
66 Ibid., 44.
67 Johan de Deckere, *Onvoorstelbaar lijden*, 181.
68 Deleuze, *Difference and Repetition*, 89.
69 Ibid., 90.
70 Deleuze, *Francis Bacon*, 45.
71 Gilles Deleuze, 'Cours Vincennes,' 24/11/1981, http://www2.univ-paris8.fr. In these lectures on cinema, Deleuze relates Bergson's *Matter and Memory* to Kant's Analytic of the Sublime and interprets the caesura, which throws time out of joint, in terms of the sublime regression of imagination, which we will turn to in the next chapter.
72 Gilles Deleuze, *The Logic of Sense*, trans. M. Lester and C. Stivale (London/New York: Continuum, 1990), 149. Cf. Deleuze, *Francis Bacon*, 46–7: 'It [inorganic life] attests to a high *spirituality*, since what leads it to seek the elementary forces beyond the organic is a spiritual will. But this spirituality is a spirituality of the body; the spirit is the body itself, the body without organs …'
73 Deleuze, *Logic of Sense*, 148–53.
74 Ibid., 149.
75 Ibid., 344, note 1.
76 Ibid., 101, 143.
77 Deleuze, *Nietzsche and Philosophy*, 115.
78 Deleuze, *Logic of Sense*, 148–50.
79 Ibid., 151.
80 Ibid., 152.

Chapter 7

1 Quote from Gottfried W. Leibniz, On Freedom (1689) in *Philosophical Essays*, ed. and trans. Roger Ariew and Daniel Garber (Indianapolis and Cambridge: Hackett Publishing Company, 1989), 95.
2 Cf. Jean Petitot, A Transcendental View on the Continuum: Woodin's Conditional Platonism, *Le continu mathématique. Nouvelles conceptions, nouveaux enjeux*, ed. M. de Glas. Intellectica 51 (1): 93–133 (2009).
3 Immanuel Kant, *Notes and Fragments*, trans. Curtis Bowman, Paul Guyer and Frederick Rauscher (Cambridge: Cambridge University Press, 2005), R4425, 17:541.

4 Kant, *Critique of the Power of Judgment*, 5:244.
5 Kant, *Critique of Pure Reason*, A25; ibid., A432/B460; ibid., A527/B555.
6 Ibid., A32/B47-8.
7 Kant, *Critique of the Power of Judgment*, 5:255.
8 Cf. Thom, *Sur la notion de Nature*, 174.
9 Friedman, *Newton and Kant on Absolute Space*, 36.
10 Deleuze, *Cinema 1. The Movement-Image*, 9, 23, 38–9.
11 See Leo Sweeney, *Infinity in the Presocratics. A Bibliographical and Philosophical Study* (The Hague: Martinus Nijhoff, 1972).
12 Deleuze, *The Logic of Sense*, 7.
13 Paolo Zellini, *A Brief History of Infinity*, trans. D. Marsh (London: Penguin Books, 2004), 5.
14 One is reminded here of Kant's reference to the veil of Isis: 'Perhaps nothing more sublime has ever been said, or any thought more sublimely expressed, than in the expression over the temple of Isis (Mother *Nature*): "I am all that is, that was, and that will be, and my veil no mortal has removed."' See Kant, *Critique of the Power of Judgment*, 5:316.
15 Sweeney, *Infinity in the Presocratics*, 8.
16 Adrian W. Moore, *The Infinite* (London/New York: Routledge, 2003), 18.
17 Sweeney, *Infinity in the Presocratics*, 58.
18 Ibid., 61.
19 Ibid., 60.
20 Simondon, *Individuation in Light of Notions of Form and Information*, 343, translation altered.
21 Moore, *The Infinite*, 19.
22 Zellini, *A Brief History of Infinity*, 3–4.
23 Cf. Deleuze and Guattari, *What Is Philosophy?*, 120.
24 Moore, *The Infinite*, 19.
25 Cf. Zellini, *A Brief History of Infinity*, 40.
26 Moore, *The Infinite*, 27.
27 Cf. ibid., 18.
28 Deleuze, *Difference and Repetition*, 59, 236–44.
29 Ibid., 36–7.
30 Deleuze, *Bergsonism*, 72–8, 91–4.
31 Deleuze, *Difference and Repetition*, 37. For a discussion of how these two opposed senses of the limit/unlimited couple run throughout Deleuze's entire philosophy, see David Lapoujade, *Deleuze, Les Mouvements Aberrants* (Paris: Les Éditions de Minuit, 2014), 292–30.
32 Deleuze, *Difference and Repetition*, xx–i.
33 Moore, *The Infinite*, 39.
34 Ibid., 40.

35 Kant, *Critique of Pure Reason,* B39. Cf. Charles Parsons, Infinity and Kant's Conception of the 'Possibility of Experience', in *Kant's Critique of Pure Reason: Critical Essays,* ed. Patricia Kitcher (Lanham, Boulder, New York, Oxford: Rowman & Littlefield Publishers, 1998); Michael Friedman, Geometry, Construction and Intuition in Kant and his Successors, in *Between Logic and Intuition: Essays in Honor of Charles Parsons,* ed. Gila Sher and Richard Tieszen (Cambridge: Cambridge University Press, 2000), 186–218; Lydia Patton, The Paradox of Infinite Given Magnitude: Why Kantian Epistemology Needs Metaphysical Space, *Kant-Studien* 102: 273–289 (2011); Daniel Smyth, Infinity and Givenness: Kant on the Intuitive Origin of Spatial Representation, *Canadian Journal of Philosophy,* December 2014, 551–579.
36 Kant, *Critique of Pure Reason,* A523/B551.
37 Friedman, Newton and Kant on Absolute Space, 36.
38 Ibid., 43.
39 Kant, *Critique of Pure Reason,* A431/B459.
40 Ibid., B40.
41 Ibid., A523/B551.
42 Ibid., A25; A432/B460; A527/B555.
43 Ibid., A32/B47-8.
44 Kant, *Critique of the Power of Judgment,* 5:244.
45 Ibid., 5:227.
46 Ibid., 5:255.
47 Ibid., 5:251–2.
48 Ibid., 5:253.
49 Ibid., 5:252.
50 Ibid., 5:254.
51 Ibid., 5:245.
52 Ibid., 5:248.
53 Ibid.
54 Ibid., 5:254–5.
55 Kant, *Critique of Pure Reason,* A169/B211. Note that magnitude (*quantum*) is not the same as quantity. The latter is the number of times a single unit is contained in an extensive magnitude. Quantity must be measured *a posteriori* in relation to a unit, that is, by comparing it to another magnitude taken as a unit of measure. This unit is in turn chosen after being compared with other magnitudes. Unlike the *quantum, quantitas* is thus not provided with an *a priori* synthesis in cognition.
56 Ibid.
57 Cf. Kant, *Critique of the Power of Judgment,* 254.
58 Ibid., 5:256.
59 Ibid., 5:252.
60 Ibid., 5:258–9.

61 Ibid.
62 Ibid.
63 Rudolf Makkreel, Imagination and Temporality in Kant's Theory of the Sublime, *The Journal of Aesthetics and Art Criticism* 42 (3): 308 (1984).
64 Ibid.
65 Ibid.
66 Kant, *Critique of Pure Reason*, B207.
67 Ibid., B210.
68 Makkreel, Imagination and Temporality in Kant's Theory of the Sublime, 309.
69 Ibid.
70 Ibid.
71 Kant, *Critique of Pure Reason*, A28–9.
72 Deleuze, *Difference and Repetition*, 246.
73 Kant, *Critique of Pure Reason*, B149.
74 Weyl developed an account of pre-extensive matter in which he suggested that the infinite-dimensional Hilbert space of quantum mechanics might be the '(transcendent) location' of matter and that the quantum mechanical projection operators might account for the causal efficacy that matter has in constituting spatiotemporal events. See Norman Sieroka, A Post-Kantian Approach to the Constitution of Matter, in *Objectivity After Kant. Its Meaning, Its Limitations, Its Fateful Omissions*, ed. Gertrudis Van de Vijver and Boris Demarest (Hildesheim/Zürich/New York: Georg Olms Verlag, 2013), 46.
75 Deleuze, *Difference and Repetition*, 241.
76 For an excellent introduction to Deleuze's metaphysical interpretation of topology and dynamic systems theory, see Manuel Delanda, *Intensive Science and Virtual Philosophy* (London/New Dehli/New York/Sydney: Bloomsbury, 2013).
77 Deleuze, *Difference and Repetition*, 230.
78 Ibid., 241.
79 Deleuze, *The Logic of Sense*, 2; Deleuze, *Difference and Repetition*, 236.
80 Deleuze, *Bergsonism*, 97–8.
81 Cf. René Thom, Postface: *La Transcendance démembrée*, in Bruno Pinchard, *La Raison dédoublée. La Fabbrica della mente* (Paris: Aubier, 1992), 583: 'The totality of living creatures composing the Biomass of our Earth is distributed throughout time following a single branching process. (…) But this process is not defined deterministically insofar as it is a spatio-temporal process, because it depends – in the sense of Cournot – of contingency, which affects the encounters that are biologically necessary (between predator-prey during predation, sexual partners in love, etc.)', my translation.
82 Cf. Deleuze, *Bergsonism*, 93–4.
83 Cf. ibid., 93.
84 Ibid., 94.

85 Deleuze, *Difference and Repetition*, 257.
86 Deleuze, *Bergsonism*, 104.
87 Deleuze, *Difference and Repetition*, 113.
88 Ibid., 258.
89 Cf. Christopher Zeeman, *Catastrophe Theory: Selected Papers 1972–1977* (Redwood City, CA: Addison-Wesley, 1977), which introduced a dynamical approach in which mental states are modelled by attractors, and the significant changes during mental processing are modelled by discontinuities, that is, bifurcations. More recently, Terrence Deacon has explored the idea that mental content is embodied as population-level dynamical attractors, in a process-metaphysical framework close to that of Deleuze. See Terrence Deacon, *Incomplete Nature. How Mind Emerged from Matter* (New York/London: W. W. Norton & Company).
90 Simondon, *Individuation in Light of Notions of Form and Information*, 278.
91 Deleuze, *Difference and Repetition*, 152.
92 Deleuze, *Cinema 1*, 38–9.
93 Deleuze, *The Logic of Sense*, 52.
94 Cf. Deleuze, *Difference and Repetition*, 139.
95 Ibid., 231. Deleuze explicitly refers to Kant's analysis of imagination in the Analytic of the Sublime as the conceptual model for this transcendent exercise of the faculties. See ibid., 146 & 321, note 10.
96 Ibid., 147.
97 Ibid., 321, 144.
98 Ibid., 187, 140.
99 Ibid., 285.
100 Ibid.
101 Ibid., 282.
102 Ibid., 183, 255, 258.
103 Ibid., 220.
104 Cf. ibid., 194.
105 Cf. Deleuze, *The Logic of Sense*, 107: 'Nietzsche's discovery lies elsewhere when (…) he explored a world of impersonal and pre-individual singularities, a world he then called Dionysian or of the will to power, a free and unbounded energy.'
106 Cf. Deacon, *Incomplete Nature*, 520.
107 Deleuze, *Difference and Repetition*, 230.

Bibliography

Abel, Günter. *Nietzsche: Die Dynamik der Willen zur Macht und die ewige Wiederkehr*. Berlin/New York: de Gruyter, 1984.
Adorno, Theodor W. *Negative Dialectics*. Translated by E. B. Ashton. London/New York: Routledge, 2004.
Andler, Daniel. 'Context: The Case for a Principled Epistemic Particularism'. *Journal of Pragmatics* 35 (2003): 349–71.
Andler, Daniel. *Intelligence artificielle, intelligence humaine: la double énigme*. Paris: Gallimard, 2023.
Andler, Daniel. *La silhouette de l'humain. Quelle place pour le naturalisme dans le monde d'aujourd'hui?* Paris: Gallimard, 2016.
Andler, Daniel. 'The Normativity of Context'. *Philosophical Studies* 100 (2000): 273–303.
Aristotle. *De Anima*. Translated by R. D. Hicks. Cambridge: Cambridge University Press, 1907.
Atlan, Henri. 'Internal Purposes, Vitalism, and Complex Systems'. In *Selected Writings on Self-Organization, Philosophy, Bioethics, and Judaism*, edited by Stefanos Geroulanos and Todd Meyers, 177–91. New York: Fordham University Press, 2011.
Atlan, Henri. *The Sparks of Randomness, Vol. 1. Spermatic Knowledge*. Translated by Lenn J. Schramm. Stanford/California: Stanford University Press, 2010.
Barwise, Jon and Perry, John. *Situations and Attitudes*. Cambridge, MA/London: The MIT Press, 1983.
Benoist, Jocelyn. *Kant et les limites de la synthèse. Le sujet sensible*. Paris: P.U.F., 1996.
Benveniste, Émile. *Problèmes de linguistique générale 1*. Paris: Éditions Gallimard, 1966.
Bergson, Henri. *Creative Evolution*. Translation by Arthur Mitchell. New York: Random House, 1944.
Bergson, Henri. *Matter and Memory*. Translated by Nancy M. Paul and W. Scott Palmer. New York: Zone Books, 1991.
Bergson, Henri. 'The Possible and the Real'. In *The Creative Mind*, translated by Mabelle L. Andison, 106–24. New York: Philosophical Library New York, 1946.
Bergson, Henri. *Time and Free Will. An Essay on the Immediate Data of Consciousness*. Translated by F. L. Pogson. London: George Allen & Unwin Ltd, 1950.
Bernet, Rudolf. *Force, Drive, Desire. A Philosophy of Psychoanalysis*. Translated by Sarah Allen. Evanston: Northwestern University Press, 2020.
Berthoz, Alain. *The Brain's Sense of Movement*. Translated by Giselle Weiss. Cambridge, MA/London: Harvard University Press, 2000.
Berthoz, Alain and Petit, Jean-Luc. *Phénoménologie et physiologie de l'action*. Paris: Odile Jacob, 2006.

Bianchin, Matteo. 'Husserl on Meaning, Grammar, and the Structure of Content'. *Husserl Studies* 34 (2018): 101–21.

Bickhard, Mark H. 'Process and Emergence: Normative Function and Representation'. In *Process Theories: Crossdisciplinary Studies in Dynamic Categories*, edited by Johanna Seibt, 121–55. Dordrecht: Springer, 2003.

Bitbol, Michel. 'Neurophenomenology of Surprise'. In *Surprise at the Intersection of Phenomenology and Linguistics*, edited by Natalie Depraz and Agnès Celle, 9–21. Amsterdam/Philadelphia: John Benjamins Publishing Company, 2019.

Blankenburg, Wolfgang. *Der Verlust der natürlichen Selbstverständlichkeit. Ein Beitrag zur Psychopathologie symptomarmer Schizophrenien*. Stuttgart: Ferdinand Enke Verlag, 1971.

Bruya, Brian. 'Action without Agency and Natural Human Action: Resolving a Double Paradox'. In *The Philosophical Challenge from China*, edited by Brian Bruya, 339–65. Cambridge, MA: The MIT Press, 2015.

Cassirer, Ernst. 'Structuralism in Modern Linguistics'. *Word* 1, no. 1 (1945): 99–120.

Chomsky, Noam. *Aspects of the Theory of Syntax*. Cambridge, MA: The MIT Press, 1964.

Chomsky, Noam. *Reflections on Language*. New York: Pantheon, 1975.

Clark, Andy. *Surfing Uncertainty. Prediction, Action and the Embodied Mind*. Oxford: Oxford University Press, 2016.

Collier, John. 'Self-Organization, Individuation and Identity'. *Revue internationale de philosophie* 229, no. 152 (2004): 151–72.

Compagno, Dario, ed. *Quantitative Semiotic Analysis*. Cham: Springer, 2018.

Corning, Peter and Kline, Stephen Jay. 'Thermodynamics, Information and Life Revisited, Part I: "To Be or to Entropy"'. *Systems Research and Behavioral Science* 15 (1998): 273–95.

De Deckere, Johan. 'Onvoorstelbaar lijden. Over picturale aanwezigheid'. In *Onheil, pijn, bloed. Voorstellingen van lijden*, edited by Marc Verminck, 143–89. Ghent: A&S Books/deBuren, 2009.

De Warren, Nicolas. 'Anarchy of Sense: Husserl in Deleuze, Deleuze in Husserl'. *Paradigmi. Rivista di critica filosofica* 2 (2014): 49–69.

Deacon, Terrence W. *Incomplete Nature. How Mind Emerged from Matter*. New York/London: W. W. Norton & Company, 2013.

Dehaene, Stanislas and Brannon, Elizabeth M. 'Space, Time, and Number: A Kantian Research Program'. *Trends in Cognitive Science, Special Issue* 14, no. 13 (2010): 517–19.

Delanda, Manuel. *Intensive Science and Virtual Philosophy*. London/New Delhi/New York/Sydney: Bloomsbury, 2013.

Deleuze, Gilles. *Bergsonism*. Translated by Hugh Tomlinson and Barbara Habberjam. New York: Zone Books, 1991.

Deleuze, Gilles. *Cinema 1: The Movement-Image*. Translated by Hugh Tomlinson and Barbara Habberjam. Minneapolis: University of Minnesota Press, 1997.

Deleuze, Gilles. *Cours Vincennes. 24/11/1981*. Available online: https://www.webdeleuze.com (accessed on 17 December 2022).

Deleuze, Gilles. *Desert Islands and Other Texts 1953–1974*. Edited by David Lapoujade and translated by Michael Taormina. New York: Semiotext(e), 2004.

Deleuze, Gilles. *Difference and Repetition*. Translated by Paul Patton. New York: Columbia University Press, 1994.

Deleuze, Gilles. *Essays Critical and Clinical*. Translated by Daniel W. Smith and Michael A. Greco. London/New York: Verso, 1998.

Deleuze, Gilles. *Expressionism in Philosophy: Spinoza*. Translated by Martin Joughin. New York: Zone Books, 2005.

Deleuze, Gilles. *Francis Bacon: The Logic of Sensation*. Translated by Daniel W. Smith. London/New York: Continuum, 2003.

Deleuze, Gilles. 'How Do We Recognize Structuralism?' In *Desert Islands and Other Texts 1953–1974*, edited by David Lapoujade and translated by Michael Taormina, 170–92. New York: Semiotext(e), 2004.

Deleuze, Gilles. 'Immanence: A Life'. In *Two Regimes of Madness. Texts and Interviews 1975–1995*, translated by Amy Hodges and Mike Taormina, 384–9. New York: Semiotext(e), 2006.

Deleuze, Gilles. *Kant's Critical Philosophy. The Doctrine of the Faculties*. Translated by Hugh Tomlinson and Barbara Habberjam. London: The Athlone Press, 1984.

Deleuze, Gilles. *Nietzsche and Philosophy*. Translated by Hugh Tomlinson. London/New York: Continuum, 2002.

Deleuze, Gilles. 'On Four Poetic Formulas That Might Summarize the Kantian Philosophy'. In *Essays Critical and Clinical*, edited by Daniel W. Smith and Michael A. Greco, 27–35. London/New York: Verso, 1998.

Deleuze, Gilles. *Spinoza, Practical Philosophy*. Translated by Robert Hurley. San Francisco: City Lights Books, 1988.

Deleuze, Gilles. *The Fold: Leibniz and the Baroque*. Translated by Tom Conley. Minneapolis: University of Minnesota Press, 1993.

Deleuze, Gilles. 'The Idea of Genesis in Kant's Aesthetics'. In *Desert Islands and Other Texts 1953–1974*, edited by David Lapoujade and translated by Michael Taormina, 56–71. New York: Semiotext(e), 2004.

Deleuze, Gilles. *The Logic of Sense*. Translated by Mark Lester with Charles Stivale. London/New York: The Athlone Press, 1990.

Deleuze, Gilles and Guattari, Félix. *Capitalism and Schizophrenia 2. A Thousand Plateaus*. Translated by Brian Massumi. Minneapolis/London: University of Minnesota Press, 2005.

Deleuze, Gilles and Guattari, Félix. *What Is Philosophy?* Translated by Hugh Tomlinson and Graham Burchill. New York: Columbia University Press, 1994.

Demarest, Boris. 'Kant's Epigenesis: Specificity and Developmental Constraints'. *History and Philosophy of the Life Sciences* 39, no. 3 (2017): 1–19.

Demarest, Boris. 'System and Organism: In Defense of an Analogy'. In *Objectivity after Kant: Its Meaning, Its Limitations, Its Fateful Omissions*, edited by Gertrudis Van de Vijver and Boris Demarest, 99–113. Hildesheim/Zürich/New York: Georg Olms Verlag, 2013.

Dennett, Daniel. *Brainstorms: Philosophical Essays on Mind and Psychology*. Cambridge, MA: The MIT Press, 1981.

DiFrisco, James. '*Élan Vital* Revisited: Bergson and the Thermodynamic Paradigm'. *The Southern Journal of Philosophy* 53, no. 1 (2015): 54–73.

DiFrisco, James. 'Hylomorphism and the Metabolic Closure Conception of Life'. *Acta Biotheoretica* 62, no. 4 (2014): 499–525.

DiFrisco, James. 'Organization and Inorganic Life in Bergson'. M.Phil diss., Institute of Philosophy, KU Leuven, Leuven (2011).

DiFrisco, James. 'Time Scales and Levels of Organization'. *Erkenntnis* 82, no. 4 (2017): 795–818.

Doran, Robert. *The Theory of the Sublime from Longinus to Kant*. Cambridge: Cambridge University Press, 2015.

Dreyfus, Hubert L. and Hall, Harison, eds. *Husserl, Intentionality and Cognitive Science*. Cambridge, MA/London: The MIT Press, 1984.

Falkenstein, Lorne. *Kant's Intuitionism. A Commentary on the Transcendental Aesthetic*. Toronto/Buffalo/London: University of Toronto Press, 2004.

Fodor, Jerry. 'Propositional Attitudes'. *The Monist* 61, no. 4 (1978): 501–23.

Fodor, Jerry. *The Language of Thought*. New York: Thomas Y. Crowell Company, 1975.

Fodor, Jerry. *The Mind Doesn't Work That Way*. Cambridge, MA: The MIT Press, 2001.

Fodor, Jerry. *The Modularity of Mind*. Cambridge, MA: The MIT Press, 1983.

Fodor, Jerry and Pylyshyn, Zenon, 'Connectionism and Cognitive Architecture: A Critical Analysis'. *Cognition* 28, no. 1–2 (March 1988): 3–71.

Forgacs, Gabor and Newman, Stuart A. *Biological Physics of the Developing Embryo*. Cambridge: Cambridge University Press, 2005.

Franck, Didier. *Nietzsche et l'Ombre de Dieu*. Paris: P.U.F., 2014.

François, Arnaud. *Bergson, Schopenhauer, Nietzsche. Volonté et réalité*. Paris: P.U.F., 2008.

Freud, Sigmund. *The Ego and the Id. Standard Edition*. London: Hogarth Press, 1923.

Friedman, Michael. 'Geometry, Construction, and Intuition in Kant and His Successors'. In *Between Logic and Intuition: Essays in Honor of Charles Parsons*, edited by Gila Sher and Richard Tieszen, 186–218. Cambridge: Cambridge University Press, 2000.

Friedman, Michael. 'Newton and Kant on Absolute Space: From Theology to Transcendental Philosophy'. In *Constituting Objectivity. Transcendental Perspectives on Modern Physics*, edited by Michel Bitbol, Pierre Kerszberg and Jean Petitot, 35–50. Dordrecht: Springer, 2009.

Friston, Karl. 'The Fantastic Organ'. *Brain* 136 (2013): 1328–32.

Gasché, Rodolphe. *The Idea of Form. Rethinking Kant's Aesthetics*. Stanford, CA: Stanford University Press, 2003.

Geroulanos, Stefanos and Meyers, Todd. 'Introduction'. In *Selected Writings on Self-Organization, Philosophy, Bioethics, and Judaism*, edited by Stefanos Geroulanos and Todd Meyers, 1–31. New York: Fordham University Press, 2011.

Guillot, Matthieu. 'Entretien avec H. Maldiney'. *L'Ouvert* 5 (2012): 79–95.

Gurdon, John B. and Bourillot, Pierre-Yves. 'Morphogen gradient interpretation'. *Nature* 413 (2001): 797–803.

Heßbrüggen-Walter, Stefan. *Die Seele und ihre Vermögen. Kants Metaphysik des Mentalen in der Kritik der Reinen Vernunft.* Paderborn: Mentis, 2004.

Heidegger, Martin. 'Der Ursprung des Kunstwerkes'. In *Holzwege*, edited by Friedrich-Wilhelm von Herrmann, 1–75. Frankfurt am Main: Vittorio Klostermann, 2003.

Heidegger, Martin. *Introduction to Metaphysics*. Translated by Gregory Fried and Richard Polt. New Haven/London: Yale University Press, 2000.

Heidegger, Martin. *The Metaphysical Foundations of Logic*. Translated by Michael Heim. Bloomington: Indiana University Press, 1992.

Hjelmslev, Louis. *Prolegomena to a Theory of Language*. Translated by Francis J. Whitfield. Madison: The University of Wisconsin Press, 1963.

Husserl, Edmund. *Cartesian Meditations. An Introduction to Phenomenology*. Translated by Dorion Cairns. The Hague/Boston/London: Martinus Nijhoff Publishers, 1977.

Husserl, Edmund. *Ideas Pertaining to a Pure Phenomenology and to a Phenomenological Philosophy. First Book*. Translated by Fred Kersten. The Hague/Boston/Lancaster: Martinus Nijhoff Publishers, 1983.

Husserl, Edmund. *Logical Investigations, Volume 2*. Translated by John Niemeyer Findlay and edited by Dermot Moran. London/New York: Routledge, 2001.

Husserl, Edmund. 'The Origin of Geometry'. In *Edmund Husserl's Origin of Geometry: An Introduction*, edited by Jacques Derrida and translated by John P. Leavey, 155–80. Stoney Brook, NY: Nicolas Hays, 1978.

Ishkhanyan, Byurakn, Christiansen, Morten H., Højen, Anders, Tylén, Kristian, Bleses, D., Fusaroli, Riccardo, et al. 'Cross-Linguistic Differences in Categorical Perception: Comparison of Danish and Norwegian' (22 December 2021). PsyArXiv. Retrieved from osf.io/qcjgt.

Jorati, Julia. 'Leibniz's Ontology of Force'. In *Oxford Studies in Early Modern Philosophy. Volume VIII*, edited by Daniel Garber and Donal Rutherford, 189–224. Oxford: Clarendon Press, 2018.

Juarrero Roqué, Alicia. 'Self-Organization: Kant's Concept of Teleology and Modern Chemistry'. *Review of Metaphysics* 39, no. 1 (September 1985): 107–35.

Kandel, Eric. *Reductionism in Art and Brain Science. Bridging the Two Cultures*. New York: Columbia University Press, 2016.

Kandel, Eric R., Schwartz, James H., Jessell, Thomas M., et al. *Principles of Neural Science, Fifth Edition*. New York: McGraw-Hill Companies, 2000.

Kant, Immanuel. *Critique of the Power of Judgment*. Translated by Paul Guyer and Eric Matthews. Cambridge: Cambridge University Press, 2000.

Kant, Immanuel. *Critique of Practical Reason*. Translated and edited by Mary J. Gregor. Cambridge: Cambridge University Press, 1996.

Kant, Immanuel. *Critique of Pure Reason*. Translated by Paul Guyer and Allen W. Wood. Cambridge: Cambridge University Press, 1998.

Kant, Immanuel. *Kant's Gesammelte Schriften*. Edited by the Deutschen Akademie der Wissenschaften zu Berlin. Band XXVIII. Berlin: de Gruyter, 1968.

Kant, Immanuel. *Notes and Fragments*. Edited by Paul Guyer and translated by Curtis Bowman, Paul Guyer and Frederick Rauscher. Cambridge: Cambridge University Press, 2005.

Kauffman, Stuart. 'Prolegomenon to Patterns in Evolution'. *Biosystems* 123 (2014): 3–8.

Kitcher, Patricia. *Kant's Transcendental Psychology*. New York, Oxford: Oxford University Press, 1993.

Lane, Nick. *Power, Sex, Suicide. Mitochondria and the Meaning of Life*. Oxford: Oxford University Press, 2005.

Lane, Nick. *Transformer: The Deep Chemistry of Life and Death*. London: Profile Books, 2022.

Lapoujade, David. *Deleuze, Les Mouvements Aberrants*. Paris: Les Éditions de Minuit, 2014.

Lebrun, Gérard. *Kant et la fin de la métaphysique. Essai sur la 'Critique de la faculté de juger'*. Paris: Collin, 1970.

Leibniz, Gottfried W. *Leibniz's 'New System' and Associated Texts*. Translated and edited by Roger Woolhouse and Richard Francks. New York: Oxford University Press, 1997.

Leibniz, Gottfried W. *New Essays on Human Understanding*. Translated and edited by Peter Remnant and Jonathan Bennett. Cambridge: Cambridge University Press, 1996.

Leibniz, Gottfried W. 'On Freedom (1689)'. In *Philosophical Essays*, edited and translated by Roger Ariew and Daniel Garber, 94–8. Indianapolis and Cambridge: Hackett Publishing Company, 1989.

Loemker, Lerry. *Gottfried Wilhelm Leibniz: Philosophical Papers and Letters*. 2nd Edition. Boston: D. Reidel Publishing Co., 1969.

Longo, Giuseppe and Montévil, Maël. *Perspectives on Organisms. Biological Time, Symmetries and Singularities*. Berlin/Heidelberg: Springer, 2014.

Longuenesse, Béatrice. *Kant and the Capacity to Judge. Sensibility and Discursivity in the Transcendental Analytic of the Critique of Pure Reason*. Translated by Charles T. Wolfe. Princeton: Princeton University Press, 1998.

Lopes, Jesse Daniel. 'How Do Mental Processes Preserve Truth? Husserl's Discovery of the Computational Theory of Mind'. *Husserl Studies* 36, no. 1 (2020): 25–45.

Lyotard, Jean-François. *Lessons on the Analytic of the Sublime*. Translated by Elizabeth Rottenberg. Stanford: Stanford University Press, 1994.

Mainzer, Klaus. *Thinking in Complexity. The Computational Dynamics of Matter, Mind and Mankind*. Fifth Edition. Berlin/Heidelberg/New York: Springer, 2007.

Makkreel, Rudolf. 'Imagination and Temporality in Kant's Theory of the Sublime'. *The Journal of Aesthetics and Art Criticism* 42, no. 3 (1984): 303–15.

Maldiney, Henri. *Art et Existence*. Paris: Klincksieck, 2003.

Maldiney, Henri. 'Existence: crise et création'. In *Maldiney. Une singulière présence*, edited by Renaud Barbaras, et al., 219–57. Paris: Éditions Les Belles Lettres, 2014.
Maldiney, Henri. *L'art, l'éclair de l'être*. Paris: Les Éditions du CERF, 2012.
Maldiney, Henri. *Ouvrir le rien. L'art nu*. Paris: Éditions Les Belles Lettres, 2010.
Maldiney, Henri. *Penser l'homme et la folie*. Grenoble: Éditions Jérôme Millon, 2007.
Maldiney, Henri. *Regard Parole Espace*. Paris: Les Éditions du CERF, 2012.
Marr, David. *Vision*. Cambridge, MA/London: The MIT Press, 2010.
Marrati, Paola. *Genesis and Trace. Derrida Reading Husserl and Heidegger*. Stanford: Stanford University Press, 2005.
Maturana, Humberto R. and Varela, Francisco J. *Autopoiesis and Cognition. The Realization of the Living*. Dordrecht/Boston/London: D. Reidel Publishing Company, 1980.
McLellan, Doug. *Bergson's Paradox and Cantor's*. Self-published at http://bergsonian.org/wp-content/uploads/2020/01/bergsons_paradox.pdf.
Mensch, Jennifer. *Kant's Organicism. Epigenesis and the Development of Critical Philosophy*. Chicago/London: The University of Chicago Press, 2013.
Montebello, Pierre. *Deleuze, La Passion de la Pensée*. Paris: J. Vrin, 2008.
Moore, Adrian W. *The Infinite*. London & New York: Routledge, 2003.
Moreno, Alvaro and Mossio, Matteo. *Biological Autonomy. A Philosophical and Theoretical Enquiry*. Springer/Dordrecht/Heidelberg/New York/London: Springer, 2015.
Moss Brender, Noah. 'Sense-Making and Symmetry-Breaking: Merleau-Ponty, Cognitive Science, and Dynamic Systems Theory'. *Symposium* 17, no. 2 (Fall/Autumn 2013): 247–73.
Moss Brender, Noah. 'Symmetry-Breaking Dynamics in Development'. *Phenomenology and the Cognitive Sciences* 16 (2017): 585–96.
Nietzsche, Friedrich. *Beyond Good and Evil*. Edited by Rolf-Peter Horstmann and Judith Norman. Cambridge/New York/Melbourne/Madrid/Cape Town/Singapore/São Paulo: Cambridge University Press, 2002.
Nietzsche, Friedrich. *The Will to Power*. Edited by Walter Kaufmann and translated by Walter Kaufmann and Reginald John Hollingdale. New York: Vintage Books, 1968.
O'Keefe, John. 'Kant and the Sea-Horse: An Essay in the Neurophilosophy of Space'. In *Spatial Representation: Problems in Philosophy and Psychology*, edited by Naomi Eilan, Rosaleen McCarthy and Bill Brewer, 42–64. Oxford: Oxford University Press, 1999.
O'Keefe, John and Nadel, Lynn. *The Hippocampus as a Cognitive Map*. Oxford: Oxford University Press, 1978.
Parsons, Charles. 'Infinity and Kant's Conception of the "Possibility of Experience"'. In *Kant's Critique of Pure Reason: Critical Essays*, edited by Patricia Kitcher, 45–58. Lanham/Boulder/New York/Oxford: Rowman & Littlefield Publishers, 1998.
Patton, Lydia. 'The Paradox of Infinite Given Magnitude: Why Kantian Epistemology Needs Metaphysical Space'. *Kant-Studien* 102 (2011): 273–89.

Petitot, Jean. 'A Transcendental View on the Continuum: Woodin's Conditional Platonism'. *Le continu mathématique. Nouvelles conceptions, nouveaux enjeux*, edited by M. de Glas. *Intellectica* 51, no. 1 (2009): 93–133.

Petitot, Jean. *Cognitive Morphodynamics. Dynamical Morphological Models of Constituency in Perception and Syntax*. In collaboration with René Doursat. Bern/Berlin/Bruxelles/Frankfurt am Main/New York/Wien: Peter Lang, 2011.

Petitot, Jean. 'Identité et Catastrophes (Topologie de la différence)'. In *L'identité*, edited by Claude Lévi-Straus, 109–56. Paris: Quadrige/P.U.F., 1977.

Petitot, Jean. 'Le Physique, le Morphologique et le Symbolique. Remarques sur la Vision'. *Revue de synthèse* 111 (1990): 139–83.

Petitot, Jean. *Les catastrophes de la parole. De Roman Jakobson à René Thom*. Paris: Maloine, 1985.

Petitot, Jean. 'Les Deux Indicibles ou la Sémiotique Face à l'Imaginaire Comme Chair'. In *Exigences et Perspectives de la Sémiotique: Receuil d'Hommages Pour Algirdas Julien Greimas/Aims and Prospects of Semiotics. Essays in Honor of Algirdas Julien Greimas*, edited by Herman Parret and Hans-Georg Ruprecht, 283–305. Amsterdam: John Benjamins Publishing Company, 1985.

Petitot, Jean. 'Mémoires et parcours sémiotiques du côté de Greimas'. *Actes sémiotiques* 120 (2017): 1–34.

Petitot, Jean. 'Morphodynamics and Attractor Syntax: Constituency in Visual Perception and Cognitive Grammar'. In *Mind as Motion. Explorations in the Dynamics of Cognition*, edited by Robert F. Port and Timothy van Gelder, 227–82. Cambridge, MA/London: The MIT press, 1995.

Petitot, Jean. 'Morphodynamics and the Categorical Perception of Phonological Units'. *Theoretical Linguistics* 15, no. 1–2 (1988): 25–72.

Petitot, Jean. *Morphogenesis of Meaning*. Translated by Franson Manjali. Bern, Berlin, Bruxelles, Frankfurt am Main, New York, Wien: Peter Lang, 2004.

Petitot, Jean. *Neurogéométrie de la vision. Modèles mathématiques et physiques des architectures fonctionnelles*. Paris: Les Éditions de l'École Polytechnique, 2008.

Piattelli-Palmarini. 'Evolution, Selection and Cognition: From "Learning" to Parameter Setting in Biology and in the Study of Language'. *Cognition* 31 (1989): 1–44.

Postarero, Tano. 'Assemblage Theory and the Two Poles of Organic Life'. *Deleuze and Guattari Studies* 14, no. 3 (2020): 402–32.

Prigogine, Ilya and Stengers, Isabelle. *La nouvelle alliance. Métamorphose de la science*. Paris: Éditions Gallimard, 1986.

Putnam, Hilary. *Reason, Truth and History*. Cambridge: Cambridge University Press, 1981.

Pylyshyn, Zenon. *Computation and Cognition. Toward a Foundation for Cognitive Science*. Cambridge, MA/London: The MIT Press, 1986.

Ricoeur, Paul. *The Conflict of Interpretations. Essays in Hermeneutics*. Translated and edited by Don Ihde. London: The Athlone Press, 2000.

Sarti, Alessandro and Piotrowski, David. 'Individuation and Semiogenesis: An Interplay between Geometric Harmonics and Structural Morphodynamics'. In *Morphogenesis and Individuation*, edited by Alessandro Sarti, Federico Montanari and Francesco Galofaro, 49–73. Cham/Heidelberg/New York/Dordrecht/London: Springer, 2015.

Sarti, Alessandro, Citti, Giovanna and Piotrowski, David. *Differential Heterogenesis: Mutant Forms, Sensitive Bodies*. Cham: Springer, 2022.

Schreel, Louis. 'Conatus and Feeling of Life: A Genetic Shift in Kant's Faculty Doctrine?' *Deleuze and Guattari Studies* 16, no. 3 (2022): 402–27.

Schreel, Louis. 'Passibility: The Pathic Dimension of Subjectivity'. In *Phenomenology, Neuroscience and Clinical Practice. Transdisciplinary Experiences*, edited by Francesca Brencio. Berlin: Springer, 2024.

Sieroka, Norman. 'A Post-Kantian Approach to the Constitution of Matter'. In *Objectivity after Kant. Its Meaning, Its Limitations, Its Fateful Omissions*, edited by Gertrudis Van de Vijver and Boris Demarest, 41–55. Hildesheim/Zürich/New York: Georg Olms Verlag, 2013.

Simondon, Gilbert. *Individuation in Light of Notions of Form and Information*. Translated by Taylor Adkins. Mineapolis/London: University of Minnesota Press, 2020.

Smyth, Daniel. 'Infinity and Givenness: Kant on the Intuitive Origin of Spatial Representation'. *Canadian Journal of Philosophy* (December 2014): 551–79.

Spinoza, Benedict. *Ethics*. Translated by Edwin Curley. In *A Spinoza Reader*. New Jersey: Princeton University Press, 1994.

Straus, Erwin. 'Die Formen des Räumlichen. Ihre Bedeutung für die Motorik und die Wahrnehmung'. In *Psychologie der Menschlichen Welt. Gesammelte Schriften von Erwin Straus*, 141–78. Berlin/Heidelberg: Springer Verlag, 1960.

Straus, Erwin. *Du sens des sens. Contribution à l'étude des fondements de la psychologie*. Translated by Georges Thinès and Jean-Pierre Legrand. Grenoble: Éditions Jérôme Millon, 2000.

Straus, Erwin. 'The Phantom Limb'. In *Aesthetis and Aesthetics. The Fourth Lexington Conference on Pure and Applied Phenomenology*, edited by Erwin Straus and Richard Griffith, 130–148. Pittsburgh: Duquesne University Press, 1970.

Strawson, Peter. *The Bounds of Sense. An Essay on Kant's Critique of Pure Reason*. London: Methuen, 1966.

Sweeney, Leo. *Infinity in the Presocratics. A Bibliographical and Philosophical Study*. The Hague: Martinus Nijhoff, 1972.

Thom, René. 'L'Antériorité Ontologique du Continu sur le Discret'. In *Le Labyrinthe du Continu*, edited by Jean-Michel Salanskis and Hourya Sinaceur, 137–43. Paris/Berlin/Heidelberg/New York/Londres/Tokyo/Hong Kong/Barcelone/Budapest: Springer Verlag, 1992.

Thom, René. 'Postface: *La Transcendance démembrée*'. In, *La Raison dédoublée. La Fabbrica della mente*, edited by Bruno Pinchard, 575–609. Paris: Aubier, 1992.

Thom, René. 'Sur la notion de Nature: la Nature et les êtres'. In *Science et philosophie de la Nature. Un nouveau dialogue*, edited by Luciano Boi, 173–6. Bern/Berlin/Bruxelles/ Frankfurt am Main/New York/Oxford/Wien: Peter Lang, 2000.

Varela, Francisco J. *Principles of Biological Autonomy*. New York/Oxford: Elsevier North Holland, 1979.

Velleman, David J. 'The Way of the Wanton'. In *The Possibility of Practical Reason, 2nd Edition*, 1–18. Michigan: Michigan Publishing, University of Michigan Library, 2014.

Visser, Gerard. 'Een nog alleen door Godheid aangeraakt gemoed. De verwijding van het affectieve bij Meister Eckhart'. *Tijdschrift voor Filosofie* 68 (2006): 691–723.

Visser, Gerard. *Gelatenheid. Gemoed en hart bij Meister Eckhart. Beschouwd in het licht van Aristoteles' leer van het affectieve*. Amsterdam: Boom, 2018.

Visser, Gerard. *Niets cadeau. Een filosofisch essay over de ziel*. Amsterdam: Valkhof pers, 2010.

Walsch, Denis. *Organisms, Agency, and Evolution*. Cambridge: Cambridge University Press, 2015.

Webster, Gerry and Goodwin, Brian. 'History and Structure in Biology'. *Perspectives in Biology and Medicine* 25, no 1 (1981): 227–43.

Weil, Simone. *Gravity and Grace*. Translated by Emma Crawford and Mario von der Ruhr. London/New York: Routledge Classics, 2003.

Willascheck, Marcus, Stolzenberg, Jürgen, Mohr, Georg and Bacin, Stefano. *Kant-Lexikon. Band 1*. Berlin/Boston: de Gruyter, 2015.

Zeeman, Christopher. *Catastrophe Theory: Selected Papers 1972–1977*. Redwood City, CA: Addison-Wesley, 1977.

Zellini, Paolo. *A Brief History of Infinity*. Translated David Marsh. London: Penguin Books, 2004.

Zuckert, Rachel. *Kant on Beauty and Biology. An Interpretation of the Critique of Judgment*. Cambridge: Cambridge University Press, 2007.

Index

A

a priori
  cognitive faculties 16–18, 20–3, 52, 77, 90, 92–3, 168 n. 10
  naturalized 17
  principles of cognition 13–14, 16–17, 19, 20–3, 25–6, 32, 52, 77, 81–2, 90, 92, 107, 110, 168 n. 2
  space 4, 6, 78, 85, 142, 158–9
  topological 75–7, 84–6
Adorno, Theodor 110, 113, 181 n. 16, 181 n. 18, 182 n. 30
affectivity 23–4, 45–7, 103, 122–3, 125–7, 134, 137, 161
Andler, Daniel 166 n. 7, 182 n. 23, 182 n. 33, 182 n. 38
apeiron 4–5, 11, 69, 139, 142–7, 157–8, 160–1, 165
Aristotle 33–4, 35–6, 38, 43, 45–6, 48–9, 58, 140–1, 143, 147–9, 171 n. 58, 172 n. 17
Atlan, Henri 167 n. 12, 173 n. 33

B

Bergson, Henri 4, 8, 55–7, 62–8, 73, 134, 141, 156, 159, 167 n. 15, 174 n. 2, 176 n. 37, 176 n. 39., 180 n. 1
Bernet, Rudolf 172 n. 17
Bickhard, Mark 60, 175 n. 10
Blankenburg, Wolfgang 131–2

C

Cassirer, Ernst 171 n. 52
causation
  circular 7, 15, 25–34
  immanent 5
  mental 37–8, 42
Chomsky, Noam 15–19, 32, 168 n. 8, 169 n. 15
Cohen, Hermann 13
computationalism 9, 59, 76–7, 90, 93–4, 169 n. 15, 180 n. 48, 181 n. 6

conatus 5, 7, 9–10, 20, 24, 30, 35–53, 113, 118, 122, 160, 162, 167 n. 12, 173 n. 17
creativity 1, 3–10, 18–20, 49, 51–3, 57, 61–2, 68, 73, 88, 100–2, 104, 108–9, 111–2, 115–19, 134, 141–2, 147, 158–9, 162–3, 165, 166 n. 10, 169 n. 14, 169 n. 15

D

De Deckere, Johan 134–5
Deacon, Terrence 190 n. 89
Dehaene, Stanislas 169 n. 10
Delanda, Manuel 189 n. 76
Deleuze, Gilles 1–11, 13–14, 16, 19, 21–4, 30–4, 35–8, 43–8, 53, 55–7, 60–3, 69–73, 75–81, 83–90, 98, 99–118, 121, 123, 127, 132, 134–7, 140, 141–5, 147, 155–65, 167 n. 15, 168 n. 6, 170 n. 47, 177 n. 2, 179 n. 25, 180 n. 1, 181 n. 6, 183 n. 4, 186 n. 71, 187 n. 31, 189 n. 76, 190 n. 89, 190 n. 95
Demarest, Boris 25
Derrida, Jacques 14, 168 n. 6
differentiation 8, 69–73, 136, 158–9, 161, 163
DiFrisco, James 176 n. 37, 176 n. 39
Dreyfus, Hubert 106–7
duration 49, 55–7, 63–9, 72–3, 100, 123, 134–6, 140, 142, 151, 159, 167 n. 15, 176 n. 39

E

embryogenesis 70–1, 85, 163
energy
  indetermination 8, 10, 62, 66–9, 73, 100, 117, 135–6, 160, 165
  potential 8–9, 57–8, 61–2, 64–9, 100, 117, 160–1, 163
  psychic 100, 160, 162–3
entropy 57, 61–2, 64, 67–8
Erewhon 147, 159, 165

F

faculty
  cognitive 3, 9, 15–18, 22, 25, 36–43, 52, 77–8, 89, 108, 114–15, 151–2, 161, 163
  doctrine 6–7, 13–15, 19, 21, 23, 25, 30, 36–8, 41–2, 48, 52, 167 n. 15, 168 n. 6, 173 n. 30, 183 n. 4
  Fodor, Jerry 19–20, 77, 84, 94, 105–8, 169 n. 15, 169 n. 18, 181 n. 6
Frege, Gottlob 13, 101, 104–6, 168 n. 2, 181 n. 6
Freud, Sigmund 83, 102–3, 180 n. 1
functionalism
  classical 58–9, 76, 84–6, 94
  computational 76, 178 n. 4
  dynamical 76–7, 85, 93

G

Goodwin, Brian 33, 71

H

Heidegger, Martin 41–2, 128–33, 172 n. 17, 177 n. 67, 184 n. 25, 185 n. 43
Heßbrüggen-Walter, Stefan 39, 173 n. 30
Hjelmslev, Louis 31–2, 80, 178 n. 11
Husserl, Edmund 14, 75, 81–2, 106–7, 121, 124–5, 130, 168 n. 2, 168 n. 6, 180 n. 49, 181 n. 6
hylomorphism 58–61

I

idea
  Deleuzian 5–6, 10, 86–8, 115–18, 162–5
  Kantian 2, 5–6, 20, 32, 139, 141–2, 151, 155
  Platonic 141–2, 146–7, 151, 155, 158, 165
  virtual 31, 78, 86–8, 115–18
individuation 3–6, 8, 9, 10, 14, 30, 34, 55, 57–63, 72–3, 88, 121–2, 127, 135–6, 142, 145, 156–63, 165
  monadic 41
  psychic 1, 8, 9, 53, 65, 77, 86, 100, 102, 105, 114, 116–19, 122–3, 126, 134, 160–1, 163, 165
  vital 8, 60–3, 65, 67–8, 71–2

infinity
  actual 10, 139, 141, 142, 143, 146, 149–51, 159
  mathematical 139, 148–50
  metaphysical 11, 139, 141, 143
  potential 10, 139–41, 143, 147–50
information 16–17, 59, 61, 77, 79, 86, 90, 93–5, 97, 98, 99, 109, 180 n. 48
  morphological 93, 97–8
  positional 71
  processing 20–1, 93–7, 106
inorganic life 10, 61, 72–3, 122, 134–6, 186 n. 72

J

Jakobson, Roman 32, 79, 91

K

Kant, Immanuel 1–4, 6–11, 13–17, 19–33, 35–45, 52, 75, 78, 80–1, 83, 86–7, 106, 108, 110, 117, 121, 139–43, 148–56, 158–9, 161–2, 164–5, 166 n. 5, 167 n. 15, 168 n. 2, 168 n. 6, 168 n. 10, 171 n. 51, 171 n. 58, 172 n. 17, 173 n. 30, 183 n. 4, 186 n. 71, 187 n. 14, 190 n. 95

L

learning 10, 15–19, 52–3, 108, 114–16, 118, 127, 129, 168
Leibniz, Gottfried W. 4, 7–9, 20, 24, 35–45, 48–50, 86, 142–3, 156, 171 n. 2, 172 n. 17, 173 n. 30
Longuenesse, Béatrice 43
Lopes, Jesse 181 n. 6

M

Makkreel, Rudolf 153–5
Maldiney, Henri 10, 123–4, 127–33, 183 n. 6, 185 n. 43, 185 n. 58
Marr, David 94–8, 180 n. 49
metabolism 8, 28, 36, 62, 65–9, 100, 112, 176 n. 37, 176 n. 39
metaphysics 4, 8, 43–4, 55–6, 58, 60, 61, 72, 131, 141–2, 144–5, 156–7, 164–5, 173 n. 30, 174 n. 2
metastability 57, 60–2, 72, 117
monad 41–3, 48
Moore, Adrian 145, 148

morphodynamic 9, 77, 84–5, 92–3, 157, 163
morphological 77, 90, 93, 95–8, 154
Moss Brender, Noah 177 n. 56
Mossio, Matteo 171 n. 58

N
natura naturans (Spinoza) 4–5, 61, 63, 73, 144–5
naturalism 8, 38, 43, 47, 83, 85, 93
naturalization 76, 77, 89
Nietzsche, Friedrich 7, 38, 45, 47–51, 53, 137, 163, 174 n. 46, 185 n. 43, 190 n. 105
nihilism 50–1, 53, 185 n. 43

O
ontic 123, 127, 133
ontological 4, 6–8, 14, 23, 38, 41, 63, 65, 78, 80, 85, 130, 134, 140, 142
    aporia of self-organization 30–3
    difference 8, 55, 72, 144, 177 n. 67
    interpretation of the affective 123, 127, 130, 135
    priority of individuation 8, 55
    reality of duration 63, 65, 67, 72–3, 134–6, 142

P
passibility 127–30, 133–4, 138
pathic 119, 123–4, 126–7, 133–4, 136, 138
Petitot, Jean 9, 17, 31–2, 76, 79, 84–6, 89–90, 92–7, 103, 180 n. 49
phoneme 31, 79–80, 83, 88–92, 94, 100
Piattelli-Palmarini, Massimo 19
proposition 94, 100–12, 114, 117, 181 n. 6
purposiveness 7, 24–5, 27–33
Putnam, Hilary 110
Pylyshyn, Zenon 77, 84, 169 n. 15, 178 n. 4, 180 n. 48

R
reciprocal dependency relations 9, 31, 76, 79–81, 86, 117, 178 n. 11
reciprocal determination 9, 26, 29, 32, 34, 71–2, 76–7, 80–1, 83, 86–9, 115–18, 170 n. 47
Ricoeur, Paul 83

S
Sarti, Alessandro 175 n. 13, 181 n. 21
self-organization 1, 5, 7, 9, 14–15, 24–6, 28–33, 72, 75, 81, 84, 118, 126, 158
sensation 15, 17, 23, 114, 121–7, 132, 134–6, 138, 154, 160–3, 170 n. 29, 180 n. 1
    pathic vs gnosic 123–7, 134–6, 138
Simondon, Gilbert 8, 56–62, 144, 160
singularity 10, 33, 47, 58, 75, 79, 84, 86, 102, 111–16, 118, 157, 182 n. 23, 182 n. 38
Spinoza, Baruch 4–5, 7, 38, 43–8, 50–1, 63, 73, 143
Straus, Erwin 10, 123–7, 183 n. 5
Strawson, Peter 13
structuralism 31, 75–8, 80–6, 89–90, 93, 170 n. 47, 177 n. 2
    dynamical 9, 76–7, 85, 89–90, 93
    in biology 33
    linguistic 31, 75, 78, 80–4, 89
    transcendental 9, 75–89
structure
    cognitive 14–19, 22, 24, 26, 51–3, 77–8, 83, 89–98, 101, 107, 109–10, 117, 124, 126, 139, 160, 163, 168 n. 6, 178 n. 4
    conceptual (Jackendoff) 90, 96
    constituent 76–9, 86, 89–98, 100, 125
    dissipative 30, 32
    ideal 9, 31, 99, 72–3, 77–8, 84–8, 99, 118, 162, 165
    individuation of 57–62, 69, 84–8, 90, 99, 101, 157, 159
    linguistic 31, 75, 77–84, 88–90, 104
    morphological (Petitot) 90, 97
    noetic-noematic (Husserl) 124, 126
    organic 3, 18–19, 26–33, 69, 72–3, 117, 163, 165
    psychic 9, 69, 72–3, 159, 163, 165
    symbolic 75–7, 84, 88, 93, 99, 170 n. 47
sublime
    Deleuzian 3, 6, 9–11, 114–15, 138–9, 142, 155, 157, 159, 161, 162, 164–5, 167 n. 15, 186 n. 71, 190 n. 95
    Kantian 1–2, 11, 139–41, 150–2, 155, 161–2, 164–5, 183 n. 4, 186 n. 71, 187 n. 14, 190 n. 95
Sweeney, Leo 144

symbolic 59, 75–9, 84, 88, 90, 93–4, 97, 99, 131, 170 n. 47, 180 n. 48
syntax 17, 19, 21, 77, 89–90, 105, 109, 169 n. 15, 169 n. 16

T
Taoism 129–30, 133
Thom, René 32, 85–6, 89, 92, 166 n. 10, 179 n. 25
Transcendental
  Aesthetic 23, 142, 148, 159, 170 n. 29
  apperception 37
  ego 75, 107
  empiricism 16, 14
  field without a subject 75, 77, 83, 99
  genesis 14–15, 17, 19, 21, 24–5, 101, 168 n. 6
  illusion 110, 113
  life 14
  logic 52
  naturalization of 17, 76
  organics (Demarest) 25

philosophy 1, 6, 9, 13–15, 19, 23, 26, 30, 37, 75–8, 80–1, 121, 156–7, 164–5, 168 n. 2, 178 n. 5
structure of thought 51, 168 n. 6
subjectivity 14–15, 75, 81, 83, 110, 168 n. 6
subjectivism 13
surface 100–1
syntax 21
topology 9, 75–6

V
Varela, Francisco 29–30
vis activa (Leibniz) 7, 39–42, 48

W
Webster, Gerry 33, 71
Weil, Simone 134
Weyl, Hermann 4, 142, 156, 189 n. 74
will to power 7, 38, 48–51, 163, 190 n. 105
wu wei 129–30, 133, 184 n. 33

Z
Zeeman, Christopher 190 n. 89

www.ingramcontent.com/pod-product-compliance
Lightning Source LLC
Chambersburg PA
CBHW052114300426
44116CB00010B/1660